THE POWER
TO CARE

THE POWER TO CARE

Clinical Practice Effectiveness with Overwhelmed Clients

JUNE GARY HOPPS

ELAINE PINDERHUGHES

RICHARD SHANKAR

THE FREE PRESS

New York   London   Toronto   Sydney   Tokyo   Singapore

The Free Press
A Division of Simon & Schuster Inc.
866 Third Avenue, New York, N. Y. 10022

Printed in the United States of America

printing number

1 2 3 4 5 6 7 8 9 10

Library of Congress Cataloging-in-Publication Data
Hopps, June G.
    The power to care: clinical practice effectiveness with overwhelmed clients/June Gary
Hopps, Elaine Pinderhughes, Richard Shanker.
      p. cm.
    Includes bibliographical references and index.
    ISBN 0-02-925285-7
    1. Psychiatric social work—United States. 2. Poverty—Psychological aspects.
I. Pinderhughes, Elaine. II. Shankar, Richard Ashok Kumar. III. Title.
    [DNLM: 1. Social Work, Psychiatric. 2. Mental Health Services. 3. Poverty.
4. Socioeconomic Factors. WM 30.5 A798p 1995]
HV690.U6H66 1995
362.2'0425'0973—dc20
DNLM/DLC   94-41532
for Library of Congress   CIP

To

ANNA FAITH JONES

President, The Boston Foundation

J.G.H.
E.P.
R.S.

CONTENTS

Foreword by William Julius Wilson   *vii*

Acknowledgments   *xi*

1. Overwhelmed Clients: Poor, Powerless, and
   Economically Entrapped   1

2. The Environmental Context for Clients   29

3. The Context for Practitioners and Clients:
   The Power Conundrum   43

4. Research on Clinical Practice: An Overview   65

5. Empirical Findings on Clinical Effectiveness   77

6. The Helping Equation: A Qualitative Analysis   93

7. Revitalizing Care: Liberation from
   Powerlessness and Entrapment   129

8. National Justice-Based Policies That Support
   Empowerment of Clients and Communities   147

Appendixes

A. Investigative Procedures and Study Implementation
   of Clinical Practice Effectiveness   167

B. Summary of Studies Cited in Chapter 4   185

C. Tables for Use in Conjunction with Chapter 5   219

   Notes   229

   Index   247

FOREWORD

POVERTY, LIKE OTHER ASPECTS OF CLASS INEQUALITY, IS A CONSEQUENCE of the differential distribution of privileges and resources. In an industrial society groups are stratified in terms of the material assets or resources they control, the benefits and privileges they receive from these resources, the cultural experiences they have accumulated from historical and existing economic and political arrangements, and the influence they yield because of those arrangements. Accordingly, group variation in resources, lifestyles, and life chances is related to the variations in access to organizational channels of privilege and influence.

If we follow T. H. Marshall's classic thesis on the development of citizenship, we see that the more this fundamental principle (the organic link tying poverty to the social class and racial structure of society) is recognized or acknowledged in Western society, the more the emphasis on the rights of citizens will tend to go beyond civil and political rights to include social rights—that is, "the whole range from the right to a modicum of economic welfare and security to the right to share to the full in the social heritage and to live the life of a civilized being according to the standards prevailing in the society."*

However, as critics of American approaches to the study of poverty and welfare have shown repeatedly, concerns about the civil and political aspects of citizenship in the United States have overshadowed concerns about the social aspects of citizenship (that is,

*T. H. Marshall, *Class, Citizenship, and Social Development* (New York: Doubleday & Company, Inc., 1964), p. 78.

the "social" right to employment, economic security, health, and education) because of a strong belief system that denies the social origins and social significance of poverty and welfare.

In 1978 the French social scientist Robert Castel argued that the paradox of poverty in affluent American society has rested on the notion that "the poor are individuals who themselves bear the chief responsibility for their condition. As a result the politics of welfare revolve around the management of individual deficiencies." From the building of almshouses in the late nineteenth century to President Johnson's "War on Poverty," Americans have failed to emphasize the social rights of the poor, "rights whose interpretation is independent of the views of the agencies charged with dispensing assistance."*

Because of the lack of emphasis on social rights, the effects of joblessness on the poor in the United States are far more severe than those experienced by disadvantaged groups in other advanced industrial Western societies. While economic restructuring and its adverse effects on lower-income groups has been common to all these societies in recent years, the most severe consequences of social and economic dislocations have been in the United States because of the underdeveloped welfare state and the weak institutional structure of social citizenship rights. Although all economically marginal groups have been affected, the inner-city poor have been particularly devastated because their plight has been compounded by their spatial concentration in deteriorating ghetto neighborhoods, neighborhoods that reinforce weak labor-force attachment and that make it difficult to locate jobs in the larger society.

In short, the socioeconomic position of the inner-city poor in American society is extremely precarious. They are vulnerable to the economic restructuring of the advanced industrial economy. Moreover, the problems of joblessness, deepening poverty, and other woes that have accompanied these economic changes have not been relieved by the meager welfare programs targeted to the poor. Furthermore, these problems tend to be viewed by members of the

---

*Robert Castel, "The 'War on Poverty' and the Status of Poverty in Affluent Society," *Actes de la Recherche en Sciences Sociales* 19 (January 1978), p. 47.

larger society as a reflection of personal deficiencies, not structural inequities.

Accordingly, a shift in the way that we approach the subject of social rights (i.e., the right to employment, economic security, health and education) in the United States would be welcome news to the inner-city poor. To facilitate this shift, we need a broader vision of the problems of poverty and welfare and of ways to address them. June Gary Hopps, Elaine Pinderhughes, and Richard A. K. Shankar's important book, *The Power to Care*, provides such a vision. This vision enables the authors to discuss their significant empirical findings on successful clinical services applied to overwhelmed clients not in isolation but in relation to the broader problems of society that affect the poor.

More specifically, it is a vision that emphasizes the need to integrate clinical interventions (that include a range of strategies to address problems stemming not only from psychological difficulties, but behavioral, social, and environmental problems as well) with macro-level interventions such as programs that enhance employment, decent housing, and the social organization of neighborhoods. Consistent with the notion of promoting social rights, it is a vision, a "justice-based" approach in the authors' words, that promotes the idea that the system is required to redistribute more social and economic resources to overwhelmed clients and to their communities.

The Power to Care is a timely book. We are in a period in which strong messages from conservative politicians, talk-show hosts, and other media outlets associate inner-city crime, family breakdown, and welfare receipt with individual shortcomings. Blame-the-victim arguments resonate with many urban Americans because of their very simplicity. They not only reinforce the salient belief that joblessness and poverty reflect individual inadequacies, but discourage support for new and strong programs to combat inner-city social dislocations as well. This thoughtful volume provides a powerful and convincing rebuttal to those arguments.

WILLIAM JULIUS WILSON
Director and Lucy Flower University Professor
of Sociology and Public Policy
University of Chicago

ACKNOWLEDGMENTS

THE AUTHORS GRATEFULLY ACKNOWLEDGE THE SUPPORT OF THE FOL-
lowing institutions in the development and realization of this project:
The Boston Foundation, Boston College and Stonehill College. We
extend special thanks to these individuals who read parts of the manuscript, offering valuable suggestions: Mary Hogan, Albert Hanwell,
Richard Rowland, Anne Freed, Tom O'Hare, Leon Williams, Thanh
Tran, Regina O'Grady-Leshane, and Demetrius Iatridis. To those
who gave assistance in the preparation of the manuscript, we also express appreciation: Mary Kelley, Josephine Connors, Catherine Ward,
Brian Moriarty, Wendy Hanawalt, June Buckley, and staff.

Finally to our editor Susan Arellano whose insightful comments
and constructive demands helped to bring this project to fruition,
and to the Hopps, Pinderhughes and Shankar families for their encouragement and endless support, we express our deepest gratitude.

J.G.H.
E.B.P.
R.A.K.S.

CHAPTER 1

Overwhelmed Clients
Poor, Powerless, and Economically Entrapped

A massive investment was made by the staff of a social service agency to intervene in the destructive, dependent functioning of the K family, which had been referred because of a disturbed relationship between Vivian, age twenty-three, and her four-year-old son, Julian. Others in the household were Vivian's husband, Fred, age twenty-four; their two sons, Freddy, Jr., age three, and Arthur, age one; Vivian's son, Oliver, age seven; and Jim, a boarder. Around the corner lived Vivian's grandmother, Ella, age sixty; mother, Winona, age forty; uncle, Manny, age forty-one; and nephew Sammy, age one. Lela, age nineteen, Sammy's mother and Vivian's sister, alternated between the two households, moving in and out after arguments and fights.

The family had a long history of contact with social services for problems related to finances, health, and coping ability. Ella, the only employed family member, received Aid to Families with Dependent Children (AFDC) for Sammy, now in her custody due to Lela's behavior as a prostitute and negligent mother. Vivian, weighing over 300 pounds at five feet, two inches tall, had many serious health problems and received AFDC for Oliver and Julian. Winona, an alcoholic with serious health problems, received Supplemental Security Income (SSI). Manny, recently discharged from a prison for manslaughter, received disability. Fred, Sr., received unemployment compensation.

Isolated from the outside world, family members literally lived within the walls of the two households. All adults exhibited extremely poor self-images, as well as impulsive, exploitative, and manipulative behavior toward

1

one another. Despite caring, laughter, and joking, their interaction was marked by intense conflict, disorganization, and violence.

Family members willingly contracted with the agency to work toward the following goals: collectively—to reduce provocative, explosive behavior; increase cohesion, support, and nurturing behavior to one another; function as a family with better organization and control; Vivian—to change neglectful, abusive behavior and lose weight; Winona—to stop drinking; all adults—to get jobs. Eventually, Ella also became a client when it became clear that as the most powerful member, she was a prime mover in the family's destructive functioning and low self-esteem. After three months, she became bedridden and never worked again.

Using eight workers, the agency spent four years and over 400 hours of intensive work with this family. Although their isolation was reduced by the use of community supports, such as after-school programs, tutoring, and camp for the children, and although the relationship between Vivian and Julian improved, an outcome effectiveness evaluation at that time would have revealed little change in behavioral, attitudinal, or motivational states. No alteration in their transgenerational pattern of dependency, conflict, abusive relationships, and poverty was demonstrated.

This family represents the classic overwhelmed client: prey to physical, emotional, and psychological problems; spotty (if any) employment; family violence, substance abuse, and child abuse; truancy, teenage pregnancy, and financially irresponsible fatherhood. Illusory escapes and maladaptive responses to devaluation related to race, gender, class, and significant life moments converge in ways that often make functioning marginal. Unhealthy living conditions spawn complex developmental problems, undermine coping capacity, and contribute to transgenerational entrapment as the dysfunctional behaviors are handed down and become further entrenched.[1]

To what extent are similar families representative of clients served by inner-city agencies in impoverished census tracts populated largely, although not exclusively, by overwhelmed people of color? Are they exhibiting powerlessness, having given up and now seeming comfortable in dependency roles? Are they involved in human capital investments such as education or work preparation? Are they working? Or do clients depend primarily on welfare—AFDC and other programs?

Additionally, what contribution did national policies make to the K's situation? What was the effect of policies that made case assistance available without expectation of work or work preparation leading to self-sufficiency? Were these policies part of the solution or part of the problem? What happens when workers fail to require addicted clients to undergo aggressive treatment for alcoholism or drugs? Has the effect of these practices and worker activity been such that they collude in keeping people dependent?

What about clinical service, even long-term services, to clients without a clear commitment from them for substantive movement toward self-improvement and self-esteem for each member? Without such commitments, do clinicians who do *not* help clients set goals and move to a higher level of functioning collude with them? Or have the helping professions, like many other Americans, written off people similar to the K's?

The literature on clinical work is not optimistic about successful interventions with this client population, citing numerous reasons for this state of affairs: poor or insufficient ideas on theories as guides to practice intervention,[2] the use of microsystem strategies—clinical intervention—to address problems stemming from macrosystem dynamics—poverty;[3] the use of methods based on stances and values that perceive this clientele as deviant, pathological, and incompetent;[4] and the fact that research capabilities for assessing interventions are still emerging.[5]

What we found in the research for this book is that clinical services with overwhelmed clients are effective. When these services are offered by caring, flexible practitioners who value education and hold their clients to high expectations and believe that they can change and free themselves from the entrapping subculture, clients can move to higher levels of functioning. In fact, the best predictor of successful client change is flexible and caring practitioners who in their practice expose clients to high goals and expect them to rise to the occasion. These clients, 71 percent of whom presented with multiple problems, are suffering not solely from psychological problems but from multiple problems—joblessness, drug abuse, domestic and street violence—that reinforce one another. The etiology of problems is not always personal and psychological but communal and environmental, compounded by systems failures. Most clients in this study received shorter-term service rather than longer term, with nearly 70 percent of cases terminated within two years. Thus, although most clients did have mental health services, they were not receiving treatment for serious personality disorders.

Clinical work nevertheless is compromised by environmental detractors—drugs, violence, communities that do not provide adequate nurturing, and national policies that do not permit a sufficient range of programs and resources to address clients' multiple problems. In fact no agency from which the sample was drawn manifested programs and activities focused on community building and such changes as safer streets and improved environs. Philosophically, agencies may not have tuned into the significance of paid work in the lives of their clients. Practically, perhaps they understand all too well the powerlessness of clinicians to have an impact on the employment picture. Thus, many of the conditions that brought clients to the clinic in the first place could not be fully addressed. This systemic process that entraps overwhelmed clients was described years ago:

> Thus, for example, we find victims of poverty and oppression caught up in a systemic process of powerlessness where the failure of the larger social system to provide needed resources operates in a circular feedback process that entraps victims and sets in motion a malignant process. For the failure of the larger social system to provide necessary supports creates powerlessness in communities. And the more powerlessness in a community due to lack of resources and nutritive supplies, the more powerless are the families within, hindered from meeting the needs of their members and in organizing to improve the community so that it can provide them with more support. And the more powerless the families in efforts to protect its members from the stress of community failure and in efforts to change its destructiveness, the more powerless are the individual members, blocked in attempts to acquire skills, develop self-esteem and strengthen the family. And the more powerless the individ-

ual in efforts to acquire skills, develop self-esteem and strengthen the family, the more powerless the community which is denied their potential for strengthening it at the same time that the community becomes itself, a stressor and a creator of even more powerlessness in people.[6]

The circular reinforcing process of these political, economic, and social forces creates a sense of powerlessness that undermines the very skills that are so necessary for coping with them. Joblessness in a work-oriented society is a major barrier to the development of effective coping. It creates serious deprivation since work serves as a psychological and developmental organizer, creating needed structure for both individuals and communities. Enhancer of independence and shaper of life-style and life satisfaction, work functions as a base of self-support and a resource for addressing human need at the same time that it becomes a reducer of isolation and a builder of self-esteem.[7]

Too often contributions to lack of success in outcomes with overwhelmed clients lie in the solutions we have fashioned, both national policies and intervention strategies and processes. To determine when the social work and mental health establishments are on target in helping to meet the needs of these overwhelmed clients, we examined a random sample of 178 cases drawn from a sampling frame of over 2,000 closed client files. The goal was to identify the interventions and worker characteristics that together operate to move clients to a higher level of functioning, characterized by greater self-esteem, greater sense of mastery, and greater self-sufficiency. This sample is larger than those in most other studies (usually 50 to 100 cases), thus increasing its generalizability. Those engaged in research efforts know that gaining access to records, let alone random selection, is no small feat.

The focus on outcomes of intervention rather than merely on the intervention process and worker activity is not only timely but vital given national resource constraints. Usually reports document service intervention plans and the process of helping, focusing on strategies, face-to-face professional time spent with clients, and even time sheets monitoring worker activities.

Without a base that would be supplied by studies such as this, far too many agencies have devised programs, carried out by hard-working, even burned-out staff, that do not interrupt these often de-structive situations and dysfunctional patterns for people but rather maintain such entrapment and even reinforce clients' collusion in it. By evaluating intervention in cases selected by random sampling procedures from agencies whose mission is to serve extremely disad-vantaged populations and by presenting analysis of a number of cases identified as successful, this book seeks to help fill the gap on strategies that hold promise for clinical work with overwhelmed clients and help change the often destructive behavior that keeps these clients enmeshed in disadvantaged circumstances and poverty, which is often transgenerational.

Women generally have been found to be more depressed than men, due in large measure to poverty, which is highly associated with single parenthood, role entrapment, early child abuse, and poor marriage, and they are more likely to seek help than men.[8] In this study, then, overwhelmed clients were assumed to be mostly women and their children. Consistent with this view about women, the sample turned out to be predominantly female; interestingly, their children were predominantly male. African Americans, Latinos (who, given their population size, were underutilizing services, as were males regardless of ethnicity), Caribbeans, Portuguese, and Caucasians constituted this overwhelmed client population. Single mothers and male children represented 60 percent of the case load. Clients were also young; 48 percent were under the age of nineteen. Yet agencies had not specifically targeted services to these groups of young mothers and their male children. How services are targeted for and marketed to needy populations is an area that requires more thought and direction as service providers are challenged by a cli-mate of diversity on a variety of overlapping levels: ethnic, racial, class, and so on. Yet the study found that as difficult as life could be for these women and their children, the most overwhelmed persons were minority males who were often jobless, homeless, moving from mother to girlfriend to girlfriend, back to mother, with a major role and occupation being the provision of sexual services. How to help them conquer "uselessness" is a tall order but one that is a pressing national poverty policy question. Wilson stated:

Thirty and forty years ago, the overwhelming majority of black males were working. Most of them were poor, *but they held regular jobs around which their daily family life was organized.* When black men looked for work, employers were concerned about whether they had strong backs because they would be working in a factory or in the back room of a shop doing heavy lifting and labor. They faced discrimination and a job ceiling, but they were working. The work was hard and they were hired. Now economic restructuring has broken the figurative back of the black working population.[9] (emphasis added)

Many clients enter treatment exhibiting a profound sense of powerlessness in relation to managing the systems (socioeconomic and political, which does not provide jobs, safe streets, decent education) that impinge on their lives as well as in managing their own lives and that of their family. Their powerlessness is ongoing, and they seldom have a respite from the threats to their mental health. The ability to set forth a course of action for even one day's survival is often threatened. The seriousness of this life predicament for mental health is reflected in the following comment: "Throughout life, the feeling of controlling one's destiny to some reasonable extent is the essential psychological component of all aspects of life."[10] J. J., a client, stated;

> After they tore down the West End and they moved us across town, my mother got sick, went to the hospital and then died. Then I had no one at home—no heat, no food, no clothes. No one to look after me. [The client's only sister, who was older, was an addict.] Life was bad every day. In a strange place without anything. I hooked up with a bunch of guys that were bad for me. We started going to Forest Hills and stealing glue. It was a better high when we stole it. Drugs became my escape and I stayed high off and on 'til I was over thirty years old.

Powerlessness that is persistent, ongoing, and intractable becomes a major factor in mental and emotional dysfunction. The magnitude for overwhelmed clients is thrown into bold relief when their realities are compared to those of victims of a major disaster. Social workers know the misery, dependence, and powerlessness that exist when a client suffers a major natural calamity such as an earthquake. They know the complexities involved in engineering and effecting a recovery. With overwhelmed clients the experience of major disaster is ongoing and seemingly unrelenting. Trapped as they are by poverty and other circumstances—drugs, violence, physical abuse, joblessness—that keep them unable to exert either personal power and control over the forces that impinge on their lives, many are pushed to respond in ways that bring some sense of power but all too often compound their state of powerlessness.

That was the situation with the K's. Their attempts to adapt to their overwhelmed plight and to survive their miserable circumstances pressed them to engage in manipulation of the system, to use dependency as a tool, to assuage pain through substance abuse, to strike out at others in violent ways, and to make relationships personal battlefields.

Others confront their adversity, using behavioral strategies that facilitate the effective use of personal power, neutralizing the consequences of entrapment. Similarly, some use social services to facilitate coping. One example of these success-oriented clients is the J family, whose outcome dramatically contrasts with that of the K's. In this instance, a massive investment was also made.

J. J., whose early life is described by his own comments (see p. XX), was now working, with full custody of his nine-year-old son, living in a successful relationship, and seeking guidance for helping his son and in his words, "our blended family." Currently in his household are J. J., his son, his girlfriend, and her four children, one of whom is severely disabled. Now a highly effective community worker with terminally ill clients, he proudly announced that patients ask for him as their worker. He described his turnaround as a several-stage process, occurring first with the judge who sentenced him after twenty-three arrests for petty crimes such as shoplifting, stealing, and more serious crimes such as muggings and snatchings.

Up to this time, he had engaged in this life of crime to support a drug habit after the death of his mother when he was eighteen. His mother's breakdown when he was fourteen had followed the demolition of the West End where they had lived, and they had been forced to move to the other side of the city. He was supported by welfare from ages sixteen to thirty-four, often claiming disability and "telling any lie I could tell." He learned that by not working he could get more resources—disability and aid for his son—and at the same time have more time for his street predator behavior. During this time when he reported no motivation to do anything except to perpetuate this life of drugs and crime, he had fathered a child with a girl who was also on drugs and overwhelmed with many problems of her own.

The arrest woke him up, forcing him to look at his life, and he was motivated to use the clinical rehabilitation services that had been mandated. He credited them as the first main source of change in his life. In the rehabilitation program he received residential care, outpatient treatment, family counseling, and parenting guidance. It was here that he first experienced the effectiveness of clinical work. Giving up drugs, he became motivated to seek work as a helping service provider, first as a successful volunteer in a program for the elderly. His competence was demonstrated to him and others. Now, in addition to his employment, he is also a board member of a community agency.

J. J. and his family recently received treatment to deal with blended family dynamics. His son's emotional problems as a result of neglect by his drugging parents during his early life had been the precipitant to this stage of help for J. J. He had admired greatly his girlfriend's stamina and management of her children and could not only look back at what his son had missed but determinedly seek assistance that would enable him to become as good a parent.

Many of the multiple problems that the J family faced are common in most of the overwhelmed cases. A common denominator in both the K and J families, and most others, is poverty. However, the J's overcame many odds, including poverty, with the help of clinicians, law enforcement, financial assistance, job training, and gainful employment. The J family's outcome is in contrast to the K's, where services were focused on support and individual therapeutic intervention using largely one theoretical approach (psychodynamic) and failure to mobilize other environmental systems, such as criminal justice, education, and effective substance abuse programs, and where expectations for movement were not made clear.

In understanding J. J.'s problems and efforts to resolve them, the codetermining role of men in the lives of many poor women and in the community may become clearer.

Poverty and Welfare

The Reality of Overwhelmed Clients

Overwhelmed clients are unlike most Americans who have income sufficient for basic material supports, but even within this cohort is a wide disparity in income distribution. The 1 percent at the very bottom of the income pyramid is the group from which overwhelmed clients were assumed to come. A client who reports monthly funds of only $400 from AFDC on the agency intake form for herself and the three children who live with her is not atypical. She receives food stamps. Trips to a food pantry and donations of food and clothing, particularly at Thanksgiving and Christmas help, but life is still hard.

Overwhelmed clients have little, if any, legitimate connection to this country's annual nearly $6 trillion economy. Their poverty constitutes more than deprivation of income; it is an inclusive life-style, a major factor in their lives, and is even maintained by government policy.[11] Like other poor people, overwhelmed clients are often deprived of nutritious food, decent housing, a safe environment, and necessary prevention, especially preventive health care. Niceties, however small, such as strawberries for a dessert, a movie for a child's birthday, magazines, and newspapers, are usually out of reach, forcing inordinate time in front of television, a much cheaper source of entertainment.

Poverty level, defined by the government, determines critical allocation for many groups. (Money income, before taxes, excluding capital gains and noncash benefits, family size, and composition, are factors used to determine poverty. The figures are updated annually in order to capture changes in the consumer price index.) For a family of four, the threshold was $11,203 in 1986, $11,611 in 1987, and $12,091 in 1989. For 1990, families were considered poor if income for two was less than $8,420; for three, $10,560; and for four, $12,700. Thus, families who fall below this determination have little in terms of cash resources and remain dependent on noncash benefits, such as public housing, rent supplements, and food stamps.

Poverty is strongly associated with single-parent households, which are predominantly female: 52 percent of poor families are female headed (a sharp contrast to 23 percent in 1959; 22 percent in male-headed households and 10 percent with both parents). Among children, one in five is poor; among those under age six, the figure is one in four; and among African-American children, one in two.[12] Among those in persistent poverty (defined as being in poverty at least eight of the last ten years), two overlapping groups dominate: African Americans and female-headed households.

Factors besides the structure of families and government policy compound the entrapment of these clients. Some are at prey for losing scarce resources since they are vulnerable to street, kin, or close (but not kin) predators, some of whom hang around for "mothers' day," when AFDC checks come in the mail.

One divorced client got off welfare, went to work every day, raised and supported her children, including two who are now working citizens and one with a disability, but was suffering from depression. In an early treatment session, the clinician discovered that her long-standing boyfriend was stealing her money, household items, and furniture and selling them in order to finance his drug habit. Unable to deal effectively with the personal and financial pressures, the client somatized them, developing assorted stress-related symptoms. This situation is hardly unusual. Nor is it unusual for a woman to seek help. Even if and when she is truly free of the boyfriend he will more than likely move to another woman who will be at prey.

Clinical intervention helped this client to give up her destructive relationship and remain in the work force. Toward the end of treatment, she commented that her "burden had been lifted." Meanwhile, the boyfriend refused to become engaged in the clinical relationship, refused all services, and remained jobless. We can predict his ongoing cycle of personal poverty, manipulation, and exploitation of others. Should there be a different national policy approach, one that recognizes the powerlessness and entrapment of these men and provides an opportunity for them through employment policy?

Too often poverty is viewed narrowly as income deficiency. In fact, its dynamics entrap clients in a multitude of problems: poor self-esteem, a sense of powerlessness, and no access to needed resources.[13] Work can help address some but not all of the issues.

The nation's attack on poverty and problems of the poor in this century has seen alternating progress and regression. In a sense this move forward and then back has been a constant since the colonial period in our national paradox of two strong values, commonweal and individual ambition, both of them compounded by attitudes about race and gender.[14] Historically, this paradox is reflected in the devaluation of women and people of color, though oppression based on color has proved more pervasive than oppression based on gender. Some white women have had deferred power because of their relationship to powerful men—their fathers, husbands, and sons. People of color, regardless of gender, could not benefit from such deferred power.[15]

Precisely because of their multiple jeopardy—race, gender, and poverty—African-American women, and other women of color, are disproportionately represented on the welfare rolls; they are often powerless and overwhelmed. Historically, ambition and individualism worked to move other groups up and out of poverty. Hard work paid off, and education yielded even greater dividends. For African Americans, ambition was a negative, and sometimes punishable, crime, resulting in beatings or even death by lynching or other means. This societal emasculation and discrimination of African-American males is widely documented. So is the resulting forced participation of women in the underpaid labor force to compensate for discrimination and marginalization of males in employment opportunity and earnings.[16] When jobs were available, they were the least attractive and lowest paying; for example, domestic service was the source of employment for 70 percent of African-American workers in 1940.[17] Many others worked in fields. The Mother's Pension, the precursor to Aid to Dependent Children (ADC) and later AFDC, provided aid to white women and children while denying it to African Americans, who were assumed to have available work opportunities and strong survival skills. Moreover, if they were not working, they would procreate. Devoid of options, African-American women were forced into often menial labor at barely subsistence wages, most frequently in other women's homes.

Later, when ADC was enacted as a component of the 1935 Social Security Act, African-American women became eligible to participate. That legislation provided a minimum floor for fatherless children. "Worthy" mothers, defined as widows, were transferred to the Old Age Insurance Programs, which, in effect, defined the remaining mothers "unworthy." (That philosophy was reinforced with action: the cash benefits for ADC beneficiaries were lower than those of other programs such as Aid to the Blind and Old Age Assistance. Even now, AFDC is not indexed to inflation, while Social Security is.) From the outset, southern states opposed ADC for undercutting the racial differential in wage rates whereby blacks were paid less than whites for the same job. Benefits were kept deliberately low so that a social wage would not compete with an earned wage and so that a welfare benefit would not be viewed as more attractive than traditional marriage.[18] Because the major social welfare program serving poor women, ADC, was more attractive than menial jobs that required hard labor, poor working conditions, and minimal wages, it entrapped them, tying them to a marginal place. Placed in this position, in part by program design that reflected national ambivalence, these women had few choices.[19] The perception of client changed from an acceptable image of deserving old, white people to one of unacceptable, immoral, young blacks.[20]

Debates over worthiness and social- and race-based wage rates created stigma and feelings of unworthiness for recipients and provided political fodder for some politicians and others who fed on public stories about how "welfare queens" cheat the government out of thousands and have babies rather than work. Early on, the concept of "suitable home" was enacted as policy in many states, with the intent to require that recipients be considered worthy or fit mothers, in keeping with the moral standards of the community. This policy succeeded in denying benefits to certain women, particularly unwed mothers and African-American mothers.[21] Many of these negative attitudes and stereotypes still hold. A survey conducted by the National Opinion Research Center found that 78 percent of whites think that blacks would rather live off welfare than become self-supporting; 75 percent of non-Hispanics surveyed think that Hispanics prefer welfare to work.[22] There is also public reaction to mothers who protect their partners by withholding information on the putative father from the state, thereby forcing the state to care for the child. Years back, searches for putative fathers created extensive controversy as several states enacted "man in the house" rules and conducted night raids on recipients' homes in the 1950s and 1960s.[23] (Civil libertarians argued that raids violated privacy rights of recipients. The opposing view was that since hard-working, moral citizens had to carry the financial burdens for offspring of able-bodied, immoral men and women, searches were within the purview of a state's rights and responsibilities.) That blacks and Latinos are overrepresented in the AFDC program, although the majority of recipients are white, exacerbates the situation, compounding the powerlessness endured daily in government-maintained poverty whereby benefits are below the poverty line in every state.

Our welfare program has become a national scapegoat, accused of supporting, even encouraging, individual weakness, sin, and laziness. This view is not new. It was the dominant theory about poverty until the depression in 1890,[24] recurring in alternating cycles during the Great Depression in the 1930s and later during the War on Poverty in the 1960s.[25]

Insufficient attention has been given to the role of structural problems in the economy, inequality in the job market, and earnings that often make it difficult for uneducated, unskilled men of color to support a family, although the moral pronouncements toward these persons were undeniably strong. Even when these men of color are educated and employed, there is inequality in wages.[26]

The low-skilled but high-paying industrial jobs that have dried up with economic restructuring in the last decade or so has played havoc with the earning power of many working-class people regardless of race and ethnic background, but black men have been dealt a harder blow, since they were employed in industries hit with the strongest long-range decline: automobiles, steel, lumber, and textiles.[27] Those who held these jobs were the backbone of their communities, providing economic stability to families and role models for the young. Once a job is lost, blacks face much more difficulty locating another job than whites.[28] The lack of skilled and semiskilled jobs has had major impact since other options—executive, professional, business—have never been as available to blacks and other people of color. Many of these people, particularly young men, have been denied connection to the legal economy.

Whether by exclusion, inadequate preparation, or poor fit, their lack of ongoing connection with the labor force contributes not just to poverty but to a decreasing pool of attractive marriage partners and to isolation, crime, and family and neighborhood destabilization.[29] Their frustration and lack of access to legitimate social roles of breadwinner or mutually respected partner encourages dehumanizing words and actions toward already overburdened women of color.

J. J. described how prior to treatment he lashed out at the mother of his child, showing her little respect and behaving in the abusive, neglectful manner characteristic of his life-style. The child's mother, also an addict, did not seem to know to expect better. Manny and Fred—the K men—were abusive and disrespectful to their women: sitting around doing nothing constructive, cursing, and playing cards.

Constraints to Clinical Work

Against this background of ambivalence and lack of national commitment to this population, clinical interventions are often constrained. Without sufficient funds for necessities, clients call on practitioners to provide more than expert clinical skill and relational support. They must also be intermediaries, helping to provide for basic human needs: food, shelter, day care, drug treatment, and locating kin in other countries or other states. Theses tasks are not simply expected of clinical professionals, but rather required.

Clients are likely to present with feelings of unworthiness, having internalized many attitudes that the public has toward them. They can be angry about their predicament, knowing that their environment is unsafe and unattractive for them, their offspring, and their older parents. They are painfully aware that moving up and out of an entrapping environment is compounded by historical discrimination in the opportunity structure that forced many unskilled men into backbreaking menial labor, and later out of employment, and women into menial jobs, and under these circumstances making welfare an unattractive necessity. Some commentators think that even more important than lack of jobs is the insidious consequence of welfare that encourages single motherhood, reinforcing the autonomy of the mother and undermining family solidarity.[30]

When needed resources are unavailable, practitioners must often compromise values that dictate certain standards. For example, when decent and safe housing is not available, they have no choice but to assist a family in taking substandard dwelling or in sacrificing a nutritious diet for children in order to stretch a wholly inadequate budget. They must take on systems that are debilitators of positive self-esteem such as schools, especially when teachers are unprepared to deal with children who bring all their issues and conflicts, as well as their perceived solutions, to school, especially when solutions too often consist of knives and guns. A young practitioner commented, "I go to the school to see my clients, but I'm scared I'll get caught in a fight. Suppose the kids have a gun that day?" Yet despite his fear and sense of personal danger, he went, risking personal harm.

Clinicians must deal with the many complexities in a service delivery system that was designed to treat specific categorical problems (food, shelter, disability compensation, financial aid) when in reality a holistic, cluster service approach is needed to address the multiple problems that burden the vast majority of clients. Eligibility for services differs from one program to another, and practitioners must spend inordinate time unraveling rules and determining what services and what benefits clients are entitled to receive. The location of programs in geographically distant parts of the city complicates access and coordination. Since there is little confidence in public transportation and clients do not usually have cars, clinicians spend hours driving clients to agencies or arranging transportation.

Respect for the individual's dignity and self-determination is a major tenet of social work, but practitioners find that they cannot honor these timeless values in the absence of essential resources. For example, lack of jobs forces them to deal with the paradox of self-sufficiency and welfare dependence in the interventive effort compromising goals and values of client dignity and self-determination (I want a job) but since there is no job, accepting welfare. Men avoid treatment because the process compounds their feelings of incompetence and vulnerability, feelings often acted out on "ma woman." In this context, jobless men in the overwhelmed client population generally manifest the same problematic behavior across racial and ethnic groups: a white alcoholic abuses his wife and rapes his child; a drug-addicted African American abuses his family; a Hispanic man whose picture is just as hopeless is just as violent. These men, jobless, cannot earn money for alcohol or drugs, so they steal it, mostly from kin, other poor people, and small storekeepers. Adept at escaping law enforcement, some brag about how many times they evade the police. J. J., for example, acknowledged theft, muggings, and robbery at least twenty-three times before apprehension. Clinicians have limited options in the absence of poverty policy that does not include: jobs, alcohol and drug treatment, and job training for people struggling to maintain a family unit and secure some equilibrium and balance.

Drugs are a phenomenon that crept up on social agencies much as they crept up on society in general. Initially, agencies were not alert in identifying the entanglement of clients in the drug scene and the destruction that brought. When they did become aware of drugs, they took steps to address the situation, usually case by case but sometimes with a wider mission. One agency, alerted in its parents' activity group about the prevalence of substance abuse in their clients' lives and in the community, supported the organization of a drug awareness group in which clients took the leadership.

Treatment of clients affected by substance abuse is far from easy. Common behaviors of lying, stealing, cheating, and acting out, including violence, can distance clients, and clinicians require concentrated time, effort, energy, and above all else, patience to engage them. Moreover, success remains in constant jeopardy as clients, free of substance abuse, are vulnerable to being sucked back into the vortex of chemical dependency. The neighborhood network of neighbors, friends, and kin, themselves users and uncomfortable with nonusers in their midst, can work with cleverness and determination to bring them back into the fold.

Practitioners are faced with a culture and ethos in which many of today's welfare recipients, including those in our overwhelmed client sample, may not understand or support values emphasizing work or comprehend why work is socially and psychologically beneficial. They may feel blocked, given lack of health care, day care, and other resources should they leave welfare for work. Generations have grown up and raised children who seldom, and maybe never, saw close adult kin or neighbors in productive, paid work roles. In the overwhelmed client caseload in our study, nearly 70 percent were not in the labor force; only some thirty percent were employed or looking for employment. A number of clients, 14 percent, were disabled with health problems (including drug addiction) or had to care for children and parents.

If learning theory has any validity it can be assumed that repeated exposure to economic dependency will create responses that leave clients no choice but to feel helpless in the absence of marketable skills, social services, and social supports. They are insecure and lack self-confidence in addition to having limited, if any, competitive skills. Some may even have found a sense of comfort consistent with the concept of learned helplessness. The K's, whose basic human needs were met, were resigned to their status. They manipulated the system that responded to them to stay in a situation they had come to accept and were comfortable in. Even critics might argue that the "culture of poverty" notion is relevant here since it suggests that the attitudes and values of the poor differ from those of society in general and are passed down over generations.[31]

Others assume, as did so many of the clinicians working with and befriending these overwhelmed clients, that when exposed to mainstream values and expectations, clients could and would opt to improve their quality of life. These clinicians assumed that when high expectations were held and clients participated in goal setting and intervention planning, they would strive to reach goals though progress was by no means easy. Practitioners were mindful that clients could relapse and regress (and some did), but still they kept progress and a better life and future in the forefront. High expectations were the key in helping to motivate clients to fight their way up and out of psychological misery and pain, to stop scapegoating and take responsibility for their lives, to give up destructive relationships and face a better future. They assumed that believing in clients, and clients in turn believing in themselves, and both believing in change, movement from entrapment would occur. They were right.

Clinical Effectiveness and Higher Client Functioning

The driving force in this study was an intent to determine what holds promise in clinical work with overwhelmed clients, the majority of whom present with multiple problems stemming from psychological, behavioral, social, and environmental difficulties. From the outset, improved self-esteem, improved self-differentiation, self-sufficiency, and enhanced social, psychological, and educational competence were defined as manifestations of higher client functioning. We found that clinicians need to use eclectic approaches to help move these clients to higher, improved levels of functioning. The predominant theoretical base used was psychodynamic, augmented by cognitive behavioral theory, family theory, systems theory, group theory, and others. This eclectic approach helped clinicians develop a range of strategies to treat the multiple problems clients presented. (Appendix A contains a full explanation of the investigative procedures and study implementation.)

Two factors were singled out as critical to successful clinical work: interventions and their subsequent outcomes, and worker characteristics. The following specific interventions showed promise in helping clients move to higher functioning:

Skillful assessment, which encompassed an accurate reading of the client's reality, including behaviors and environment

Advocacy, the worker's standing up for the client and getting resources, and the client's learning to do same

Empowerment, or the enabling of clients so that they could take
charge of their lives by helping them see their uniqueness, their
strengths, and their capacity to grow

Individual treatment, whereby clients demonstrated that they
had learned to value themselves as worthwhile and learned
parenting skills, communication skills, and hygiene and personal health care

Group treatment, in which clients demonstrated they had learned
certain day-to-day life skills

Group treatment provided the most effective outcome and was
particularly dramatic in work with youth, helping them learn about
grooming, dating, safer sex, AIDS, nonviolent activities, and avoiding violence. For a slightly retarded, shy teenager, the group he became engaged in after referral was an ideal beginning service point
at which clinician leader helped him focus on these pressing queries:
"Tell me about dating. What do you do? What do you pay for?" The
worker then led the group through a discussion about dating, safer
sex, and AIDS, topics that became the focus of several sessions.
Safer sex discussions were candid, with clients being taught how to
protect themselves from disease and unwanted parenthood.

In another group, teenage boys were helped to address their fear
and anger arising from the violence and mayhem in the streets. The
emotional outpouring after loss through murder, so much on the
youngsters' minds, was as painful and difficult for the worker to
process emotionally as it was for the teenagers. Some educational
groups became therapy groups as youngsters were helped to deal
with physical abuse, sexual abuse, and self-esteem issues. Outreach
efforts were important as well. However, whenever resources were
not available, these worker efforts were thwarted.

Skillful assessment, advocacy, empowerment, and individual and
group treatment were not in themselves sufficient to bring about
successful outcomes and improved client functioning. Critical to the
client change process was the clinician. Clinicians who importantly
demonstrated that they cared about their clients and that they were
with them through hard times, believing in them and their capacity

to change and to step away from any engulfing subculture and overcome psychological problems, could motivate change. These clinicians manifested flexibility, being available when and where the client needed help—responding to a call after Saturday midnight, going to a housing project or a schoolhouse, teaching clients how to locate resources to supplement an inadequate welfare check—and through it all respecting the uniqueness of the client and her struggle. Worker characteristics of caring and flexibility—the interventions above and their corresponding outcomes—constitute the personal attributes and practice skills that yielded successful or effective outcomes.

The results point to the inadequacy of single theoretical approaches and interventions to address the multiple problems that these clients had experienced and wanted or needed help with. A single theoretical approach is insufficient to inform work with the various systems (intrapsychic, cognitive, environmental) that need to be addressed in order to reach a successful outcome with this clientele.

Let us look at J. J. once more. The eclectic approach employed for him used multiple programs (inpatient hospitalization and outpatient services): individual and group treatment, job apprenticeship, supervision and work referral, family therapy, parenting guidance, and child therapy. Caring workers who could see the intelligence and potential in this young man at all times accorded him dignity and hung in there with him, not allowing him to regress while keeping a positive and brighter future in front of him and emphasizing responsibility for self and family. Of note is the fact that an angry, fed-up judge set this recovery process in motion. His toughness sobered and frightened J. J., who did not want a life in prison, which is where he felt he was headed.

No effective outcome will result if clinicians do not believe in clients' capacity for change and hold out high expectations. Surprisingly, workers' professional power, control, and cultural indoctrination can drive them to focus on weakness and dysfunction. Clinicians, with and without graduate degrees, who had achieved mastery of traumatic experiences similar to those of overwhelmed clients manifested unusual empathy and served as role models. One clinician traced her experience from welfare recipient to service provider; another reflected on her own struggle with drug addiction and poverty; yet another had overcome a background of incest.

With the diversity of clientele, culturally sensitive approaches to clinical work are imperative. For example, a client stood at her window in the presence of her practitioner who had come to help her through a domestic crisis. Before any talking therapy took place, the practitioner respected the client's ritual of plant worship. Afterward, attention was given to the relational problem leading to the battering that precipitated this call for help, referring back to earlier issues and trying to help the young woman understand the seriousness of her problem and ongoing threats to her mental and physical well-being. The extra time in the home, a housing project, demanded an approach that required more than a fifty-minute hour. (One concern in this approach is the growing mandate for managed care and economic capping of services, prompting many practitioners and administrators to question future work with this clientele under time-driven clinical approaches.)

In another situation a young teenager referred for acting-out behavior was helped by his clinician, who understood that his problem was partly related to the institutional racism he was experiencing in school. One of the treatment goals, which was effectively achieved, was to teach him how to cope with racism The clinician used role play to reconstruct the teacher-student interaction and facilitate better anger management. By playing both roles, the student became more knowledgeable about the dimensions of the situation. In another instance, a clinician helped a teenage lesbian client address a sexual identity crisis and to deal with a relationship she was unprepared to handle.

Culturally sensitive approaches can be carried out by bilingual clinicians, who will be increasingly in demand as the client population becomes even further diversified. Agencies are already employing bilingual practitioners but comment that the supply of such workers is thin. Institutions that educate and prepare clinicians for practice must add language and communications skills to the curriculum.

Clinicians understood the saliency of education for this clientele. They knew that most clients could finish high school (most of them usually got to tenth to twelfth grade), and they encouraged them to pursue associate degrees. A tacit assumption was that the way out of welfare or other forms of dependency was education and job training. Yet they typically faced a systems dilemma: jobs were not forthcoming for their clients, and especially for their clients' male companions, and necessary social supports such as day care remain out of reach. This state of affairs perpetuates the stereotype of the unproductive, procreating recipient and judgments of immorality that blames clients for their entrapment when current unemployment and poverty policy narrow their options. Reforms in poverty policy and welfare will strengthen clinical effectiveness only if the change provides for useful work and thereby decreases the stigma related to unproductivity. Options for men must be included since reforms will not be effective if the earnings of mothers who work are taken away from them by the unemployed companions. A young client who was referred for treatment concerning her aggressive outbursts in the workplace was helped to pinpoint the major sources of her anger, incest and financial exploitation. She learned to control her anger and remained employed, but the pain was so deep-seated that scars remained.

In the absence of expansionary macroeconomics and a tight labor market, which would provide needed jobs for all sectors of the populace, young men in this needy population face a work resource vacuum;[32] in attempting to deal with their sense of powerlessness, they turn to empowering themselves through maladaptive processes. For example, peer pressure to join 20/20 clubs (twenty babies by the time one is twenty years old), and in the absence of a source of self-esteem such as that supplied by meaningful work and other productive ways of providing a sense of competence and mastery, will push teenagers and young men to deal with their sense of powerlessness and empower themselves through the number of babies they father. Peer and societal expectations must be modified to require more from them: completion of school, work competency, employment, and financial responsibility for themselves and their offspring.

With such opportunities, the playing field of men would be more level to that of women, who do receive welfare, job training, health care, and other services. But they too need jobs.

Justice-Based Clinical Work: A Model for Client and Community Change

Success or effective clinical outcome was more ensured when caring and flexible workers used the interventions of assessment, advocacy, empowerment, individual treatment, and group treatment in their work. Theories that were shown to drive and inform interventions were a combination of psychodynamic, cognitive-behavioral, family theory, systems theory, group theory, and others. Thus, the approach used effectively with this clientele is eclectic.

The specific outcomes of interventions include self-efficacy–personal mastery dimensions of clinical work, demonstrated by movement to minimal scapegoating, the use of personal power, increased self-esteem, more effective communication and parenting skills, improved health and personal hygiene, greater self-differentiation, greater self-sufficiency, and overall competence. Certain competence–behavior for action dimensions of clinical work were also demonstrated, such as effective coping, obtaining resources, making decisions, and pursuing personal goals. Others were making connections (with agencies, resources) and managing resources, including time (implying the need for structure). Together, these self-efficacy–personal mastery and competence–behavior for action dimensions provide for overall improved functioning and a higher level of life satisfaction (figure 1-1).

Given the determination of the workers and their capacity to motivate clients even with limited resources, there is potential for greater clinical success, providing that deficits in the community and neighborhood and in national policy can be addressed.

John Rawls suggests a way to test for our readiness and commitment to justice-based policies: If we would not choose to work and live as overwhelmed people do, then we must commit ourselves to whatever it takes to improve their lives.[33]

Justice-based policies are called for where corresponding and simultaneous attention is given to structural problems in the econ-

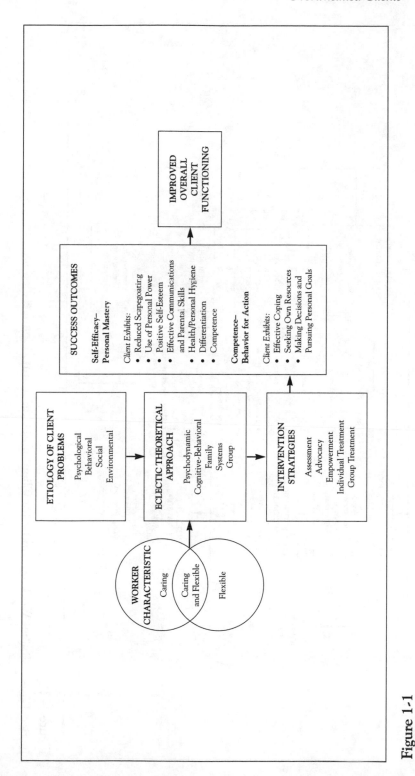

Figure 1-1
An Empirically Derived Model of Clinical Effectiveness in Work with Overwhelmed Clients

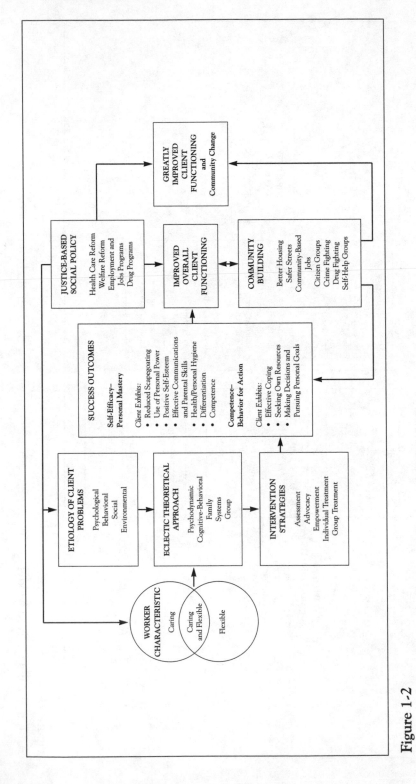

Figure 1-2
Justice-Based Clinical Work: A Model for Client and Community Change

omy, evidenced by the lack of jobs and other resources, which have a devastating impact on personal and family relationships as well as neighborhoods. Any serious national intervention must address problems faced by men (not only women) since their joblessness is a codeterminant of poverty.[34] In other words, whole neighborhoods and entire groups of people must be targeted for action.[35] At the same time, clinical work must be continued and expanded. Without community building that eliminates drugs, addresses the "uselessness" of unemployed men and joblessness of both men and women, refurbishes housing, and makes streets safe, the success formula outlined here will be compromised (figure 1-2).

A justice-based approach, whereby the system is required to redistribute more to this population and to their communities, will begin to neutralize the debilitating forces of joblessness, drugs, violent streets, and inadequate and uncoordinated services that compromise clinical work. Community building will empower clients to become shareholders in the community, and clinical work as a source of education and a force for enabling and promoting advocacy and empowerment becomes a facilitator of justice and equality, helping to bring the full stream of opportunity within grasp of those who grow stronger and less overwhelmed.

CHAPTER 2

The Environmental Context
for Clients

THE LARGE NUMBER OF DEBILITATING FORCES THAT CONSTITUTE THE context for clinical work—poor neighborhoods, social isolation, joblessness, and economic entrapment—produce major constraints to effectiveness.

The K's lived in a poor neighborhood where houses were rundown and many boarded up, streets littered, vacant lots filled with garbage and trash—a breeding ground for rats and other rodents. Yet some houses were well kept and some streets were presentable, showing pride that many residents still hold despite the overwhelming forces of blight and decline.

By contrast, J. J.'s family now resides in a modern facility in an inner-city neighborhood. The housing unit is clean and well maintained and also occupied by middle-income residents. In this blended family, children see their own father/stepfather and other fathers as participants in the labor force. This opportunity has been made possible not only by clinical intervention but also by environmental support.

Today most Americans participate in a multifaceted environment—encompassing work, school, home, and neighborhood. Central to all of these, with a pivotal influence on the others, is the work environment. Opportunity to participate in a productive work environment stems from one's educational experience, which itself is highly influenced by one's parents' work, residence, and access to opportunity for achievement. Residential environments tend to be stratified by social class, if not also by race, so that the people who reside therein tend to have similar backgrounds. Responsibility for community increasingly is viewed by those most capable of sharing and contributing as responsibility to their immediate neighbors rather than for the total good. As the wealthy and comfortable retreat into private habitats, public places do not fare as well, and public protection is not nearly as available or complete. Those with the capacity to buy what they wish may not share community or solidarity with others.[1] In contrast, few of the overwhelmed poor live in safe, secure environments. As cities continue to face mounting financial problems, they no longer can afford to deliver the protection or services that are needed.[2] The dollars passed to cities from the federal government declined from 18 percent in 1980 to 6.4 percent in 1990.[3]

The Environment of Overwhelmed Clients

Overwhelmed clients live in neighborhoods and go to schools characterized as poor, and often violent and unsafe. The buildings, streets, and sidewalks that are crumbling are the most visible problem and theoretically the easiest to correct. But there are others as well.

One is the decline, if not absence, of positive role models—of daily encounters with those who work hard, get their children off to school, and enjoy respect in the community. This rather recent phenomenon is a by-product of civil rights laws, fair housing legislation, and the push for nondiscrimination in housing and job markets that has led to an exodus of middle-class families of color from the old neighborhoods into suburban and exurban areas, both racially integrated and segregated. Many middle-class African Americans are moving to homogeneous areas. Middle-class Latinos and other people of color are following the same pattern of moving beyond the central city as soon as they can. The communities they left in the past had known sociological and economic—if not racial—diversity and stability. The so-called Old Heads—fathers and father surrogates who transmitted culture and socialized many youths to the values of work, family, community, and respect for laws—have become victims of social change.[4] The social organization of these communities changed as the former leadership was replaced by the young and rootless, who are often affiliated with the drug trade. Under these circumstances, practitioners in social agencies and mental health centers who work with this population find their roles very demanding. In this growing vacuum of leadership and positive examples, these professionals are among the scarce role models available.

An expanding culture of drugs, crime, and quick, dirty money is filling the vacuum of leadership and dedication to work, family, and community left in the absence of older, stable men.[5] One commentator writes that "the communities of the underclass are plagued by massive joblessness, flagrant and open lawlessness and low-achieving schools, and therefore tend to be avoided by outsiders. Consequently, the residents of these areas, whether women and children of welfare families or aggressive street criminals, have become increasingly isolated from mainstream patterns of behavior." Legitimate jobs are replaced by welfare and the underground economy.[6] The same author argues "that neighborhoods plagued with high levels of joblessness are more likely to experience problems of social organization. The two go hand in hand. High rates of joblessness trigger other problems in the neighborhood that diversely affect social organization, ranging from crime, gang violence, and drug trafficking to family break-ups and problems in the organization of family life."[7]

A director of professional services in one of the agencies participating in this study went to a middle school to review progress on services being offered to a client family. The student support worker at the school described a young boy who started dealing drugs for his mother when he was seven years old. The child had learned the trade and rationalized that the money was worth the risk taking with full knowledge of the potential for violence. Without supports and strong families to offer guidance to a child, a pattern of behavior develops. When similar patterns develop among families, multiplying from one block to the next, a new norm is created. Drugs mean fast money, and the otherwise scarce dollars provide the incentive that keeps the underground economy moving.

Historically in poor communities, folk can get money hustling goods, and not always illegally. But as examples of and opportunities for productive work have decreased, there is corresponding escalation into clearly illegal behavior: pimping, dealing drugs, stealing and dealing food stamps, and engaging in serious exploitative behavior such as armed robberies and street muggings. Incentives to sell drugs are stronger when opportunities for legitimate employment decrease.[8] Young men especially need to prove they can produce dollars. Regardless of the amount, the money-obtaining activity is costly in terms of increased drain on tax-supported services: police, rescue, ambulance, hospital, and court operations. Isolation is fueled by the underground economy, and vice versa. The cycle is hard to break. But for this population, there are few other employment options when in both good economic periods and bad ones the overall unemployment rate for African Americans has stood at roughly double the rate for whites.[9]

Legitimate businesses suffer in the face of gangs, crime, and vandalism, and most have boarded up and moved elsewhere, leaving residents without access to grocery or drug stores. Just as important as these blows to access and convenience is the loss of both low- and moderately skilled jobs that could build the legitimate economy, weaken the illegal economy, and reduce isolation. Despite program initiatives of the Nixon administration of the 1970s, businesses sponsored by blacks under black capitalism have fared no better than others in these neighborhoods.[10]

Clinical work under such circumstances—poor neighborhoods, a job vacuum, illegal activities, guns, violence, weakened formal and informal social control—taxes the psychological stamina of practitioners while requiring a repertoire of eclectic approaches. Use of interventions based on psychodynamic or cognitive theory alone could not bring the necessary focus to address drugs, illegal earnings, and street violence. In fact, clinical work today is even more difficult than it was during the time the K's were in treatment. Even then the men had guns. Vivian's clinician stated:

> When attention to Vivian and the offer of multiservices for her and the children angered her husband, Fred, Sr., because he felt left out, word reached the agency that he was threatening Vivian with a gun. It became the worker's task to approach him in order to convince him to get rid of the gun and to assure him of the agency's interest in him also.

Clinicians today are more physically vulnerable because of the arsenals stockpiled in overwhelmed communities. Some agencies in these neighborhoods, wary of those carrying guns, have limited walk-in access by installing buzzers. Most clinicians can escape this environment after work, but the clients live where the ring of gunfire and mayhem are constant and an ongoing threat, not just to mental health but to life itself. Clinicians helped clients with physical safety concerns and helped teenagers become aware of street knowledge and skills vital to their survival. In such a precarious environment, clinicians who are helping clients cope must direct attention to what clients can and cannot control. In one situation, a woman being treated for anxiety and depression who had been making observable progress was caught in gun crossfire. When she recovered from her injuries, her treatment had to begin all over again since the trauma had caused her to lose the ground she had recently gained.

Mean Streets and Decline in Authority

Streets are mean in overwhelmed communities. Juvenile homicide is high and continues to soar. One troubling projection suggests that greater numbers of brutal homicides will take place in the future due to a number of coalescing forces: major substance abuse among youth and adults, increasing rates of child maltreatment, greater access to guns, larger numbers of juveniles growing up in poverty, and

a projected resurgence in the number of juveniles. Of those juveniles who do kill, 85 percent are between ages fifteen and seventeen
years; fewer than 1 percent are under fifteen, although concern is
growing that youths under the age of fifteen are engaging in more violent crimes.[11] African Americans and Latinos are overrepresented
among those arrested for murder or nonnegligent manslaughter.

Too few agencies have directly targeted preventive services to this
youth cohort. One agency in the study was successful in organizing
female teen groups and preteen groups, but the males were all lost
by the time they reached age fifteen. In the struggle against gangs
and mean streets, the agency won little. Its next attempt is to organize mother and son activities and plan adult male groups that
might help attract teenagers.

Streets have a deadly pull that some cannot escape. Public housing areas are dense and harbor all manner of dysfunction. Although
only seven years old, Datrell Davis, a resident of Chicago's 7,000-
resident Cabrini-Green Housing Project, was experienced at running and hiding at the crack of gunfire. One October morning while
he walked to school with his mother, a sniper in a tenth-floor window pulled the trigger that took his life. The suspected gunman was
reportedly aiming for rival gang members when the first grader
walked in harm's way. The chairman of the city's housing authority
called for the National Guard to protect residents. Mayor Daley
opted for a police sweep of the project, stating, "We have seen a
complete breakdown of society."[12]

In clinical work, the violence that takes a toll on neighborhood
residents threatens to compromise outcome. In our study a nine-
year-old boy was referred by his teacher for withdrawn behavior following his father's sudden death; he was fearful of also losing his
mother. His clinician noted that the violence and recent shootings in
his community had exacerbated these fears so much that the child
was intensely preoccupied by them, and his anxiety was out of control. Resolving his loss of father became mandatory for his ability to
cope with his fears of violence. There was also work with the mother.

In desperation, residents of apartments in some of the poorest
neighborhoods in Brooklyn have turned to hiring private police,

who are reported to be as violent as the drug dealers they are expected to combat. One private crime fighting company, SSI Patrol Services, is licensed by New York's secretary of state. Its services are costly, and public funds have been allocated to purchase them. SSI is considered effective, based on records of arrests and first-hand reports from neighbors who describe how the guards have helped to reduce drug activity using tough action—reportedly violence and intimidation.[13]

In the absence of effective institutions—families, civic and community organizations, recreational facilities, businesses, shops, and churches—some authority is considered necessary to protect the young and to prevent increases in crime, especially homicide. In Atlanta, community breakdown became so severe that in November 1990, the city council voted to establish an 11:00 P.M. curfew for youth under age seventeen.[14] Loss of authority in contemporary society is a seriously undermining force. Nisbet sees it as the cause of societal atomization, fragmentation of community, the increase in unreason, and the decrease in respect for due process, privacy, and individual rights.[15]

Atlanta is not the only city where lack of familial authority has been exhibited. Dallas, for one, has moved to enact a curfew and in spring 1994 Orlando, Florida, established one. In Detroit, past Devil's Nights (Halloween Eve celebration) resulted in so many fires and extensive destruction of property that residents and police organized surveillance to help combat crime and deterioration.[16]

But a curfew is a quick fix; it does not address the need for deeper and more demanding work with the family. Both nurturance and moral education are needed if young people are to develop the capacity to function and participate in a democratic community. The breakdown in families and parental authority, like the absence of role models, adds yet more pressure to the role of practitioners who work with this population. As the primary contacts with these victimized, overwhelmed families, it is to them that families and clients turn for someone to function in loco parentis. They help explain culture, morality, and decency—expectations that citizens should respect.

One ten-year-old youngster whose single mother was unable to manage him in the family was referred for oppositional defiant behavior in school. Although he made rapid improvement in anger management, the ability to be empathic, and comfortable interactions with his teacher, his daily reality tempered these changes. His worker noted with concern his growing use of "stud" behavior, his eager anticipation of moving into a housing project so he could learn "new stuff" about fighting, his refusal to consider his behavior as bad and to care about breaking the law. He was angered by his social worker's efforts to find a summer camp for him. Claiming that she deceived him because his teacher promised he would have the summer off, he admitted wanting to "get back" at her for spoiling his summer.

The breakdown of familial authority that is characteristic of so many overwhelmed families stands out in a comparison of the form and functioning of families today with their seventeenth-century counterparts. Glaringly different in these two unlike family structure and process models are the socialization experiences of the young. In colonial times, the family constituted the basic unit for economic, political, and religious needs, and its relationships were based on authority. A new family ideal based on affection and mutual interest emerged in the twentieth century: the companionate family, which is thought to be the creation of professionals (legal scholars, social workers, educators, and social scientists). A direct outgrowth of this model is the family of today, labeled the minimal family, which is the product of two factors: steadily expanding consumption stimulated by a growing economy and the salience of egalitarian and democratic values as the basis for how people should behave toward one another.[17]

Industrialism's market economy was key in these changes. Its need for the market rather than family interdependence to be the source of meeting people's needs pushed private as well as public sectors toward policymaking that led to less connectedness between them and their families to allow for geographic and social mobility. Parents can no longer expect to be as authoritative as parents once were, nor can they expect to interpret the world or to prepare their children for it on the basis of their own skills, aptitudes, and past experience. The primary bases of interaction between child and parent have become love, intimacy, and emotional dependency, and these too frequently have become conditional. With no clear economic role and fewer opportunities to prove themselves, while at risk for losing love (because of its conditional nature), children now have fewer opportunities to build self-esteem.[18]

The goal of child rearing has moved from discipline directed toward obedience to one of socialization to encourage choice and flexibility. In middle- and upper-class communities, structures and family supports are stronger and more likely to be in place. When they are not, many of these well-off families are able to purchase guidance and structures, such as parental substitutes and programs that promote growth, development, and competence. Day care, camping, and after-school programs are valued and utilized. They are also pricey. Overwhelmed mothers, like middle-class mothers, also recognize the need for support. That is a reason why they become engaged with clinical services in the first place.

In an effort to learn street youths' perception of the issues confronting them, former Boston mayor Raymond Flynn held a series of meetings with some of the city's leading professionals and businessmen along with a group of high-risk street youth seventeen to twenty-five years old. The leaders noted the youths' connections to crime and drugs but especially their lack of access to role models, advocates, and structures to help them move on.[19] Some of those who could serve as role models are afraid to do so; they go home after work and lock up. A community activist explained recently that for the first time ever, she was afraid of "her people." Hard working, intensely committed to helping the community, and having raised two daughters, an engineer and a social worker, as a single, widowed mother, she obviously has much to give to troubled families.

Violence in neighborhoods where overwhelmed clients reside finds expression with individuals as well, manifest as suicidal attempts, among both young and older clients. One client, diagnosed as a borderline personality with delusions, had made at least thirteen serious suicide attempts and was only nineteen years old. In another situation, two young teenage girl lovers made a suicide pact and ran away from home. In this encounter, one was harmed (cut or stabbed) trying to block the partner's suicidal behavior.

Drugs

It is increasingly difficult to sort out the effects of drugs on the overwhelmed population in distressed neighborhoods. Drugs are a part of the quick-fix scene and widely available and used. Many poor, young people are especially attracted to and identify with what they view as success—athletes, stars, and other high-visibility personalities who flaunt drug usage. Drugs provide the illusion of security that many want, but in fact the population under discussion is the victim group. Yet even minimal participation in the drug trade gets them something in the short run: the sudden appearance of more money than they ever had for new clothes and gold jewelry, free drugs, and sometimes both, which they often share with their families. It takes them longer to see the victim status.

Overwhelmed clients describe to clinicians how extensive and widespread drug usage actually is and how for many its use constitutes a socially and psychologically acceptable pattern of behavior.[20] Drugs help mothers, lovers, and youths through treadmill days and nights. Peer pressure is exerted to keep neighbors and friends on drugs. Those trying to be drug free are often suspect, held in contempt, isolated, and treated as traitors. Will they tell public housing authorities, police, or social workers?

One client living in a housing project who was addicted to crack cocaine worked hard in her treatment sessions, using therapy and supportive services to become drug free. The social worker was available late nights and early mornings to offer support and guidance as the client went through the pain and agony of withdrawal in an effort to have a better future. Once drug free, this client's neighbors in the housing project said hurtful and accusatory things to her and put drugs under the door to her apartment and in the mailbox to tempt her. Her children were rejected by their friends under the influence of drug-hooked parents. The young woman resisted but knew she would eventually lose ground unless she moved to a new environment. The social worker helped facilitate a move to another apartment in another neighborhood, where she remains drug free. This courageous and lucky young woman was able to break out of an entrapping environment with help. She was also able to trust enough to use the available helping resources.

In another case, a social worker explained to a very young client the problems of crime and violence. The child responded that in his neighborhood "*drugs* are the big problem." Children see the devastating impact of drugs on their parents, older siblings, and neighbors. They know neglect first-hand because a mother is pumped up and spaced out, oblivious to their needs. They also know danger first-hand and that drugs and guns are an explosive combination.

Yet another example from the study illustrates how clients and their workers when dealing with drug-based problems suffer trauma and burnout. A Latino mother of a retarded fifteen-year-old daughter sought help when her daughter was raped. The mother, depressed and overwhelmed as a result of years of physical abuse, had murdered the child's father, a drug user. The mother served no time but had received no help to deal with the emotional consequences of her abuse and the murder. The worker invested extensively in resources and intervention strategies, and the daughter was placed in a residential center. There, failure to coordinate plans for home visits and family treatment resulted in the teenager's pregnancy. The mother received treatment for her rage and depression; this worker, and others, were burned out from attempting to cope with large caseloads of similar overburdening problems.

Improved Neighborhoods and Housing Options

Years ago it was observed that residents in some public housing units referred to the maintenance department as the "Maintain-Us" department. Initially, this was viewed as dialect, but one must question why so many used the term and whether it carried a more significant understanding of the depths of despair. In addition to being "maintained" in public housing units with all of its attendant crime, filth, and drugs, overwhelmed clients are also "maintained" by institutional welfare benefits. No one would deny that most residents would be even worse off without public housing and other forms of public assistance, but the debilitating aspects of these programs are nevertheless arguably a part of the problem today.

This situation presents major contradictions for clinical workers who work with these clients since in some instances their initial priority upon intake has to be to find housing and financial support. Often public housing, with all its attendant problems, including massive, segregated projects that isolate people by both race and social and economic strata, remains the only option. To set up an intervention program that would address their clients' needs entraps practitioners in a value dilemma: their task to help their clients cope better and improve the quality of their lives is compromised by the pathogenic options that are available. With options so limited for housing choice, clients' visions of possibilities in their lives are also narrowed. This was the case with the ten-year-old Puerto Rican youngster who wanted to "get back" at his teacher for "spoiling his summer" because she planned an enriching experience at summer camp for him; he looked forward to moving into a housing project despite its reputation as a breeder of crime in order to learn "new stuff" about fighting.

Given the interplay of drugs, guns, poor neighborhoods, and exodus of middle-class families, opportunities for neighborhood betterment and housing options are minimal. Limited access to credit prevents the purchase of homes or improvement of property by many people of color who reside in the community, and the consequences are evident in neighborhood blight and deterioration. Limited access to funds also obstructs the opportunity for some middle-class persons to stay, purchasing and supplying rental property. When property remains vacant and abandoned, crack dens have a greater chance of moving in. Although the terms of the Community Reinvestment Act of 1977 oblige banks to serve all neighborhoods in a given banking area, helping to meet the credit needs of all citizens, this is not the case. A Federal Reserve Bank study showed that African Americans and Latinos are twice as likely as Caucasians, with income held constant, to be turned down for mortgages.[21] In many cities, high-income African Americans have

more difficulty getting loans than lower-income whites. The dispari-
ties in rejection rates for blacks and whites are further convincing
evidence of the institutional racism that feeds into troubled neighborhoods.

Considering neighborhood conditions and financial constraints,
where can poor, overwhelmed clients expect to live? How can clinicians help improve the quality of these clients' lives under such conditions? From all indications, this society has moved away from
major tenets of the National Housing Act of 1949, which embraced
the goal of a "decent home and suitable living environment for every
American family." Since 1980, funds for federal housing programs
have been slashed by some 75 percent. By the mid-1980s, Section 8
rental assistance was the major resource for provision of housing for
low-income persons.[22] (Under this program tenants pay 30 percent
of the rental, with the remaining market rate subsidized by the government up to $1,000 per month.) However, a study that addressed
implementation of Section 8 in Boston determined that nearly half
of those with an eligibility certificate were unable to locate housing.
Those most likely to be successful were white, single mothers with
small families who did not have great expectations, voicing limited
preferences for better housing. Those least likely to be successful
were women of color who had several housing needs and high expectations for moving to a better environment. In other words,
those following the tradition of duplicating the public housing location pattern by not moving away from the poor area have the
highest success. Consequently, the conditions that Section 8 was designed to negate are perpetuated.[23] Still, Section 8 does allow for
flexibility when housing units are available and clinicians can successfully advocate for clients and help arrange financial supports.
This happened in J. J.'s case.

In poor neighborhoods, with poor housing and always at prey and
vulnerable to violence, it is small wonder that residents' self-esteem,
competence, and self-sufficiency are nourished at all. With greatly
reduced federal assistance for aid to cities for services and better
housing and documented discrimination in the banking industry,
which is the intended resource for critical loans to upgrade and ex-

pand housing for inner-city populations and joblessness, clients and clinicians are trapped. One solution is to document and validate the threat to family stability and individual mental health that is constituted by these poor neighborhoods, poor housing, high drug usage, violent streets, and lack of jobs—all connected in a circular reinforcing process. A way must be found to address these entrapping, isolating problems beyond the case-by-case approach.

Currently no interventions focused on community change are being undertaken. This is not to say that clients who have improved personal functioning do not contribute to stronger communities. They do. The point is that such improved functioning as was found in this study was not connected to community change nor was any agency demonstrating such a programmatic thrust. A focus on neighborhood and community change and rebuilding must gain greater attention.

Community-based program goals can be developed. One way is to rethink the use of practitioners' time, possibly allocating more to engaging neighborhood groups and community organizations in empowerment-oriented work.[24] Some practitioners may reside and raise families in these neighborhoods. They can, along with other natural leaders, join forces and push for drug education and violence reduction programs. Second, agencies must develop resources to facilitate neighborhood groups and community organizations. Funding from foundations can be important since many service contracts are case specific. Third, practitioners, agencies, foundations, and clients should join forces and advocate for gun control and jobs. During group discussions for this research, it was noted that youths are not likely to give up guns unless they have jobs to replace them. Marion Wright Edelman of the Children's Defense Fund stated, "Without adequate investment in jobs for youths and parents, we can neither end violence nor welfare as we know it."[25]

CHAPTER 3

The Context for Practitioners and Clients:
The Power Conundrum

NOT LONG AGO A SOCIAL WORK STUDENT IN A CLASS EXPLORING HOW to work with black families asked in desperation, "How do I help black families when I feel so helpless myself!" On another occasion a well-known family therapist made the comment: "The problem in working with Black families is that the therapists feel incompetent because they get as overwhelmed as the families."[1] The confusion and sense of entrapment manifested by these two social work practitioners has been a common response in work with overwhelmed clients.

In working with these clients, the issues of power and lack of power are indeed paramount, affecting practitioner and client, for power and powerlessness are critical factors in behavior at all levels of human functioning. Power and powerlessness relate to practitioner-client roles, cultural process, and the behavior of practitioners, overwhelmed clients, and their families.

Defining Power

Defining power makes clear its complexities and the various levels on which it exists: individual, interactive, family, group, and soci-

43

etal.[2] Wrong, Heller, and Pinderhughes define it as the capacity to produce intended and foreseen effects on others. Goodrich defines it as "the capacity to gain whatever resources are necessary to remove oneself from a condition of oppression, to guarantee one's ability to perform, and to affect not only one's own circumstances, but also more general circumstances outside one's intimate surroundings."[3] Power thus involves the capacity to influence for one's own benefit the forces that affect one's life space; powerlessness is the inability to exert such influence.

Power is gratifying.[4] Basch has stated that "the feeling of controlling one's destiny to some reasonable extent is the essential psychological component of all aspects of life."[5] This means that a sense of power is critical to mental health. Everyone needs it, and everyone strives to acquire it in some way. Powerlessness is painful, and people defend against feeling powerless by behavior that can bring them a sense of power.[6]

Experiences of having or lacking power occur in many areas of people's lives. Power (or lack of it) is a systemic phenomenon, a key factor in human functioning, from the individual level, where "submission to power is . . . the earliest and most formative experience in human life,"[7] to all other levels, including family, group, social role, and cultural adaptation.[8] Power thus is internal, being manifest in a sense of mastery or competence on an individual level, and external, being manifest on environmental levels. And since power and powerlessness operate systemically, transacting both macrosystem and microsystem processes,[9] the existence or nonexistence of power on one level of human functioning (for example the interactional) affects and is affected by its existence or nonexistence on intrapsychic, familial, community-ethnic-cultural, and societal levels.[10] For example, the power that exists in the interaction between people is reflected in dominance-subordination or equality. These styles of relationship in turn are affected by role assignment related to status within one's group or within the larger society and by the value attributed to that role. Power or lack of power emanating from cultural group status assignment and from the status assignment of other groups from which one derives identity and meaning (sex role, sexual orientation, class status, etc.) thus become factors in the dynamics of relationships.

Within families, other groups, and organizations, the power dimension also exists in terms of authority, decision making, and control and is similarly affected by systemic processes. Historically, the provider role in families has been joined with that of authority-decision maker. In most white families, this has been the primary province of the male, whose power in relation to others in the past could be threatened only by other men above him in rank.[11] In other cultural groups, by contrast, for example in many African-American families, the female role has been endowed with more power. African-American women have contributed proportionately more as providers than their white counterparts and thus have been accorded higher status within the family. Problems related to employment access (or lack of it) have also served to undermine the male. At the same time, the subjugation of both the white female and the African-American male, along with the manipulation of the African-American female, have served to consolidate the power of the white male as dominant in both his family and the social system. Although that dominant position is being challenged by the movement of women into politics and commerce, it remains well entrenched.

In other groups of color, the female role has not been as dominant as in the case of African Americans. Moreover, American discrimination and traditional role subjugation operate in such a way that their realities are vastly different from those of the white female:

> The situation for women of color is worse and more hopeless than for white women. White women may have been excluded from the financial and power centers, but many have enjoyed derived power and material gains in their roles as daughters, wives, and mothers and thus are reluctant to face change. Although the problem of sexism is still prevalent, changes are occurring that have enabled white women to move well ahead of all people of color. The double income earned by white families widens this gap. Thus, women of color are in multiple jeopardy, facing as they do the combined forces of racism, sexism, and in many cases, poverty.

What this means is that more white women are in a socially advanta-
geous position. Because of their individual and collective relationships
to the power structure, they are able to exercise leverage that people of
color, regardless of their gender, do not have.[12]

Yet another example is the power dimension on the societal level
whereby poverty has functioned to control and victimize large
groups of people, many of them overwhelmed clients.

Power is also implicit in the practitioner role. Derived from the
professional mandate that endows that role with knowledge and expertise, and the privilege to manifest both in practice, this license to
diagnose, teach, and treat establishes a clear power differential between practitioner and client. Effective outcome and empowerment
for the client who comes in in a state of powerlessness because he
cannot solve his problem requires clinical activity that can neutralize and equalize this inequity in power.[13]

Power, Practitioner Entrapment,
and Need to Control

The complexity of issues to be addressed, the depth of need to be
met, given clients' usual economic, emotional, and psychological deprivation, the growing societal constraints and blocks that bar access to the resources that overwhelmed clients need, can push
practitioners into feeling as overwhelmed as those they seek to help.
The energy needed to deal with these constraints and to extend
themselves in order to join their clients, plus the effort needed to
present themselves as empathic and eager to be of assistance, to
convince clients that they as practitioners are trustworthy and de-
pendable, easily generate a sense of entrapment, anxiety, and fatigue. One practitioner described her fear of her clients' pain and
awesome realities: "I was really afraid to be important to her. I was
afraid to see her pain and experience it with her. I was afraid if I got
too close, I'd feel the helplessness of her life and become as immobilized by it as she was."[14]

At such times there is real susceptibility to overinvolvement.
Consider the effort, energy, and commitment required to intervene
with the K family. Convincing them initially that the agency was in-

terested in the family required six months of outreach. There were failed agency appointments, and home visits as an alternative, so that help, once trust was developed, could be extended to every family member who expressed a need. And this help embodied persistence in working with them despite repeated failures to follow through with services that they requested: the long-time preparation of Vivian for the weight loss program she wanted (which required hospitalization for evaluation and regulation of diet and exercise) and which she thwarted by having relatives secretly bring in snacks; working intensively with rejecting, disapproving teachers who had written off Vivian's children in order to engender from schools and teachers more support and positive expectations; offering support to Fred when attention to Vivian and other family members mobilized such jealousy that he was threatening them with a gun; assistance with parenting and impulse control so that Vivian could manage the children, especially Freddy, without being abusive; counseling for the intensely negative relationship that existed between Vivian and Fred, and between Lela and Vivian, whose jealousy of Lela was based on her belief that Lela had sexually seduced Fred (she even claimed that Lela's child was fathered by Fred); assistance for Vivian in securing medication for depression and in complying with the doctor's instructions; assistance to Winona for alcoholism treatment and job referral, and referrals for Lela and Manny to psychiatric treatment and job training, referral (and support for follow-through), for the children to after-school programs and special education programs, and others. That such extensive activity, especially in the face of very limited gains, might generate for the practitioner anxiety, fatigue, and a sense of entrapment should not be surprising.

Under such circumstances, the unaware practitioner can be seduced by the client's reality into behavior that compounds the entrapment. At close range, perspective may be lost compromising the assessment process. Anxiety aroused by recognition of clients' overwhelming needs and limited external resources can press the practitioner into self-comforting behavior that will ease his or her own anxiety, allowing rescue fantasies to take hold. One could ask, for example, whether the interventions with the K's, in which the workers were so involved, were illustrations of conscientious practice or worker-rescuing behavior. Moreover, despite repeated requests of different family members—for assistance with job training, schooling, health care (weight loss), and alcoholism treatment—such services when offered were not used; yet the agency continued to work with the family, possibly giving the message that no change was really expected. Rescue behavior is not only reinforced by practitioner anxiety and sense of powerlessness stemming from the effect of systemic processes upon the client; it can be doubly determined if the practitioner has an exaggerated personal need to be helpful, that is, to be in control. The need for a sense of power is universal, but it creates for every practitioner a vulnerability to exploiting the intervention activity for such personal need. When there is exaggerated practitioner need for power or control, such as when it grows out of developmental experience or reference group role, that vulnerability is compounded. Pleasure or gratification will be sought in the clients' apparent need for the practitioner's expertise. A sense of power and comfort will be sought through the demonstration of that expertise, and it will be used to ease the discomfort concerning the client's reality and any general sense of entrapment about the work.

Practitioners who are middle class, white, and male or who occupy any ongoing powerful social role are far more vulnerable to engaging in rescue behavior and to using their clinical activity with clients who are poor, female, of ethnic minority, to relieve personal discomfort than we may think. Both groups, those in more powerful social roles and those in less powerful ones, are trapped in a societal process that victimizes the client while automatically conferring benefits on the practitioner, making their encounter in the clinical process one that can reinforce their power differential roles.[15] Bowen defines this process as one in which the dominant group in a society, through perceiving another group (the victims) as inferior or incompetent, is able to enhance its own functioning while reducing tension and relieving anxiety in themselves. Identified as victims of the societal projection process are delinquents, mental patients, alcoholics, minorities, and the poor. Bowen comments:

These groups fit the best criteria for long-term, anxiety relieving projection. They are vulnerable to become the pitiful objects of the benevolent, over-sympathetic segment of society that improves its functioning at the expense of the pitiful. Just as the least adequate child in a family can become more impaired when he becomes an object of pity and oversympathetic help from the family, so can the lowest segment of society be chronically impaired by the very attention designed to help. No matter how good the principle behind such programs, it is essentially impossible to implement them without the built-in complications of the projection process. Such programs attract workers who are over-sympathetic with less fortunate people. They automatically put the recipients in a "one down," inferior position and they either keep them there or get angry at them.[16]

Thus, overwhelmed clients, large numbers of whom are poor and minority and whose problems identify them as substance abusers, delinquents, mental patients, or prisoners, constitute victim groups whose relatively powerless positions require them to serve as a balancing mechanism for the systems in which they and the practitioner exist. In being excluded and kept separate and in being the recipient of much of the tension, conflict, contradiction, and confusion that exists within the system, they provide stability for the dominant group. For confirmation we need only to look at ghetto communities and suburbs, prisoners and jailers, some mental patients and caregivers. Practitioners thus must ask about the extent to which the mere presence of their victim client serves to reduce anxiety and relieve tension for themselves as beneficiaries in this process. They must also ask whether their efforts to help clients do not instead actually maintain the social system equilibrium that victimizes their clients. For example, by not engaging in the necessary documentation or advocacy that leads to community building for betterment of the environment, jobs, and good schools that can free clients from their systemic entrapment, are not practitioners who are working with this population reinforcing instead while benefiting personally and professionally?

The operation of the societal projection process can further press practitioners whose repeated encounters with overwhelmed clients and their complex realities do spell exhaustion and burnout, to exploit their clients for personal need. When behavior is calculated to ease the practitioner's discomfort, sense of anxiety, and sense of powerlessness and fails to address the client's need, the client is disempowered and victimized. In one instance, a professional dealt with a personal sense of burnout and powerlessness in relation to the complexity and exhausting demands of the overwhelmed client caseload through inappropriate romantic behavior with a client, who reported the behavior. But such dynamics can go unchecked and, worse, unrecognized. To face the gravity of the client's situation and the seeming intractability that it embodies also forces the practitioner who exists at the nexus of two worlds, living with haves but working with have-nots, to cope with the tension and guilt that stems from the contradictions implicit in the two environments. Exhausting to many practitioners, such dilemmas push them to use the clinical encounter to ease their sense of personal discomfort. Under these circumstances, the power embodied in the practitioner role exists no longer primarily for the benefit of the client. The practitioner, in the role of helper and the powerful one, is automatically placed in the position of being able to manipulate the clinical process to suit personal needs. This means that personal need for power and esteem that is not adequately met elsewhere in the practitioner's life may be addressed through the clinical relationship or process. When this kind of activity does occur, power that intends to enhance the image of the practitioner can be the most infamous of therapy abuse.[17]

Although the clients showed little progress, a widely known practitioner respected for her theoretical expertise tended to maintain clients on her caseload for extensive periods—as long as ten years. In this situation cited above, the worker clung to her overwhelmed clients, seeing them as character-disordered dysfunctionals, while she herself was seen by colleagues as using her clients to relieve anxiety and guilt related to being white and affluent. At the same time, she was using her cultural group identity as white and upper middle class and her professional status to provide a sense of power, entitlement, and expertise that satisfied some personal need. When these privileged positions mobilize anxiety to the degree that practitioner need for comfort becomes a driving force to ease personal anxiety, practitioner power, time, money, and expertise can be as harmful as they can be useful. Practitioners must learn to manage the pain of their clients' realities, discomfort concerning their own more privileged position, and their own power needs so that they do not further victimize or disempower their already disempowered clients.

When the relationship between the practitioner and the client is a cross-cultural one, all of these dynamics can become compounded since the power (or lack of power) embodied in the clinical role is reinforced by that implicit in the cultural group role of practitioner and client. The power implicit in the helper role can then be reinforced by the aggrandizement that is associated with his or her cultural group identity. In the case of the K's, the cultural variable was not exclusively race or ethnicity but social class. Several of the practitioners were African American, and all were middle or upper middle class. The practitioners saw Ella's loss of her capacity to work and taking to her bed as clearly associated with their intervention; the attention directed to her because she was viewed as pivotal in the family's negative view of itself had caused her to regress and give in to strong dependency needs that were mobilized by the work. Then her behavior became consistent with the role of poor, dependent, black female.

Power becomes not only significant to the creation and maintenance of those designations of cultural group belonging and the value assigned; it is also critical in the value assigned to roles on other levels of human functioning, which are directly affected through systemic process. The degree to which individuals, families, and groups perceive themselves as having or lacking power is critical to their manner of functioning. Thus cultural group status, which is a direct consequence of power, affects these other levels of functioning (and vice versa), becoming a factor in such self-perceptions.

Power and Powerlessness
in Overwhelmed Client Families

Powerlessness is significant in individual and family functioning, and on both levels its dynamics are similar. A major factor affecting a family's sense of power and mastery is its fit with the environment. When there is a good fit, the environment offers support, security, protection, and supplies, and in using them the family can create for itself an effective organization that enables members to reach individual and group goals. When the fit is poor and support is lacking, the family must compensate. The traditional source of compensation for many families has been the extended family and the neighborhood, which often includes the church. When these have been absent or deficient or when other supports have been nonexistent, the family has been forced to rely on its own inner resources. Being isolated and with few, if any, supports creates extreme stress for families, with a profound effect on all aspects of their functioning: their values and beliefs, how they relate to family members and other societal institutions, rules, role relationships, and communication patterns. Values are the standards that guide behavior. When families and groups must cope consistently with powerlessness, they embrace values that ease their frustration, such as conflict, instant gratification, trickiness, cleverness, and beating the system, and give them a sense of power, as manifested by the K family and J. J.

Other values ease frustration and bring a sense of power: fatalism, high spirituality, living for today (since the past is seen as painful and the future hopeless), and cooperation (bonding together to achieve some sense of power). When the stresses become extreme and families are totally overwhelmed, they learn to function in an autonomous fashion. This comes not from an expectation or intention to achieve self-actualization and realization but from a sense of aloneness, with no help anywhere. Other values that families (and groups) must contend consistently with are strength, toughness, struggle, cunning, and power itself.[18] Dominating behaviors, bravado, and gun toting become valued; when exercised by the young, inexperienced individuals and gangs, mean streets became the norm.

Many groups that are struggling to overcome isolation, oppression, and poverty have embraced these other values. Although they enable survival and convey a sense of power, some of them—autonomy, fatalism, struggle, toughness, and power—create other problems since they do not tend to encourage harmony, cooperation, and the working together that is necessary for effective family group and neighborhood functioning. Rather, they make the family or group process vulnerable to conflict and dysfunction. Again the K family is instructive. Conflict in relationships, despite family members' affection for one another, was rife. Additionally, Ella's control of the family, Winona's alcoholism, Vivian's eating disorder, Manny's striking out could be seen as maladaptive attempts to exert some sense of personal power. The isolation of the family fed into its boundary rigidity; there was little effective connection between the family and any supportive system.

Especially significant is the lack of connection or access to an employment system. The K family also exhibited a deficiency in the capacity for work. Although the grandmother, Ella, was employed in the beginning of the contact, other family members did not use her as a role model, relying instead on public aid and falling more deeply into a dependency pattern in which practitioners colluded by undermining her capacity to work and reinforcing her tendency to give in to her dependency needs.

Family boundaries can easily become dysfunctional due to the powerlessness stemming from external sources and members' societal roles. As the family closes off to protect itself from the noxious external influences, it becomes vulnerable to isolation and rigidity, which means that even if there is a source of support, the family cannot or will not use it. The isolation of the K's was apparent in their lack of connection with persons outside the family and their refusal to interact with the neighborhood. They even kept their shades drawn all day. There can also be the opposite effect, whereby boundaries become extremely open when the family struggles to extract some nutrients from the external environment and this results in the family's inability to keep out destructive forces. J. J. had no family as a result of his mother's death and sister's addiction and turned to a gang.

Most of the clients in this study are women of color. A special caution on the role of women must be noted. In their multiple powerless roles—as women, as minority, and as poor—these women experience realities that embody unique complexities and constraints. Not only must they cope with the confusion and contradiction inherent in their position as members of a minority cultural group that functions at the boundary of society, but they also must cope with the traditional woman's role of nurturer and supporter of others. This role pushes them to compensate for societal undermining of the minority male in their traditional role of provider and protector by fulfilling the roles from which they have been blocked. At the same time, minority women are expected to nurture and to cope with their reactive anger, as well as to nurture and support their children's efforts to thrive in a hostile environment—very stressful expectations. One client, frustrated because her husband could not find work and was beginning to drink and become depressed, was pushed to compensate by procuring resources for the family from an agency. When her efforts to get food and more adequate housing met with resistance from the agency's resource contact and she found her energy so depleted that she was unable even to help her children with their school difficulties, she became even more depressed. But instead of withdrawing and becoming passive as do so many overwhelmed clients, she attacked the punitive agency response, yelling, "I'm tired of feeding my family potatoes and onions with ox water [bouillon] over them."

Women are often expected to relieve tension and reduce anxiety within their families, but minority women generally have fewer material resources with which to do so. Furthermore, the beneficiaries of their nurturing and supporting efforts, their mates and children, have far greater need of their services because of the effects on them, both as a family and as individuals, of the structural limitations imposed by society and the overwhelmed isolated communities in which they live.

In understanding their role of systems balancers in the larger social systems, the subtleties and nuances characteristic of the realities experienced by various people of color groups must always be kept in mind. For example, while entrapped in the overfunctioning role, African-American women have historically had more power in relation to their men than Latina women. Further, African-American women, who historically had closer affiliation to the labor market, have not experienced the same value conflicts concerning work as white or Latina women. Latina women, and Native American women, deserted by men, widowed, or single parenting by choice, may find raising a male child alone a formidable task. A Latino mother faced with rearing her son alone after the murder of her lover could not cope with the demands at hand. Because of her feelings of inadequacy, she sought the social worker's intervention to place her son in residential treatment.

Low self-esteem is a major consequence of the overwhelmed client's position that reinforces powerlessness and victimization and requires practitioner intervention. Limited opportunity to participate in power-negotiated arrangements, along with feeling no control or sense of power, reinforce poor self-concept. Self-esteem and self-worth are manifested in competence, resilience, a sense of control over events, a sense of significance, a notion of self as attractive and approved of by others, and finally by the capacity to test reality and evaluate the self.

Self-esteem can be seriously undermined by poverty. For clients who sustain poor mastery of life tasks and are trapped in dependency, the lack of opportunities to develop a sense of competence inevitably leads to poor self-esteem. Limited role options are barriers to opportunity for developing mastery and skills. Additionally, living and being forced to participate in communities where they are always at prey and vulnerable to rape, stabbing, gunshot wounds, murder, beatings, or self-destructive drug and alcohol activity severely compromise positive self-esteem.

Those who are very poor can have difficulty acquiring the necessities that help them to act, look, and feel attractive. Societal isolation and the poverty of many overwhelmed clients means that primary sources of communication to the outside world are limited. Positive reinforcement is not forthcoming from the outside world, which finds its stereotypes of this population hard to give up. It is for this reason that debates concerning welfare reform are so highly charged.

Low self-esteem is tenacious, creating a vicious cycle whereby low expectation leads to diminished effort, pessimism, and apathy, which are seen by the self and others as indicative of inferior ability.[19] In reality the social and economic isolation so characteristic of the circumstances of overwhelmed clients blocks their access to supportive systems, leaving them exposed to debilitating, destructive systems that are permeated by drugs and crime. In this type of environment, self-esteem is more readily eroded. Low self-esteem presses people to attribute failure to internal causes (lack of ability), blaming themselves and pushing them to put in less effort because they have lower expectations of success. Ella, the grandmother in the K family, demonstrated the family's extremely low level of self-esteem in describing her husband and the family they produced: "Nothin' from nothin' equals nothin'." J. J. said; "I had nothin'—nothin' to do and nothin' to lose."

Poor self-esteem helps maintain depression, self-defeating behaviors, and psychiatric problems, all of them common within this population group and represented in the overwhelmed client sample.

Mediating factors in poor self-esteem development are supportive family, neighborhoods, jobs, churches, and other networks. In the absence or near absence of these, clinicians become substitutes. A client struggled with a negative sense of self-worth by her drug-dealing, addicted husband. Her questioning of his source of income made him angry. His reactive complaints about the household, her child-rearing practice, and her attractiveness caused her to doubt herself, attractive and competent though she was. Her isolation, because of her husband's need to protect his drug-dealing activities and the absence of family, reinforced her self-view. Finally, with the help of a friend, she left her husband and secured help from the agency. With support, she clarified her thinking about the relationship and her future and the child's future. Stronger and not overwhelmed, she left the marriage, went back to school (with help from AFDC and job training), and is now employed, with plans to move away from the inner city.

Dynamics of Culture and Power

In becoming systems balancers and tension relievers in the social system, overwhelmed clients must learn to live with stress, conflict, and contradiction. They must find ways to cope with a sense of powerlessness. Coping responses vary from time to time and from overwhelmed client to overwhelmed client, but they become the essence of the culture that the group develops. And since culture represents people's response to the political, economic, and social realities they face, these responses, which take the form of values, social roles, norms, and family styles, grow out of people's efforts to get a sense of power. Such an understanding of culture and power allows appreciation for the creativity and complexity involved in cultural responses. The many variations, often subtle and elusive, that characterize rich and varied cultural differences then become understood in terms of the strength they embody. For example, overwhelmed clients frequently are manipulative, oppositional, passive-aggressive, or autonomous, often viewed as stubbornness; they use reaction formation (demonstrating behavior that is opposite to what is felt), are overcontrolling or dominating, or they strike out, often seen as violence. All of these responses could be observed in both the K and J families.

The K family is again instructive. As African Americans, their situation of poverty and lack of access was responded to by behaviors calculated to bring them some sense of power: by becoming overly dependent and extremely manipulative, as demonstrated in their long-term connection to welfare, dependency on alcoholism, and manipulation of practitioners. In the case of Winona's alcoholism, there were requests for assistance and efforts to enroll her in substance abuse programs, with which she never followed through. Similar observations were noted in relation to referrals for jobs and job training, enrollment (and even hospitalization) in weight loss programs, and joining a mother's parenting group.

A client in this study who was incapacitated after an illness, from which full recovery was expected, received assistance from an agency that included services in the home. For a period of time, several professionals were involved, and a continuing pattern developed: each morning, she was assisted to the living room couch by her employed husband; later in the day, more helpers would arrive, to counsel and assist her; even later, neighbors sat with and checked on her. She obviously was enjoying the attention and the sense of power she experienced.

Pinderhughes suggests that poor people frequently use manipulation. A social worker describes the lessons in manipulation she learned from her client:

My client educated me on survival mechanisms in poor neighborhoods. "You get a buck any way you can," she told me. I had found myself worrying about the games she played with people because I could see the trouble she could get into. I was also getting overwhelmed by her manipulation with me; she would tell me horrendous stories of seemingly unsolvable problems, and I stayed overwhelmed.[20]

Another practitioner discusses her understanding of the adaptive use of manipulation:

I was no longer worried about the games my client played with people and the trouble she might get into because I was able to validate her behavior of manipulation as adaptive to the powerlessness she experienced and at the same time to show her the price it cost her.

I could see the pervasive powerlessness of my client meant that with few choices externally and an internal sense of being powerless, the one choice she had was to say "no" to me. And thus I could wait patiently sending messages that she could return whenever she was ready.[21]

Another practitioner who described her battle with a poor black client noted her client's adaptation to poverty, the stressful family situation, and her contradictory behavior; the client refused to use available preventive sources (which included support, medication follow-up, socialization, and skills training) but persisted in using hospitalization and her family in a kind of revolving door solution:

The client would arrive in crisis at the hospital when she had to get away from the stress of the family and, after a brief stay, would then demand to be released because she now felt her family needed her. . . .

I entered the treatment arena with her, armed with my problem solving strategies, my individualistic values and need for success. And she retaliated by "yessing" me to death, undermining any constructive plans we made, being as withholding as possible and intensely determined not to let me help. What I didn't see was that by this behavior she was enabling herself to feel as empowered as she knew how to be. I couldn't see that. Caught as we were in this paradox, neither of us found satisfaction in our relationship. My goal was to help her stay healthy and hers was to maintain her cyclical pattern. I could not understand why she kept up such destructive patterns; it made perfect sense to me that she'd stay out of the hospital. Evidently my goal was just that—my goal, not hers. She had absolutely no desire to change her pattern of living and I honestly believed she gained quite a sense of satisfaction that I was running around, beating my head against the wall and getting nowhere. She even *told* me that she had no intention of changing, but I didn't believe her. I needed to believe that I could step in and change her life to the way it "should" be. No wonder we got nowhere.[22]

These behaviors serve a useful purpose—easing the pain and helplessness endemic to the state of powerlessness and conveying some sense of power—but they block the capacity to act affirmatively instead of react, to take initiative, or to assume leadership and responsibility for one's self, in one's family, and in one's community.

Another behavior that brings a sense of power but extracts a costly toll is that of identification with the aggressor. The price it exacts is that of self-hatred. Overwhelmed clients even assume stereotyped projections upon themselves such as being dependent, incompetent, crazy, being a stud or a "sapphire" (read: bitch) or, as in the case of youngsters in school, playing dumb in an attempt to gain some sense of power. Sometimes they believe such behavior is necessary to extract resources from the social system. Years ago, McClelland noted that dependency is not a state that anyone desires but is embraced primarily to get a sense of power and to be close to persons who actually possess power.[23] Overwhelmed clients may also get a sense of power by embracing negative attributions upon themselves in an exaggerated way—being a super-stud, super-crazy, super-dumb, super-helpless—and then valuing such behaviors positively. The 20-20 club noted earlier is a manifestation of the super-stud syndrome. The sense of power that people experience in using this exaggerated behavior derives from the fact that the stereotype they are powerless to change is responded to in a way that stems from *their* initiative. For example, one client told her social worker that she advised her son, "If you are going to be a sonofabitch, be the best damn sonofabitch there is." He followed this advice, to the extent of becoming a criminal and overdosing on drugs. The K family evidenced super-helplessness; J. J. too manifested super-dependency and super-thievery.

Chestang's early formulations about African Americans' response to oppression explain these dynamics.[24] He discusses how blacks often turn powerlessness into power by using such responses as aggressive accommodation and aggressive passivity (responses characterized by an exaggeration of the behavior that is accommodating, to the state of being powerless) and victory in having pride as opposed to pride in having victory. These mechanisms, he suggested, are used to defend against the inconsistency, injustice, and oppression faced by powerless people. For adequately functioning African Americans, such behavior "results in a psychological unity."[25] Humor, paradox, and subtlety are also adaptations to their powerless roles, which assist them in managing large amounts of rage and negative feeling while simultaneously struggling to maintain affectionate relationships and family solidarity.

Openness, mutuality, reciprocity, and self-disclosure are strategies practitioners need for work with overwhelmed clients. They require practitioners to be patient, flexible, and comfortable with themselves and with persons whose values may differ from theirs. The ability is needed to be patient with the tendency of overwhelmed clients to size up and check out practitioners, testing them to prove their trustworthiness, competence to do the work, and capacity to understand where the client is coming from. For practitioners who need the power embodied in their clinical and societal roles, being tested on interpersonal competence will be intolerable; having to engage in a family-like relationship will be unacceptable. These behaviors require an alteration of the power inherent in these clinical roles.

Self-disclosure is a way of equalizing the relationship, of assuming a nonpower, nonhierarchical stance. It is often necessary for work with clients who bring experiences of rejection, denigration, and deprivation, a consequence of societal and family dynamics. Competence is determined by practitioners' ability to diminish the perceived power differential between themselves and the client, where the client can see himself or herself as a peer and collaborator. Failure to develop these capacities means practitioners are exploiting their clients and using them to protect themselves.

Practitioners who use stereotypical thinking cannot focus on strengths because stereotypes usually prompt them to have low expectations of their clients. To expect incompetence or deficiency can be deadly, for it can seduce clients into adopting behavior consistent with such expectations, thus setting in motion the process of the self-fulfilling prophecy. Expectation is the key not only to recognizing strength but also to bringing about change. Only if clinicians believe a client can change can they hold out high expectations. Such a belief can be maintained only when practitioners are free of stereotypical perceptions of clients that are based on their own societal roles and on their own need to maintain them.

A focus on strengths in work with populations whose realities have forced them to cope with extreme powerlessness credits their struggle to survive the contradictions inherent in their societal position and conveys the message that the solutions they have sought to their problems show how hard they have worked to do the best they can. Identifying strengths and relabeling certain behaviors, such as opposition, stubbornness, reaction formation, passive aggression, manipulation, domination, striking back, and even dependency and passivity, as maneuvers to be strong give credit to the adaptability, creativity, and resilience that the use of these mechanisms can represent.

For example, relabeling a black mother's controlling behavior, her overly central role that made her children feel smothered (but which she used to compensate for the failure of support systems to do their job) as an exhausting yet heroic effort to organize her family enhances her strength.

Telling a Puerto Rican wife who was tolerating abuse that she is trying too hard to show her love reduces victimization. Similarly, suggesting to an underfunctioning father that in the face of a disorganizing, nonsupportive, even racist external system, his backing off and leaving may be his way to reduce stress in the family can reinforce positive family interaction; and while it shows how much he cares and wants to make things better for his family, his family needs him to be more involved.

With a focus on strengths and adaptations, clients can learn that in some instances it is not they or their adaptive mechanisms that are at fault but the degree to which these have become exaggerated and the inflexibility that marks their use. Hard work, toughness, struggle, strength, persistence, determination, adaptability, creativity, and caution may be critical strategies for managing their oppressive societal position. Under stress, however, adaptability can easily slip into inconsistency, toughness and strength into abuse and power behavior, persistence into stubbornness, caution into immobilization, and hard work into driven dedication.

Class in Client-Practitioner Interactions

Client-practitioner interaction is keenly affected by both parties' cultural backgrounds in which the dynamics of power play a role. Class status and position based on economic resources also greatly influence communication style. We know, for example, that upper-middle-class clients tend to be more facile and comfortable in communication, more readily focusing on feelings and ideas, and because of this are viewed as ideal clients by practitioners.[26]

The power differential between middle-class client and practitioner exists to a lesser degree than that between the practitioner and the poor client. With their similarity in outlook, the middle-class practitioner and middle-class client are usually able to move more readily to problem identification and problem solving. By contrast, the situation of overwhelmed client and practitioner differs greatly. Although there is considerable economic disparity among them, nearly all practitioners subscribe to middle-class values. This means that more time and more effort and negotiation in the beginning phase of the professional encounter may be needed to reduce or bridge differences in values, life, orientation, to build trust, and to reach clients from poor backgrounds. Some practitioners can work with no clients other than those who are overwhelmed; others can never work with overwhelmed clients. The task for the profession is to help both practitioner types understand the sources of their motivation and ensure that their personal power needs do not undermine the professional role. Personal self-knowledge, achieved through professional clinical education, practice wisdom, continuing education, and scientific evaluation of one's own practice, as well as through reflection and assessment, can help the practitioner to keep the goal of client progress uppermost.[27]

Practitioners who are self-aware and understand their own cultural biases, including their power needs and responses, will have no problem in considering environmental support or insufficiency as a factor in the etiology of the problem to be addressed. The stresses related to deprived minority group status are frequently related to socioeconomic factors, not cultural ones. Practitioners must recognize the effects of the societal projection process on both their minority clients and themselves. Knowledge of these realities will not threaten and immobilize them. Relationships to the wider society will be assessed to determine the degree of exposure to negative valuation (and thus to the hazards of developing feelings of powerlessness) that can occur as a consequence of cultural group membership. Central to the goals of overwhelmed client empowerment are strategies that enable clients to exert their own power to secure needed resources.

Given the seductiveness of the power intrinsic to the practitioner role, the vicissitudes faced by clients in their paradoxical societal position, and the often maladaptive efforts to get a sense of power, which lead to further entrapment and powerlessness, it is no wonder that some clients stay overwhelmed. Nor is it surprising that practitioners succumb to the vulnerability to exploit their powerful clinical roles in work with these clients. Vigilance and competence are mandatory for controlling this vulnerability if practitioners are to assist their clients toward effective clinical outcome.

CHAPTER 4

Research on Clinical Practice
An Overview

THE STAGE OF KNOWLEDGE CONCERNING WHAT WORKS WITH, OR holds promise for, overwhelmed clients is vastly incomplete. Reviews of research evaluating the effectiveness of social work practice offer limited evidence of unequivocal positive outcomes. A majority of reviewers point out that a lack of specificity—in defining presenting problem, in theoretical explanation of the problem, and behaviors to be changed, in methods to be employed to change behavior, in expected behavioral outcomes associated with method used, in instruments to measure outcomes, and in worker characteristics—may explain why social work interventions have failed to demonstrate more effectiveness. Cautioning against a proliferation of research evaluating practice effectiveness, Rubin suggests instead a focus on more methodologically credible experimental research.[1] Hopps challenges social workers to "find the will to document what we know of the ways that meet human needs, of what works in helping people and to relinquish comfortable but inadequate approaches, acquiring a readiness to explore in a responsible manner alternatives to ways that have failed."[2]

As early as 1931, social workers were admonished to assess the significance of their practice processes and to determine the effectiveness of their interventive efforts.[3] Not until some forty years later did social work practice begin to act on this concern. In the 1970s, there was expansion of the profession's knowledge base, a proliferation of new practice modalities, and a recommitment to the value of direct practice.[4] With new service possibilities, social work began a critical examination of its effectiveness, which was fueled by the ferment of the 1960s, dissatisfaction with the existing program models, and the new consciousness that poverty could be eliminated. In what became "the age of accountability,"[5] critics challenged the profession to evaluate empirically all its professional interventive endeavors.[6] By 1985 Hopps commented "that the message has become increasingly clear: 'Good' motives and good goals are not 'good' enough for an increasingly critical electorate that is opposed to or skeptical of social reform and wants assurance that those programs it funds are working."[7]

Questions regarding whether social work interventions are effective remain unresolved. Mullen and Dumpson,[8] for example, analyzing the first controlled studies evaluating the effectiveness of therapeutic interventions conducted between 1937 and 1945, reported that outcome ineffectiveness of psychotherapy and counseling with predelinquent and multiproblem families was related to methodological problems of evaluation (table B-1).* The failure of these studies to reach their goals was identified as a failure to consider such questions as on what basis and toward what end who will do what to whom, for how long, with what effectiveness, at what cost, and with what benefit; a failure to explain adequately why a change took place in projects with positive outcomes; a failure to include specification of and measurement of the intervention; and an inconsistency between the problem definition from a systemic perspective and the intervention strategies employed to test them. Also noted was the need to target problems like poverty at a macrolevel rather than at the microsystem level.

Geismar too identified methodological shortcomings associated with unfavorable outcomes (table B-2): an absence of a coherent theoretical framework for study design, development of methodol-

---

*The tables referred to in this chapter are in appendix B.

ogy, and interpretation of results; inconsistency in assessment processes; and lack of a representative accidental or convenience sample, which severely limited generalizability to other similar practice methods.[9]

Segal's review of evaluative studies of interventions undertaken by nonsocial workers, which also failed to demonstrate effectiveness, provided evidence of a connection between therapist characteristics and outcomes (tables B-3 and B-4).[10] For example, clients whose therapists offered high levels of unconditional positive warmth, genuineness, and empathy exhibited significant, positive personality and behavioral changes. Segal even concluded that the literature indicates that treatment can have negative effects. For example, treatment groups receiving therapy showed significant decrease in mental health on the TAT (Thematic Apperception Test) projective test, and the delinquency prevention program did not reduce the number of court appearances in the treatment group.

Segal's review of delinquency prevention studies, which explored the effects of intervention on delinquency rates of a welfare population, demonstrated the ineffectiveness of interactive therapeutic interventions in preventing delinquency. Segal questioned the effectiveness of this intervention for this population and suggested that the use of psychologically based intervention for a population with social problems may be inappropriate (table B-5).

Fischer's critique of casework effectiveness in evaluative studies using two control groups (one other treated, a second untreated) was published in 1973.[11] (See table B-6 for untreated control groups and table B-7 for other treated control groups.) Fischer, noting greater effectiveness from control groups over experimental groups, concluded that "the lack of effectiveness appears to be the rule rather than the exception across several categories of clients, problems, situations and types of casework."[12] Years later he listed deficiencies associated with casework interventions.[13]

In a review of major controlled studies of delinquency, Wood reached conclusions similar to Fischer (table B-8): that group work with delinquent adolescents "is likely to be ineffective at best and harmful at worst." Finding practitioner failure to assess clients' perceptions of their problems and the nature of help they sought, she

also found that practitioners imposed their own theoretical and ideological orientation on their clients, assuming that they "knew what
ailed their young clients and what was good for them."[14] Such behaviors on the part of practitioners may be associated with a lack
of motivation on the part of the clients to modify their delinquent
behaviors.

Wood's review of studies on interventions with preadolescents
linked the ineffective outcomes to a lack of clarity in problem focus
(table B-9). She noted that neither a formed-group experience nor
one-to-one insight-oriented therapy is effective in itself in changing
the course of children's problems.

Wood's review of studies on public welfare recipients and clientele
of other programs to aid the poor found little or no useful data concerning what is helpful and what is not (table B-10). She cited lack of
clarity or specification of variables such as intervention, workers,
clients, presenting problem, and circumstances as factors that may
severely undermine the significance of the evaluative endeavor.

In contrast to these negative outcomes, Reid and Hanrahan
found greater promise for clinical work, citing positive outcomes in
the controlled studies they reviewed (table B-11).[15] Specifically,
increased effectiveness was attributed to clearly prescribed interventions, task-oriented methods guided by the client-centered approach, and a learning theory model, all directed toward specific
outcomes. The researchers, who were also the practitioners, implemented interventions and observed the client changes. The model
that demonstrated success shows the specificity of intervention (behavioral contract), dependent variable or outcome of intervention
(school achievement), and measurement of outcome (GPA for
school achievement).

The data in table B-10 provide a base for optimism, although,
upon closer scrutiny, the summary seems less than decisive due to a
methodological shortcoming (internal validity), which diminishes
the believability and generalizability (external validity) of the conclusions. Reid and Hanrahan concede that it is somewhat problematic
to generalize about the studies reviewed; however, the implication inherent in their analysis is that "these small successes of the present
are better than the grand failures of the past."[16]

More grounds for optimism in practice effectiveness were reported by Rubin (1985), who reviewed thirteen controlled experiments on the effectiveness of direct social work practice in community-based care for the mentally ill (table B-12).[17]

Ezell and McNeece challenged Rubin's conceptualization of social work practice since in the studies he reviewed, social workers reported on outcomes but were only minimally involved in the intervention process.[18] Thus, the critique of Rubin's review raises the important issue of what constitutes social work practice and what is the intervention that makes "social work" social work. The need is critical for the social work profession to define clearly and specifically the parameters of its practice, identifying both intervenors and interventions before any study of its effectiveness can appropriately be implemented. Without such specificity, can meaningful assessment of practice effectiveness be adequately undertaken? Ezell and McNeece raise a broader issue regarding the relationship of intervention effectiveness and knowledge advancement since Rubin's review of studies reports positive outcomes that have offered little to advance practical knowledge, thus begging the question, What can direct practitioners of social work learn from these studies? Issues of external validity must be a primary and critical concern in any research evaluating practice outcomes. Rubin did declare that the evidence of practice effectiveness does not warrant euphoria.

Clinical Practice Effectiveness with the Overwhelmed Population

Conclusions derived from some of the early studies on social work practice with overwhelmed clients suggest that the failure of clinical work is associated with lack of an integrating theory or lack of specificity in theory or inappropriate use of theory.[19] For example, strategies to address poverty, a social problem, have been based on treatment models for individualized psychological problems. The literature is replete with anecdotal accounts of what appears to work with overwhelmed clients. However, influenced by a deficit or deficiency model—the view that poor people lack personal attributes necessary for successful life and living—traditional research and social work with the overwhelmed population have made little use of this information, basing its approaches on premises that have inappropriately identified and defined the target problem of the poor and overwhelmed population. Prior to the 1950s, such models were based on the notion that renunciation of one's ancestral culture in favor of the behavior and values of the Anglo-Saxon core group would greatly improve the life chances of a culturally different population.[20] Failure to make this transition was viewed as deviance and further interpreted as an innate inability to emulate the values and life-styles of mainstream society.[21] The 1960s reconceptualization sought to view the overwhelmed population as victims of malevolent forces external to them.[22] These perceptions or beliefs about the overwhelmed client are consistent with Tidwell's formulation of culturally deviant and culturally equivalent approaches to assessing black family functioning, which have had some impact on social policy and social work practice.[23]

Many social policy and social work practice processes reflected the deviant-pathological or equivalence-opportunity paradigm, the latter derived from the premises that an expansion of opportunities and the development of compensatory programs and services would minimize or at least neutralize the debilitating effects of discrimination and economic deprivation. The tacit assumption underlying the former was that the individual's personality, character, and values must be transformed to approximate the majority middle-class norm. While well-intentioned national policy and programs during the 1960s sought to expand job training and job opportunities, decent education, and community development, ultimately the individual was still held accountable for his or her predicament.[24] Persistence of poverty in spite of such programs has been linked to the ideological biases structuring such policies and programs.[25]

These two ideological perspectives remained the dominant paradigms guiding research of the poor and overwhelmed population well into the 1980s. The 1965 Moynihan Report, *The Negro Family*, Banfield's 1974 publication of *The Unheavenly City Revisited*, the publication of IQ studies by Jensen and Herrnstein, and the 1986 CBS Special Report, "The Vanishing Family" have produced an analysis of the problems of the poor that is isolated from their historical context or from the larger frameworks of social and racial stratification.[26] By ignoring how social conditions may trap individuals and groups in poverty, social policies may make certain groups of people especially vulnerable to being poor.[27] Myths and inaccuracies reported about the overwhelmed population must be dispelled in order to develop programs and direct public policy intelligently.[28]

Thus, with misperceptions of overwhelmed client functioning and its relation to social conditions dominating practice explanatory theory, a macrosystem problem has been defined as a microsystem problem, and interventions have been developed accordingly. In fact, Mullen and Dumpson, Geismar, and Segal's reviews on clinical effectiveness found that clients with macrolevel presenting problems—jobs, education, and housing—were being treated with a microlevel intervention—clinical work (individual or family-focused change). Indeed, treatment and interventions consistent with a microsystem definition of the problem have produced discouraging results when implemented in work with the poor.

What would help? As Jones and Borgatta suggest in their assessment of interventions of large-scale programs on total population groups and their impact on the community, better theories to explain the effect of community structure and institutional change on individuals and their behavior are needed in order to determine which variables to consider and what data to collect.[29] Theory development and refinement are indispensable links to improved measures of effective practice and accurate outcomes. Grounded theory, such as empowerment theory, appears appropriate for assessing the impacts of community structure and institutional arrangements on the behavioral and attitudinal patterns of the overwhelmed population.[30]

Although theoretical models have been developed and clinical practice with the poor and overwhelmed populations has been guided by newer conceptualizations and reconceptualizations—family preservation models, ethnic-sensitive practice, and the empowerment model—scanty data exist to validate their effectiveness. Preliminary reports appear to suggest that interventions derived from such models hold promise in work with overwhelmed clients, but these strategies must be subjected to more rigorous testing and continued monitoring. In fact, results of recent experiments with innovative family-focused intervention programs appear to generate some cause for optimism for social work practice. One model, intensive family preservation services, was conceived in its broadest sense to ensure continuity of care for children at risk for out-of-home placement. Highly intensive family-centered social services were delivered in the client's home for a relatively brief period of time.[31] The ultimate goals of preventing out-of-home placement, improving family functioning, and providing needed clinical services are reached through the use of short-term, crisis-oriented treatment models. Enthusiasm for early family preservation service projects has been reported by Maybanks and Bryce and Bryce and Lloyd.[32] Assessments of service effectiveness indicate that an impressive 70 to 97 percent of children serviced by family preservation–type programs avoided out-of-home placement.[33] Countering these early reports of service effectiveness by intensive family preservation providers are critics who maintain that variations in family preservation models and service intensity without the use of control or comparison groups, to establish the reliability and validity of effectiveness of these programs, are problematic.[34]

With very limited evidence of successful social work practice with overwhelmed clients, business as usual appears to characterize the profession. Moreover, a survey of recent (1980–1989) literature shows that minorities are only a marginal concern for social work and that much of the intervention with minority clients continues to be driven by the deficit-deficiency model despite the fact that practitioners have developed a more culturally sensitive approach.[35]

Identifying Measures of Effective Evaluative Practice with Overwhelmed Clients

The first step in evaluation research requires a clarification of both the formal and stated and the nonformal and unstated goals and objectives of a program or intervention. To achieve such clarification, there must be a clear delineation of the problem. Accurate assessment helps to identify or clarify the client's presenting problems, including the behavioral systems involved in the problems—individual, family, community, or societal. Precise documentation of the client's situation serves as a baseline against which outcomes will be measured and evaluated.

Practitioners must take care to ensure that their own cultural lens is not the basis of assessment. Since clinical work includes improving social functioning, facilitating people's ability to cope with their realities and improve the quality of their lives, achievement of these outcomes requires the practitioner to consider the significance of culture throughout the clinical process.[36] Culture must be considered as a factor in problem formation, problem resolution, the engagement phase of the intervention, and the formation of the clinical relationship itself, requiring the use of approaches that respect the client's culture and do not conflict drastically with client expectations.[37] Also significant to assessment are the nutritive quality of the social context and the strengths it embodies. Tidwell, for example, in reference to practice issues with black families, emphasizes the cultural-variance perspective of the black experience in America.[38] This perspective provides unconditional respect, integrity, and dignity to the black family life experience, focusing on strengths, emphasizing the continuities in the structure and functioning of black families in relation to their African heritage, and illuminating the interplay between African-based family life-styles and the black experience in America.

The theoretical conceptualization of the client problem determines the goals and objectives of intervention. Therefore, identification of the theory or theories that provide an accurate orientation, stance, or view of the presenting problem and the target population is key. Goldstein reports that there is not much evidence substantiating that social worker practice is driven by the theories presented in professional education.[39] Overwhelmed clients present multiple problems, and it may be assumed that various theories should be used to inform intervention with this population.

Since intervention strategies must be based on theories explaining client problems, there must be clear articulation of these guiding theories. For example, a client's dysfunctioning may be due to disempowerment and explained by differential power theory. Thus, to improve client functioning, a specific set of interventions or program activities must be designed to empower the client. Interventions must clearly specify and list the precise nature of activities to be implemented. One possible strategy to empower the client may consist of increasing his or her positive self-esteem through individual work. Once an intervention strategy has been designed, the next step is to articulate the desired outcomes for that particular strategy—that is, the specific behavioral and attitudinal patterns that can be expected (consistent with the problem theory) if the intervention is to achieve its goals and objectives.

Measurement of outcomes rests on a base for determining outcome, that is, how it will be determined that improved self-esteem has occurred or that the client has secured external resources. Such outcome measures must be expressed in concrete terms. For example, improved self-esteem can be determined by the number of positive statements about self that the client makes in a paper-and-pencil measure, such as the Index of Self-Esteem (ISE).[40] Finding and retaining a job or a housing unit can constitute a criterion measure for securing external resources.

All outcome measures must be evaluated in terms of their reliability and validity. Do these measures measure consistently and accurately what they purport to measure? For example, interventions or specific strategies to empower the client should be based in power differential theory and become the basis of evaluation. That is, did the intervention or treatment program (individual work to increase positive self-esteem) make a difference (empowering client to improve functioning)?

Also influential in success outcomes are sociodemographic or client variables and noninterventive factors, such as worker characteristics and the content and the manner of service delivery.[41] Specification of such noninterventive factors must also be clearly delineated, and questions of internal validity must be addressed to determine if the outcomes produced are attributed to the intervention strategies and the extent to which they may be linked to noninterventive variables.

Evaluation requires multiple sources of information and multiple methods of data collection:

Program records and service files, on whether the client accomplished the goals and objectives of the treatment or intervention and successfully met the predetermined performance criteria.

The clients themselves, who are in an excellent position to evaluate many aspects of the intervention and are most knowledgeable about their current state, especially at the follow-up interviews.

The practitioner, trained to assess the degree of the client's dysfunction and any improvement.

The agency director, since decisions made at higher administrative and policy levels can impact practice effectiveness.

Measures of effective practice require both qualitative and quantitative methods, what Cheetham called pragmatic eclecticism, to determine the extent to which the particular intervention was effective in producing the desired outcomes.[42] Research characterized by the needed specificity, that clearly delineates how, under what circumstances, and with what strategies the powerlessness and entrapment of this population can be interpreted, remains in its infancy. This book helps move forward practice effectiveness research with overwhelmed clients.

CHAPTER 5

Empirical Findings on Clinical Effectiveness

THE FOLLOWING DISCUSSION PRESENTS SOCIODEMOGRAPHIC DATA ON overwhelmed clients, information on interventions and their outcomes as well as on duration of agency service and practitioner characteristics.

Overwhelmed Clients: A Sociodemographic Profile

The records of 178 randomly selected cases from a sampling frame of over 2,000 cases drawn from four agencies that provide services to overwhelmed clients in the greater Boston area were critically assessed.[1]

The majority of clients, nearly 58 percent, were women, while slightly over 40 percent were males, of whom 68 percent were under age nineteen.[2] Consistent with other findings on utilization of services, this study found that adult women were using services to a much greater degree than adult males: 70 percent and 32 percent, respectively.[3] The largest client categories in this study consisted of mothers and their male offspring, both children and teenagers.

Although the racial and ethnic identity of all clients was not known, the majority were African Americans and Latinos (primarily Puerto Ricans), representing 44 percent and 39 percent, respectively. The remainder were whites (9 percent), other racial and ethnic groups (5.2 percent), and Caribbeans (3.4 percent). Of note here was the underutilization of services by Latinos, especially in view of their poverty status.[4]

Clients are young. Nearly 48 percent were under age nineteen; 13 percent were between ages twenty and twenty-nine, and 19 percent were between ages thirty and thirty-nine. The few clients over fifty years of age were usually seeking services that would help them in their roles as primary caregivers to the offspring of their adult children who were suffering from problems such as addiction, joblessness, homelessness, and serious illness. No clients over sixty years old were found. In comparison with city-wide demographic data, this study found a larger number of children receiving services than their numbers would suggest.[5] Fifty-eight percent of overwhelmed clients in this study were single. Twenty-six percent were married, 20 percent were divorced or separated, 38 percent were never married,[6] approximately 3 percent were widowed, and 12 percent of clients had "other" nondefined marital status. Most families had an average of three children, a finding that fails to support the stereotype assumption that poor people have a large number of children.

The findings suggest that at least 26.5 percent of clients are employed, with another 3 percent seeking employment (table 5-1). That employment status is tenuous and precarious is not at all surprising given the vulnerability of these clients to joblessness, discrimination, and problems stemming from restructuring of the economy and globalization. Even when overwhelmed clients were employed, the wages they received were not sufficient to provide an adequate level of well-being or support for a family, forcing them to use food pantries, subsidized rentals, and other financial supports.

Forty-eight percent of clients had received between ten and twelve years of education; 15 percent reported thirteen or more years. The median level of education for the sample was between ten and twelve years, indicating at least some secondary education. Reports showing that African Americans and Hispanics with the

same educational attainment as whites receive lower economic rewards do not support the assumption that given the tie between
earnings and educational attainment, education becomes the greatest equalizer in the American social system.[7] What exists is a reflection of discrimination in both the larger society and in the educational
system. Despite the fact that education and job training do not yield
the same rewards for this population as for others, they surfaced as
important goals in clinical work.

Thirty-two percent of households were intact, comprising a wife
and a husband (or couples assuming these titles, even when not
legally married),[8] children, and/or other relatives; 27 percent were
single parent, and 32 percent were nondefined "other" or nontraditional. These facts are consistent with expectations that African
Americans and Latinos are more likely than whites to live in extended or nontraditional households that "transcend and link several different households, each containing a separate (or seemingly
so) family."[9]

Seventy-one percent of the clients presented multiple problems
at intake: psychological, behavioral, environmental, medical, and
substance abuse. Even when clients were not referred for multiple
problems, multiple diagnoses were made following the initial assessment process, underscoring the complex, circular, and reinforcing
nature of the problems experienced by this clientele.

Intervention

Length of Service by the Agency

Interventions tended to be short term rather than longer term.
Sixty-nine percent of clients were officially terminated within a two-
year period, although a few were terminated in less than six months.

The Practitioners

Among the professionals who worked with overwhelmed clients
M.S.W.s constituted the largest number (50 percent), followed by
M.D.s (psychiatry), Ph.D.s, and Psy.D.s (32 percent); those remain-

ing held M.A.s, no professional degree, or no college degree. In a number of instances, direct clinical services were delivered by non-professionals as well as professionals. When nonprofessionals are used, professionals more frequently function as supervisors, planning and directing services without always becoming directly involved in front-line delivery. When client need or educational programming required it, however, highly credentialed professionals were on the front line.

Practitioners reported that they spent an hour or two in each meeting or session with a client; however, more extensive contact, follow-up, case planning, and referral and counseling were indicated in recording. Actual records reveal that the following activities consumed much of their service time to clients: telephone calls on behalf of clients, transporting clients to appointments, completion of application and intervention monitoring forms, meeting with school officials, and availability according to need, sometimes twenty-four hours a day, for support. The total time expended on behalf of these clients suggests that practitioners who commit themselves to working with overwhelmed clients put in a countless number of hours, far greater than that reflected in the workers' time accounting. This finding has ramifications for newer managed care restrictions in relation to client activity and use of the traditional fifty-minute hour, as well as other changes occurring in agencies today whereby full-time workers are being replaced by part timers.

Client Behaviors Resulting from Interventions

The following discussion examines client behaviors which are associated with successful outcomes. Changes in client functioning are indications of the relative success of a given intervention. These changes were also linked to worker characteristics, and agency mission. (See Appendix C).

Assessment

The intervention process starts with assessment to determine the nature of the client's problem or situation in the context of the environment. Successful engagement—the client's joining with the worker or participating in discussion and contracting for services—is critical to accurate assessment, which in turn helps structure the treatment plan. During the assessment phase, important information about the dynamics of individual and family functioning, including all significant relationships and life events, are ordered and given meaning. The more skillful the assessment and the consequent treatment plan are, the more likely will the intervention outcome be marked by success. Moreover in the process of assessment, some insight and motivation are provided such that these may effect change or improved functioning.

Effective Coping. The use of the genogram or sociogram may help the client to visualize the configuration or patterns of relationships in his or her situation and thus lead to more effective coping and movment to a higher level of functioning (table C-1).* For example, after assessment, a grandmother previously immobilized was able to put her drug-abusing daughter out of her house so that her grandchild could have a better life and a chance to stay and succeed in school. She took this action after seeing the problem for what it was and realizing that the needs of her grandson were paramount. Accurate assessment was instrumental in producing positive outcomes in this case.

Extensive data gathering is not always necessary in assessment—for example, when the problem is to secure resources for material needs, such as food or housing.

Reducing Blaming and Scapegoating. Successful engagement and skillful assessment can initiate movement toward effective coping, but only occasionally does it initiate movement toward reduced blaming and scapegoating (table C-2). In another case, a young man denied personal responsibility, blaming his spouse for their marital problems. The clinician assessed the client's contribution to the conflict in the relationship, particularly his neglect of his partner and his scapegoating of her. After assessment, his combatant stance reduced markedly, and he agreed to assume some responsibility for the quality of the relationship and to return for further work with his spouse. Assessment thus led to identification and clarification of the individual's responsibility, which helped him to begin to recog-

---

*The tables referred to in the balance of this chapter are found in appendix C.

nize and then accept responsibility for self, initial steps for reducing blaming.

Advocacy

Seeking Own Resources. Advocacy refers to the practitioner's activity and pressure to obtain resources for clients from community institutions that may not have otherwise been available (table C-3). The practitioner's activity to obtain resources, explanation of entitlements, and sharing of information concerning services increases the client's opportunity to learn to seek her own resources, advocate for self, and protect self from victimizing circumstances. As workers become involved in negotiating food orders or other provisions and services, for example, clients learn from, emulate, or model such worker behaviors in their subsequent encounters with community institutions. Examples of successful advocacy were found where clients could, on their own, "handle the welfare department," get their own emergency food order, and procure services for a child in school or day care.

Of significance in this study is that when housing or drug treatment was needed but no units or programs were available, neither workers nor the clients were successful.

Empowerment

Empowerment enables clients to develop behaviors that improve the use of personal power, foster self-esteem, take charge of personal problems, and set and pursue personal goals (tables C-4, C-5, C-6, and C-7).

Use of Personal Power. B manifested use of personal power by leaving her abusive, drug-pushing husband, learning to feel better about herself and being able to say, "I am not unattractive; I am smart; I can go to school." The practitioner helped her believe in herself and take steps to make personal goals become realities: attend school regularly, use day care for her child, and secure transportation and appropriate clothing. As well, the clinician helped the client to understand the issues that contributed to her sense of powerlessness: the marriage failure, the husband's inability to hold a job, the role of drugs, the significance of painful early childhood experiences related to an alcoholic, abusive, and abandoning father who had kidnapped the client and her siblings, placing them in the care of his relatives.

Ability to Make Decisions and Pursue Personal Goals. As B took charge of personal problems and set and pursued personal goals, she implemented her decision to go to school, she made arrangements for day care for her child and secured appropriate resources, including considering the purchase of a car. The worker provided necessary clarification and, above all, support.

Positive Self-Esteem. The capacity to view oneself as a worthwhile and valued individual is another facet of empowerment. B not only learned to view herself as "not unattractive" and "not incompetent" but also developed the sense of mastery that is critical to self-esteem when she successfully completed her training and achieved her personal goals. The clinician's activities here centered on support, encouragement, clarification of options, and resolution of impediments to positive actions such as her guilt over taking her son from his father and her expectation of abuse and abandonment.

Individual and Family Work

Communication and Parenting Skills. For parents who were provided instruction in these two areas, 60 percent exhibited effective communication skills with family members and others. They made progress as well in parenting skills, which had a positive effect on family functioning. Often development of these skills was connected with mastery in other areas.

One client had been unable to give up drugs and a destructive relationship with her boyfriend, who was a pusher. Moreover, her family dynamics were marked by poor communication and poor household management. The clinician's intervention activities initially focused on changing this communication and management style. The first tasks were to get family members to be quiet and listen to one another, to address one another with more respect, to organize the household (pick up clothes and trash, wash the dishes, sweep the floor, etc.), and to develop a budget and understand the range and limitation of available household resources. This meant learning not to waste funds and to use resources for family betterment. Through counseling, the client learned that she had been using drugs to deal with a sense of powerlessness and entrapment that she felt in relation to her boyfriend, whom she clung to because of a sense of emptiness. With support, she was able to give up drugs and the destructive relationship with her boyfriend. Here, the clinician's activities included visiting the home daily to confront the drug abuse, and teaching and modeling effective parenting (the family was under a child protective order) to offer support, insight, and encouragement to change. A sometimes tough and confrontational process led to better parenting, including appropriate limit setting, and more effective communication, an outcome that contributed to the client's sense of personal power, improved self-esteem, and better family image.

Personal Health and Hygiene. In cases in which health and hygiene were of some concern and clients were instructed in such matters, 73 percent exhibited improvement. The simple task of organizing the household was the first step toward personal health and hygiene: picking up clothes, washing dishes, doing the family laundry, understanding and using sanitary toileting procedures.

Many of the housing options available to these clients are dilapidated, roach and rat infested, trash littered, and odor filled. The energy needed just to fight roaches, for example, is considerable. The capacity to organize oneself and family members, one aspect of which is caring for self, making self valued and acceptable to self and others, is a strength and a demonstration of personal and family pride and evidence that clients were not beaten down, no matter how hard life was. When children and their mothers looked good, they felt uplifted and hopeful and said so. People need to see beauty somewhere, to nourish the soul.

Positive Self-Esteem. Assisting the client to become effective in individual support and problem solving will be manifested in clients' experiencing themselves as worthwhile, valued individuals who demonstrate improved self-esteem, self-mastery, and self-sufficiency. A majority of clients who received individual treatment exhibited positive self-esteem.

Differentiation. Successful outcome of individual treatment can be manifested in clients' progress to a greater sense of self-differentiation. In at least 58 percent of the cases, clients exhibited a clearer sense of themselves as capable of intimacy with others, able to set goals and maintain personal behavioral intent, and capable of having positive and productive interaction with others.

The mother of a sixteen year old dealt with her depression after abandonment of her drug-abusing boyfriend through encouraging her daughter to become pregnant. Enmeshed with her daughter, through whom she was living out her own needs, including wishing her daughter to give birth so that personal needs for nurturing could be met through the presence of an infant, she and her children were embroiled in serious role conflicts (Who is in charge of household? Who is parent? Child?), and all were attacking one another. Through individual treatment, the mother became more differentiated and better able to address her own needs, take charge of the mother role, let go of the boyfriend, see herself as attractive and valued, and understand the strengths of her children. The children were supported in their need for growing independence and self-sufficiency (going to school, preparing for a job, taking some responsibility for the household by picking up their personal space), and all family members were helped to communicate appropriately with one another, to show respect to one another, to relate as a family unit, and to pursue personal and family goals (school every day, job hunting, support relationships with drug-free friends). There was growing insight into the family enmeshment, the role of drugs in the destructive functioning of family, how the perceived need for a man came from a void in the mother's life, and how the unborn child was becoming a substitute object.

In another case, a child living amid violence and mayhem in the inner city was so petrified of death that he was literally immobilized. The clinician determined through assessment that his intense anxiety was related to incomplete mourning of his father's death and to fears of losing his mother—fears compounded by his mother's own fears following her husband's death. Helping the mother to complete her mourning and supporting her through assumption of responsibilities as head of household, the worker ensured that the mother's need to overburden the child and keep him afraid and in panic was reduced. This case is a good illustration of the interaction between individual and family functioning and the community. It crystalizes the need for multilevel change: at the family and individual level and at the community level, where violence must be reduced.

The clinical intervention took place in the context of neighborhood-environment dynamics that were often unsupportive and even obstructive of the work for both family and practitioner. Over and over again, the critical need for macrolevel interventions such as jobs programs, availability of decent housing, and community programs that facilitate residents' joining together to initiate changes in the environment, were evident.

Competence. Evidence of movement toward a greater sense of competence—that is, a higher level of coping and sense of task mastery—was demonstrated in a majority of cases (52 percent), suggesting that clinical intervention may have accounted for this change in client functioning. The variety of strategies that clinicians used in the facilitation of clients' movement toward competence are examined in the next chapter.

Group Work

Group work, which assists clients through group support and problem solving when successful, leads to positive self-esteem, differentiation, and competence (tables C-12 through C-14). It is not the preferred intervention strategy, perhaps because it is not consistent with one-on-one, highly individualistically oriented clinical intervention, the preferred mode. Emerging from the societal value of autonomy, this mode constitutes the dominant orientation of professional training and preparation of those in powerful agency roles.

When group work is practiced widely, success rates can range from 75 percent for improved differentiation to 88 percent for improved self-esteem and progress toward task mastery or competence. Groups initially tend to focus on education (safety in the streets, hygiene, responsible dating, nonviolent behavior, and problem resolution, among others) and sometimes psychological problems.

Where group was the intervention, improved client functioning was evident through skill development and better management of behavior within the group, which then transferred into home and school settings. For example, a youngster who was acting out in class and referred by his teacher was determined upon assessment to be also acting out at home. He was assigned to group intervention where the peer support, limit-setting, and educational focus enabled him to process his anxieties related to father abandonment, problems with peers on the street ("Am I going to get beat up?"), concerns about mother ("Who is going to take care of me?"), and his enmeshment conflicts with her. Learning appropriate survival skills, anger management, and self-assertive behaviors, he manifested more differentiated, less enmeshed behavior within the group, improved capacity for peer relationships, and ability to focus on instrumental tasks. These gains are reflected in better school performance and family relationships.

Because group work holds promise, efforts must be expanded to increase its implementation in work with overwhelmed clients. Priority must be given to resource allocation for the variety of group interventions that can address the problems of this client population.

Community Change

Also assessed was evidence of client action to effect change at the community level. Practitioner tasks to facilitate such activity involve teaching clients advocacy for community building and improvement and helping them to work toward changes in policies or programs that would benefit groups of residents. There was no evidence of clients' involvement in such activities, suggesting that agencies' did not or could not address community change.

The findings reported here point to interventions that hold promise in work with overwhelmed clients. Over 50 percent of clients exhibited evidence of positive self-esteem, which was connected to empowerment; clients' exhibiting effective communications and parenting skills, personal health and hygiene, positive self-esteem, greater differentiation, and greater competence was connected to individual and family work; and clients' stronger competence was also connected to group work. The success of group work was greater than that for individual and family work, although its incidence of use was limited largely to children, adolescents, and young mothers. It was not the preferred intervention among the agencies.

Forty percent of the cases also revealed evidence of effective coping, which was connected to assessment; advocacy, workers' activity and successful pressure to obtain resources for clients from community institutions that may not have otherwise been available, and clients' learning to do likewise; and empowerment, improved client capacity to use personal power, make decisions, pursue personal goals, and move toward self-sufficiency.

In a third set of interventions, there was some, though limited, evidence of reduced scapegoating attributed to assessment and positive self-esteem and greater differentiation attributed to group work. Group treatment appeared effective with this population in facilitating the hypothesized success outcome.

Only one agency reported evidence of client functioning connected to community change, and we can only speculate about why. Funding is doubtless a major issue, as may be the complexities involved in effecting larger systemic change.

Intercorrelations of Success Outcomes with Worker Characteristics

The extent to which worker characteristics were associated with successful outcomes of interventions was computed for each intervention, its success outcome(s), and worker characteristics (table C-15). There appears to be a moderately to very strong positive linear correlation between interventions, success outcomes, and workers who exhibit characteristics of flexibility and caring. In other words, success or effective clinical outcome is more assured when caring and flexible workers were involved in the lives of overwhelmed clients.

Factor Analysis of Dimension
of Overall Functioning

By demonstrating and documenting significant association between intervention strategies and worker characteristic variables, we can determine which worker characteristic variable is significantly associated with which intervention. But overwhelmed clients are characterized by multiple presenting problems, so rarely can implementation of a single intervention effectively address the complexity of their environmental and psychological gestalt. Depending on the assessment, a combination of intervention strategies needs to be implemented.

Successful clinical work with overwhelmed clients promotes changes that manifest themselves in positive self-esteem, social and psychological competence, educational competence, and movement toward self-sufficiency and dignity.[10] Thus, improved functioning is connected to several client changes occurring at about the same time; that is, there is an interconnectedness among successful outcomes. A factor analysis performed to determine if any outcomes were highly correlated with one another but have little or no correlation with others found strong intercorrelations among two sets of success outcomes (table C-16).[11] Factor 1 is labeled the self-efficacy–personal mastery index of overall functioning stressing thinking and obtaining of insight. It reflects:

Minimal blaming and scapegoating.
Use of personal power.
Positive self-esteem.
Effective communication and parenting skills.
Health and personal hygiene.
Differentiation.
Competence.

Such capacities and client characteristics are intrinsic to empowerment, and acquisition of capacities and readiness to cope constructively with the forces that have entrapped him or her.[12]

Factor 2, the second set of strongly intercorrelated success outcomes, is the competence–behavior for action index of overall functioning involving acting on one's own behalf. It reflects:

Effective coping.
Seeking own resources.
Making decisions and pursuing personal goals.

These outcomes represent a client's capacity and mastery of skills to influence the external social system. This factor may be interpreted as an expression of the client's empowerment to exert his or her own power to make the surrounding systems more responsive to his or her growth and development. (Tables C-17 and C-18 show what interventions cluster together, and thereby constitute the self-efficacy, personal mastery, and competence-behavior for action indexes.)

Together, these two factors provide a good way of summarizing overall improved functioning of overwhelmed clients. This scheme tells us that successful outcomes are interconnected; a positive outcome in one aspect of functioning will probably produce similar results in other areas of functioning. Thus, successful outcomes are ensured when multiple interventions are implemented. Clinicians need to know the significance of multiple interventions when working with overwhelmed clients. Results of factor analysis both provide a theoretical conceptualization of overall improved functioning and offer practical approaches in clinical work with this population.

Table 5-1
Employment Status of Clients

Employment Status	Distribution (%)
Unemployed, not seeking jobs	27.0
Unemployed: Child caring, disabled, and health problems	14.5
AFDC and other reasons	29.0
Employed	26.5
Searching for employment	3.0

Regression Analysis of Overall Functioning
by Worker and Program Characteristics

To determine the most effective predictors (worker characteristics were treated as independent variables) of overall improved functioning (dependent variable, Factors 1 and 2 combined), a regression analysis was performed.[13] There was a very strong positive association between worker characteristics of flexibility and caring and overall improved functioning. Furthermore, the variables in the equation show that worker characteristics of flexibility and caring together are very strong predictors of overall improved functioning. In other words, a very large portion of the changes in the overall improved functioning in clients is explained by the combination of these two worker characteristics.

Analysis of the findings suggests as well that overwhelmed clients have the capacity for self-development. The interventions we have identified have the potential of helping clients in improving their self-esteem, their sense of competence and differentiation, and skills that facilitate self-sufficiency and greater dignity. The cases examined in this study are reflective of larger populations of overwhelmed clients, and so the results and findings lend themselves to the general population of overwhelmed clients.

CHAPTER 6

The Helping Equation
A Qualitative Analysis

THIS RESEARCH WAS DRIVEN BY THE INTEREST TO DETERMINE WHAT holds promise for successful clinical work with overwhelmed clients and to translate the findings into information that can aid clinicians in their practice. In this study success is not defined as merely positive outcomes that are "more salutary than would be the case without professional services."[1] Neither is successful intervention defined as a totalistic approach, meaning total systemic change. For at least a decade and a half, a period in which resource poverty has marked the circumstances of overwhelmed clients, such an approach is neither possible nor realistic. Rather, success means movement toward social functioning that manifests improved self-esteem, social and psychological competence, educational competence, and the capacity to develop skills that lead to self-sufficiency and dignity. These skills represent the embodiment of empowerment. Moreover, acquiring them facilitates change in individuals, families, and the neighborhood environment that ensures clients' ability to function so that they can take advantage of educational opportunity, job training, or employment or parent at a level that facilitates a child's achievement of educational, psychological, or social competence.

Many clients have access to direct social work practice intervention, and the total social work helping enterprise could benefit from some feedback on various modalities and their effectiveness with this particular client group. At the same time outcome effectiveness and accountability have long been viewed with skepticism, and workers are usually more comfortable with process accountability.

The cases analyzed in this chapter show the depth of the dysfunction, the strengths amid the awesome realities, the coping capabilities of clients, the commitment of the helpers, and some paths to successful outcomes. To deny these realities or to fail in appreciating their meaning in the context of the clients' desperation because of vulnerability to be labeled as politically incorrect or culturally insensitive would do little to help focus thought and action where it is needed. Clinical intervention begins with the engagement of the client, moves to assessment and treatment planning, treatment implementation, and then to termination. In every agency, such work requires engaging and staying connected with clients whose problems are characterized by drugs, gangs, violence, and other inner-city troubles.

Initial Contact and Engagement

The initial contact and engagement determines whether helper and client connect, a relationship that is vital to change. Differing approaches were manifest in the agencies' engagement of clients, some using methods based on practice approaches common to settlement house work and others typifying 1990s upper-middle-class private agency practice. Agencies are acknowledging the need to address language barriers, which were minimized during initial contact and engagement by capable translators and interpreters, even including telephone reception, no small feat in view of dialects or the absence of English-speaking capacity. Given changing demographics, much more effort is warranted to make sure the entire process of service corresponds with needs of particular ethnic groups, particularly Hispanics.

There are doubtless questions of practice-agency-client fit and philosophy of helping. One agency in particular demonstrated creativity and sensitivity in reaching and engaging this clientele. Its initial contact occurred primarily through a child's participation in an activities group, and only later were the parents engaged. The goals of such groups consisted of teaching children relationship competency, hygiene, and recreational skills. Groups were offered for many age ranges; none was coed. The activities were traditional and nontraditional and included educational tours, introduction to the world of work and to top area athletes, and group discussion on issues such as school, sex, drugs, friends, and family. Also organized was a reading group. A particularly innovative activity was the teen incest theater group: female teens made a videotape growing out of their own personal experiences.

Parents were then involved through their interest in their children's growth and development. As concerns and needs became known and as trust developed, individual parents were offered an opportunity to work toward meeting these needs through joining an adult group organized by the agency and also through participation in individual or family counseling. A major focus in both group activity and individual counseling was on parenting skills and preparation for work or further education. A focus on the families' problems emerged only as a result of the initial activities with children and was a philosophy based on the premise of client empowerment, the guidepost of this program.

Another effective agency engaged clients through follow-up referrals from a number of sources but primarily the Department of Social Services. There is no doubt of the staff's commitment to outreach; they rendered in-home services, accompanied clients to health delivery systems, and visited schools to meet with school personnel. Follow-up on missed appointments, reminders of future sessions, and notes to clients were further indicators of commitment to them. Staff were also conscientious and dedicated and did not turn away from difficult clients. Sometimes communication was not as clear as needed and sometimes clients did not respond, but there is evidence that workers were on the cases.

In yet another agency the engagement of clients was not as effective as appeared in presentation by the staff; of the fifty cases reviewed, in only ten was there evidence of engagement. In all likelihood, lack of engagement occurred because of cultural dynamics.

The outreach needed to work with the agency's culturally diverse clientele did not seem forthcoming. Many of the clients were from populations that seek help not from mental health services but through spiritualism, superstition, folk medicine, and reliance on helpers who are family members or traditional healers. In trying to nail down why a highly educated staff failed to use the necessary strategies to make and sustain contacts—Is it training? Economics? Attitude?—we decided that the culprits are probably attitude and cost. Perhaps outreach activities (going to the tenement and knocking on doors, going to the neighborhood bar, etc.) are not valued by these highly trained professionals. These engagement strategies were not demonstrated in the records.

Successful engagement appeared to be uncorrelated to amount of training possessed by workers. It was found in agencies whose workers were highly trained and skillful but not highly lettered. Of particular interest was the role and effect of untrained workers. Because the financial rewards were small and their education was limited, with the consequence that professional status and recognition eluded them, they were in their commitment "truly their brother's keepers." They were motivated to help, and understood the meaning of the old casework directive, "Begin where the client is." They were available in times of crisis and understood that a crisis might occur at midnight on Saturday on the top floor of the housing project with the elevator out of operation. It meant extending themselves when weapons were numerous, walking up smelly stairwells and through littered hallways. It meant meeting a client at 9:00 A.M. Monday for coffee at a local hangout or visiting in a well-kept apartment. The point is that the workers were effective engagers, working around physical and environmental barriers and time constraints, and taking calculated personal risks.

Assessment, Treatment Planning, and Treatment

If and when engagement was successful, assessment was the area where professional training and commitment converged across all the agencies. In most instances, clients were beneficiaries of high-quality, thoughtful, well-organized analyses of their behavioral-situational predicaments. Assessments of their functioning offered evidence of staff and agency commitment to understanding the client and her context. These analyses drew from theories of behavior, personality, and environment. Workers were often alert to behaviors stemming from psychological, physical, and sexual abuse, economic deprivation, and victimization on a variety of levels. In fact, more than 70 percent of cases had multiple presenting problems. A variety of theoretical approaches were used: In most cases the intervention used an eclectic blend of strategies based on these and a few other theories.

In one agency every case was assessed through the use of a genogram, which facilitated a reality-based systemic perspective. All family members, including significant others such as boyfriends, girlfriends, caretakers, neighbors, and extended relatives in other locations such as Puerto Rico, southern states, and other urban areas, were duly identified. The transient relationships in some of the cases were also shown (figure 6-1). In another agency, body diagrams were

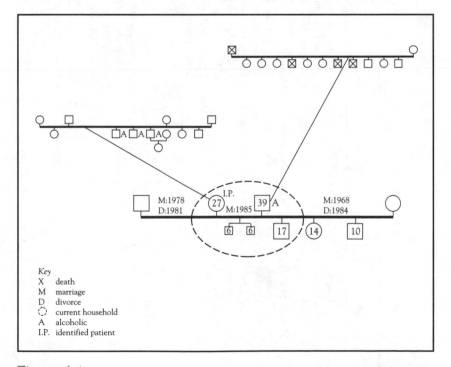

Key
X   death
M   marriage
D   divorce
◯   current household
A   alcoholic
I.P. identified patient

Figure 6-1.
Genogram used to facilitate understanding of family dynamics

Table 6-1
Components of the Success Equation

	Strengths	Problem	Treatment Focus	Theoretical Approach	Outcome
Case 1	Competent, personable, church affiliated	Acting-out issues with father	Aggressive management Coping with racism Processing family dynamics	Ecological-cognitive system Psychodynamic	Improved functioning in academic and family systems
Case 2	Mother: Self-referral, aware Child: High energy; cognitively capable, aware, intelligent	Mother: victim of violence, poor parenting skills Child: depressed, oppositional, bed wetter, aggressive behavior, learning disability	Mother: Parenting skills Trauma therapy Suicide management Process depression and rage Child: Process family dynamics, father abandonment, Aggression management	Family Mother: Psychodynamic Psychoeducation-behavioral Child: Family Psychodynamic Behavioral	Improved individual and family functioning Depression lifted Mother's parenting improved Child's bed wetting ceased
Case 3	Supportive mother	Suicidal behavior, sexual identity confusion, relationship problem with lover	Problem solving Aggression management Suicide management Processing dynamics re family sexual abuse and sexual orientation	Psychodynamic Behavioral	Improved self-esteem Problem relationship terminated Employed
Case 4	Employed mother, caring relationship between mother and daughter	Job in jeopardy, victim of sexual abuse, STD, schizophrenic, lacks GED	Daughter's problem behavior Family functioning	Psychodynamic Family systems with one person Cognitive	Improved functioning Maintained job

Case					
Case 5	In school, role in family	Deprived mourning, depression, parentification, developmental barriers	Developmental needs / Family functioning / Reaction to father's death / Understanding alcoholism	Psychodynamic / Cognitive	Improved functioning / Mourning completed / College bound
Case 6	Caring relationships	Mother: poor parenting, depression, alcoholism / Daughter: ambivalent about pregnancy, unkempt household	Parental skills / Processing family dynamics / Alcoholism	Psychodynamic / Family system / Cognitive-behavioral	Mother: alcoholism checked / Daughter: motivated to graduate high school / All: improved family functioning
Case 7	Talented, family connectedness	Client alcoholism, poor self-esteem, victim of abuse, poor relationship with boyfriend / Mother: alcoholism	Mother: / Grief work / Alcoholism and drug awareness	Family / Educational / Mother: / Psychodynamic / Educational	Daughter and mother employed / Mother's alcoholism checked / Family functioning improved
Case 8	Protectiveness, coping skills	Child's functioning / Negativity	Daughter's drug problem / Child's needs	Strategy, problem solving	Child: symptom free / Daughter evicted; environment improved
Case 9	Attractive child, verbal capacity and desire to trust	Responses to traumatic losses, depression, family disruption, learning, self-esteem	Problem feelings / Self-assertion / Coping with school	Electic; used problem-solving approaches / Psychodynamic	Higher level of functioning sustained in school / Improved self-esteem / Better living arrangement

*No indication in record of focus on learning disability.

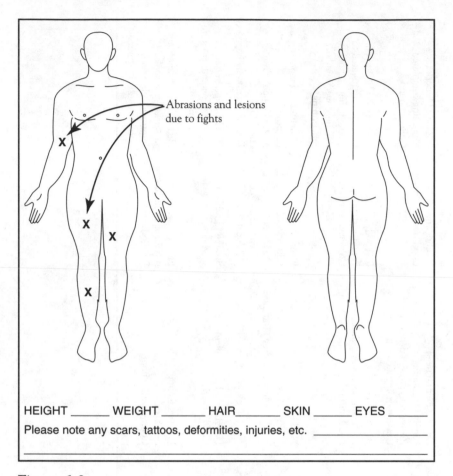

Figure 6-2.
Body Diagram

used to show physical injuries such as knife wounds and scars (figure 6-2). Some specific examples of successful or quasi-successful intervention follow. The cases, which constitute a purposive sample, focus on aspects of the intervention process, including treatment focus, theoretical approaches, or treatment strategies, and they help illuminate the clinical work. In all of the cases there was found improved self-esteem and an enhanced sense of self-differentiation, that is, the ability to make appropriate choices, set goals, and cope effectively for self-sufficiency, all necessary for achieving personal power. Clinical intervention, knowledge, and skills contributed to and may be even determined by the enhancement of these, thus playing a part in successful outcome. Table 6-1 contains a summary of the cases.

Case 1

Because funding for schools in Massachusetts is linked significantly to property taxes, wealthy towns and suburbs allocate more dollars per capita to schools than can poor or less-well-off areas. (This process has been successfully challenged in the state judiciary system.) To moderate the imbalance, some communities support busing to better school districts as a vehicle for improved education in cross-cultural, integrated settings. The assumption is that white children in well-off school districts benefit from the cross-cultural exposure, and children of color from poor school districts benefit from a better curriculum, better facilities, and the middle- or upper-class milieu.

A teenager in a busing program who was exhibiting extreme acting-out behavior was referred to a worker who, upon assessment, determined that the etiology of the behavior lay in the youngster's inability to cope with problems in the school setting, a middle school in an affluent suburb. The treatment plan was designed to teach the child coping strategies for handling institutional and individually directed racism. This approach is an example of the use of successful application of ecological and systems theories.

The fourteen-year-old boy had been referred by a pediatrician in a community health center because of his mother's concern about truant behavior. The client was seen four times before his mother was informed that her insurance (Medicaid) would not cover the costs. During the four sessions a number of issues surrounding the boy's behavior in school and at home was explored. It was learned that he was a personable, competent youngster who lived with his mother and older sister; his father had left the family suddenly on two occasions. The family had a strong affiliation with their church. His acting-out behavior, which included whitewashing a teacher's car, was "in response to expectations of people in school that he would behave that way."

Treatment goals targeted several problem symptoms and behaviors for change. In response to peer pressure, the worker explored both the boy's behavior in school and his reasons for acting out and racism in the school. Then they role-played appropriate responses to deflect or manage institutional racism and supported his strengths (his positive self-esteem, college goals, and positive relationships with his mother, peers, and role models). They explored as well the relationship between the boy and his father and the boy's disappointment and anger about their relationship.

This work illustrates success in helping a child to cope with racism and stay in school, an empowerment imperative for people of color. The strategy is particularly significant since education is a pivotal variable and a goal to be achieved if these clients are to break out of their entrapment in poverty, sometimes transgenerational poverty. The significance of education as a tool for empowerment must be understood by practitioners. Many cases demonstrate evidence that practitioners provided positive reinforcement for education: 66 percent of these clients moved toward improving their educational level.

Case 2

The next example shows how the worker focused on client-family strengths in the assessment-treatment plan and in intervention.

The mother of an eleven-year-old boy sought help when he began acting out by defying her and hitting his sisters, ages thirteen and eight, upon learning that his parents would divorce. The client was an energetic child, eager to please but not listened to very well. Shy and stuttering at times, he was seen by the worker as an intelligent, sensitive child. Although his speech was unclear and his thoughts seemed unorganized, he was deemed cognitively capable of insight. Also determined to be depressed, oppositional, and a bed wetter, he was evaluated as learning disabled (a condition that his father has). His parents had a violent relationship; his father had beaten his mother in front of the children. The family was on Medicaid.

Treatment planning had two prongs. One was to exteriorize the client's problem to the whole family system (to help it understand how the functioning of the entire family played a part in the problem) and modify each individual's response to the boy. Second, home-based family therapy explored the feelings and unfinished business associated with the separation of parents. The targeted behavior, bed-wetting and aggressive behavior toward siblings, was approached through family and individual therapy with the child, which allowed him to express his feelings and frustration about his father, and to examine his bed-wetting and the factors that contributed to it: the fighting between the parents, their separation and eventual divorce, the family's fear of fragmentation, and the purpose of the child's behavior, which was to draw attention away from the parents' conflict.

In family sessions, the mother was taught techniques in limit setting and management of the child's acting out. The mother became depressed and in individual sessions began to have flashbacks of childhood sexual abuse, finally becoming suicidal. A suicide contract—an agreement between client and clinician that the mother would not commit suicide and when such ideation became strong would call for help—was made along with cognitive restructuring of thoughts, acknowledging that rage hides shame. In family meetings again, the children discussed the mother's rage, and its effect on the family unit and the children, and especially the son's sadness about his father loss.

Family and individual therapeutic modalities were used to deal with a transgenerational problem of sexual abuse and violence. As the mother's depression was targeted in the treatment phase, her childhood experiences of sexual abuse were revealed, with the consequence that she became suicidal.

As this difficult case became more difficult with the mother's suicide threats, the worker was called upon to use inner strengths (stamina, commitment, persistence) along with therapeutic skills. [Earlier, we alluded to workers' power in the treatment relationship, but there is also worker burnout, and several cases of this nature help focus on the demands of the role and the fatigue that ensues.]

The eclectic approach in this case drew on psychoeducational, behavioral, psychodynamic, and family theory over the year's treatment and netted several positive outcomes: the boy ceased bed-wetting; the efforts to in-crease the mother's parenting skill led to an exploration of her depression and rage based on childhood abuse; and the mother became able to man-age suicidal tendencies and master intense feelings. Everyone in this fam-ily moved to a higher level of functioning. Of particular note was the mother's improvement in parenting skills, which at the point of termina-tion was facilitating the children's increasing social and psychological com-petencies and educational readiness.

Case 3

A seventeen-year-old female was referred for outpatient treatment follow-ing brief hospitalization pursuant to her running away with a girlfriend and being apprehended by the police. The girls, young lovers, had made a suicide pact, and the client stated that she had sustained an injury at-tempting to keep her friend from stabbing herself. Of note was the fact that this client had been abused sexually by her father, who also abused her mother physically.

Upon exploration, the worker secured a suicide contract and set goals to help this young woman understand herself within the context and func-tioning of her family and aid her in problem solving and in acceptance of her preferred sexual orientation, thereby addressing her sexual identity cri-sis. In the sessions, the worker underscored the strengths of the supportive mother, who, albeit overprotective, had at one point been viewed as ne-glectful (she had been found drunk and ignorant of her daughter's where-abouts when apprehended by police). During twenty-four sessions over six months, the worker drew on psychodynamic approaches and behavioral techniques.

After several sessions, the suicidal impulses diminished, and despite am-bivalence about treatment, the client became well engaged. She examined in detail her confusion about her sexual identity and the hostile relation-ship with her lover, which was marked by battles over whether to reveal the relationship or to keep it a secret. The client appeared unable to set limits in the relationship or to be clear about what level of revelation was tolerable for herself. She made great progress in managing her anger and frustration and in her ability to problem solve and in the clarity she ob-

tained concerning her sexual identity. She was able to end the destructive relationship in which she was caught and remain in school. At termination she was gainfully employed.

Case 4

In this study, work was viewed as a self-organizer and self-esteem builder; the case that follows used work as a constructive force for client growth. Clinical intervention was a condition for continuing employment, with the expectation that the client could achieve some mastery over her problematic behavior. Both the client and her mother worked as electronic assemblers at the same worksite.

The client, who suffered from schizophrenia and sexually transmitted diseases, was a twenty-one-year-old who was able to maintain employment despite her impairment. She was referred by an employee assistance program because of her explosive, aggressive behavior in the workplace.

Forced to drop out of high school to join the work force in order to help support the family, the client had been raped by her father. Currently she and her mother left the housing project early each morning for the twenty-plus-mile drive to a suburban manufacturing company. While the mother manifested strength in helping her daughter remain on the job, at the same time she colluded with the father, her husband, to get her daughter to drop an investigation to substantiate parental abuse or neglect for sexual abuse against the father/husband.

The worker used extensive therapeutic skills and arranged for additional help from a psychiatrist, and during the course of treatment, the client was able to maintain employment. The treatment approaches were psychodynamic, cognitive (focusing on helping the client to reduce delusional, paranoid, and impulsive behavior), and family systems (with one person) whereby the client's role in the family was clarified and targeted for change. The client made progress in directing her rage appropriately in the family and in rejecting the role of family scapegoat.

Progress is the key in treatment, and it is used in distinction from "total change." The intervention, although painful, had not fragmented the family unit and the client, and the mother gained insight on what triggered the explosive workplace behavior and how to control it. This intervention did not engage the father. Whether he refused services, if offered, or whether there was tacit understanding that it would be of no benefit to try to engage him is not known. In either event, the marginalization of the male is clear from both the family perspectives and the larger societal view, which tolerates the unemployment or unemployability and largely reduces the male role to that of sex mate. The male adaptive process in this context is often to seek power through violence, sexual exploitation, and/or drugs when the positive outlets of adult education, work preparation, and employment are unavailable. And even if employment and other resources were available, was the father/husband in this case ready to take advantage of them?

Case 5

A seventeen-year-old girl was referred by her teacher because of decreased capacity and functioning brought on by the death of her father who resided in a southern state. The client had not known that her father was ill because of his alcoholism. In her home, she functioned as an adult caretaker for her older siblings and her mother, although she was the youngest child and obviously the most parentified. Assuming this role prevented her from adequately mastering the adolescent task of self-consolidation. She presented as depressed and overwhelmed from her enormous responsibilities and unable to manage her intense sadness and rage.

In the treatment plan, the worker assisted her with identifying her own needs associated with adolescent maturation and helped her to see that her role in the family was blocking her from meeting these biological and psychological developmental demands. The worker also facilitated identification of feelings related to her father's death and encouraged their expression. The worker sustained her through this mourning process.

The theories used were largely psychodynamic and cognitive, with an emphasis on the former. Feelings were explored and insight used to facilitate behav-

ior change. Working from clearly articulated goals, the worker relied strongly on the therapeutic alliance to give the young woman the courage to explore the feelings and experiences that had so immobilized her. The work centered on feelings of loss and abandonment and educational exposure to the disease of alcoholism and its effect on the family, particularly the children.

The client made ample progress toward greater self-esteem, self-confidence, and competence, and she was able to complete high school. Upon achievement of this important milestone, she expressed an intention to take an extended vacation or break where she would rest, have no demands made upon her, and be taken care of. The worker helped her to expand her horizon and move beyond this dependency position to a sense of her own ability to change her life and experience her personal power. They explored part-time employment and college options, and at the point of termination the client was headed to college.

Good clinical movement and a successful outcome, assisted by the strong positive relationship between worker and client and the respect and caring shown by the worker, were demonstrated.

At the point of engagement this client had been so depressed that she was unable to identify any positives in her life. The worker's strategy of requiring that she pinpoint whatever she could think of that made her feel proud helped her to reframe her destructive, cognitive self-definitions. After repeated sessions and discussions on values, beliefs, and pride in herself and family, the client was able to acknowledge the strengths that the worker saw from the beginning. This sharing, bonding, and growth occurred between a white worker and a teenager of color.

Case 6

The need for intimacy is critical. Often the relationship with a child is clung to as the only hope for closeness.

The mother of a sixteen-year-old became severely depressed when her pregnant daughter revealed plans to have an abortion. The worker had been concerned when she sensed the mother's pleasure in this pregnancy and her role in encouraging it. Later, the mother had shared her feeling that there was nothing for her in life since her boyfriend, who had been pushing drugs, had stormed out of the household and the relationship following pressure from the worker that the mother get off drugs. Seeing her daughter's baby to be the only thing that would give her life meaning, she asserted, "I don't need a man if she [the daughter] has that baby." The daughter, however, was extremely ambivalent.

This crisis was used to motivate the mother and the daughter toward goals for self-development as an antidote to their sense of meaninglessness. Contracting for intensive work with the client and her family, the worker met with the client daily around organizing her household and financial resources and also developing her parenting skills (there were two other children). The dramatic change in the family functioning subsequent to the following interview which was held with the whole family is noted in detail for its clinical and heuristic value:

Worker; mother, Alicia; son, Pepe; fourteen; and daughter, Gina, eight, attended in addition to pregnant daughter, Maria. Mother's boyfriend, Jaime, who had been invited, was absent. Alicia started off freely acknowledging how much better she felt now that the house was straight and things more organized. When the worker asked what the family wanted to accomplish, Maria said she wanted the family to get along and respect her; Pepe said he wanted the family to move and start all over; Maria said she wanted help for her mother to stop the drinking. When the worker asked what it's like when mother gets drunk, Pepe confessed he gets angry and began to cry. The worker asked if she could speak to the mother for him. Turning to Alicia, the worker [as Pepe] said "it's hurting me to see you this way, I'm afraid you might die." Alicia was asked her reaction to seeing her children's pain. She hung her head and said "it makes me very sad." The worker then asked Alicia why did she drink to which she answered, "It helps me fight for myself, I can tell Jaime how I really feel. But after I do that, we have a fight and then he leaves, so I take it out on the kids." The worker asked if she wanted help to change the relationship with Jaime and do better with the children, to which she agreed.

Through individual work with mother and family meetings that at first in-cluded Jaime, who then dropped out of treatment as the work required a commitment for change from him, the mother developed a greater sense of competence and self-value and became less dependent on alcohol and a male relationship for self-esteem. Eventually she stopped drinking, found a job as a day care assistant, and encouraged Maria's plan to finish high school and go to college after her miscarriage. Improvement in the home environment and household organization and better use of financial re-sources were evident.

The theories underlying the strategies used in this intervention were psychodynamic, cognitive-behavioral, and family systems, with an emphasis on the last. The teaching of communication skills, parent-ing skills, health care and hygiene was not unlike that which oc-curred in a majority of cases.

Case 7

In the following case the clinician successfully intervened with a mother-daughter dyad. Here, the worker drew on psychodynami-cally based short-term strategies to facilitate problem solving and grief work and also drew on family therapy theory.

First known to the agency three years earlier, this twenty-eight-year-old woman had dropped out of school when pregnant. The worker then had helped her to return; she received a high school equivalency diploma (the GED) and had enrolled in a professional college program during which she organized a fashion show with some of the mothers from the agency. Suddenly she had dropped out of school and treatment. When a year later she returned to the agency (the worker, who had been very disappointed, had not reached out), she confessed that her boyfriend had become upset by her achievements. Now, he was beating her when he was drunk. She again set goals of becoming independent financially, finishing her educa-tion, and furthering her career and did so, terminating her contact with the agency.

Her mother, meanwhile, had become a client after the death of her son, the former client's brother, age twenty-six, which had precipitated the mother's addiction to alcohol. After joining a drug awareness group upon the urging of her daughter and attending family sessions with her other son, who had been placed in special education classes by the worker who supported his getting into a life guard swimming program, she stopped drinking and got a job. Both women became self-supporting and off the welfare rolls as a result of these interventions, clearly examples of client empowerment.

Case 8

In much of the helping literature over the years, African-American families were identified by their weaknesses and exploited in these perceptions. Since the 1970s, a positive opposition literature has appeared. The following case is consistent with the focus on positives, strengths, and exercise of personal power.

An employed black grandmother purchased clinical services when she brought her seven-year-old grandson for help with his nightmares and worrying. She was caring for him because his mother, who currently lived in the home, was a drug addict and frequently disappeared from the home for long periods of time. The grandmother's strengths and the worker's effectiveness were joined when after two sessions the grandmother took action, evicting her drug-using daughter. The child's symptoms then ceased.

The worker helped to focus on the problem, bringing reality to the situation and freeing the grandmother to find a solution, however painful. Additional supportive services for the child were not deemed necessary, although the grandmother, resourceful and assertive, stated that she would return with the child should the need arise. The child, as the grandmother's focus of attention, had support to master the multiple competencies appropriate for his age, laying the groundwork for sound functioning in the years ahead.

Herself a good role model, the grandmother refused to allow her daughter's incapacity to block her grandson's opportunities.

Confronting a problem of this nature is far from easy for parents who live in disadvantaged communities. Deciding to evict an off-spring conjures up frightening possibilities to many parents—homelessness, drugs, physical harm, even death—and immobilizes them. In one of the agencies in the study, the director of professional services reported a case (not within the study sample) in which a teenager was enraged with his mother when she gave him an ultimatum to get a job or go to school by a certain date. He persisted in his unproductive behavior, siphoning resources from the family and not respecting the home. The mother followed through with the ultimatum, evicting the son from the home. For weeks the boy slept in his car, trying in various ways to make his mother feel guilty. His sister subverted the mother's action by secretly bringing him food, which the mother blocked when she realized what was happening. Today (eight years later), this young man, now married, working, and a father, verbalizes his appreciation of his mother's behavior although he is still angry. Of interest and importance to this discussion is that this working-poor mother was employed at a human services agency, where she received support and direction for her bold solution to her son's problems. In this case the mother's limit-setting and tough love strategy were appropriate because the teenager was reality-focused and healthy enough to accept these limits.

Case 9

Another successful intervention occurred in the case of a biracial child fathered by a white male in relationship with a woman of color. Both parents were now absent from the child's life, although the child remained connected to the mother's family.

This eleven-year-old boy was seen for depression and history of losses along with feelings of powerlessness consequent to multiple placements: with an aunt, then a foster home, then another foster home. He responded by withdrawing, developing feelings of worthlessness, and showing prob-

lems with learning. Individual play therapy was the intervention of choice, and from all indications the child responded.

Adoption planning became an initial focus of intervention. The aunt could not provide care because she was a drug user, and the first foster home placement had been disrupted when the family's son became the target of gang activity. Through these disruptions, the worker helped the child to manage his problematic feelings, including responses to the many losses he had sustained, and gradually he became more expressive and comfortable with himself and appropriately assertive, with much improved behavior in school. The worker engaged in a number of concrete services, such as arranging for transportation to school and facilitating camping plans during summer vacation. The boy obviously trusted the worker, who helped him to reach a decision to reject adoption, thereby encouraging a sense of personal power. In addition she helped sustain him in school through supportive therapy based on problem-solving approaches.

Schooling is important because mastery contributes to self-esteem. The future of this child is connected to his education, and although the social services were costly, in the long run they may well be cost-effective.

As much as the worker cared about this child and as effective as this outcome appears, the absence of attention to the child's biracial heritage, along with his experience of abandonment by his white father, is to be noted. Though biracial children are identified by society as black, they are in reality connected to their white parent as well. The connection to both parents, already jeopardized by societal denial of the white heritage, is compounded for biracial children in one-parent families. Especially when the child is the same sex as the absent parent, sexual identity may be in jeopardy. In this case, the child remains connected with his black heritage through his mother; the absence of his white father means both that he is cut off from his white heritage and is at risk for disconnection from maleness as well, with no connection to black males in the community. Therefore his source of sexual identity must come from these males. When a black child, particularly a boy, is being raised by a white mother, the loss of the black parent, whose presence helps connect the child to his cultural group and facilitates social definition and sexual identity as a part of self-identity development, is also serious. This discussion illustrates the interrelationships and some of the ensuing complexities attendant to racial and sexual identity in the family structure of biracial children.

An Innovative Therapeutic Strategy

An intervention that worked with an overwhelmed, depressed, and dependent client deserves comment: that of a clinician sharing a personal experience that mirrored that of the client.

Incest was an issue. The worker, suspicious that incest was at the base of the client's depression and immobilization, encouraged a discussion of the client's relationship with her father. Observing the client's terror at approaching the subject, the worker shared the fact that she had been a victim of abuse by her father and thus understood the pain and sense of despair such memories evoke. In the processing of the client's recollections, the worker used her personal experience several times in assisting the client to feel joined by one who understood what she felt and believed that the pain could be transcended. As a result of the work that followed, the client came to view herself as a worthwhile, valued individual, demonstrating improved self-esteem and sense of individuation along with self-mastery and development of strengths enabling her movement to self-sufficiency.

Working with Male Clients

With few exceptions, the males who were served were primarily children and adolescents. Rarely did an older teenager or adult male commit himself to individual counseling. The following case is one of a few exceptions, with successful intervention achieved with a white male over fifty years old who had been institutionalized at age three for retardation.

The client had been referred for depression following the death of his mother. Although he had attended a sheltered workshop and other training programs at a transitional employment shelter, he was unemployed and living alone in a supervised apartment. He was evaluated as able to benefit from therapy addressing his depression. Once the depression lifted, the focus of the work became employment. At termination, the goal of movement toward self-sufficiency was reached as the client prepared to start a new job. Resources, agencies, programs, and staff had been available to this client over decades, and such support continued in the abatement of his depression and subsequent job acquisition.

Some men were involved in family counseling as father, boyfriend, or husband, but longer-term involvement was not usual. A larger number were involved in a drug awareness group organized by one agency. Many of these fathers were unmarried; some were homeless and did odd jobs around the immediate environment (project or neighborhood) and serviced women sexually. It was not uncommon for a young male to live with a girlfriend until kicked out after a brawl, then to move back to mother or friends, only later to return to girlfriend and for this to become an ongoing pattern. A large number of these men had been stripped by society of any significant value except a sexual one. This has been the state of affairs for African-American males since their arrival on these shores. Records of slave children listed the name and the slave owner of the mother but omitted any recognition of the father, or even his owner, an example of the institutionalization of the nullification of the black male and how it has been maintained in this society.[2] As a result of slavery, colonization of the Caribbean, and current societal dynamics, Latino and Caribbean males also suffer consequences similar to those endured by African Americans.

More concretely for the female partner, the male who has no job or steady job, and therefore no cash resources or health benefits, and who is not connected to mainstream institutions with which he can negotiate for benefits and resources, is not an attractive marriage partner—thus, the on-again, off-again relationship found in several, but by no means a majority, of these cases.

Social workers must understand that caring and relational experiences are fundamental needs even in the absence of concrete resources and benefits, and perhaps even more so. In this connection, too, the lack of contact with agencies experienced by these males mitigates against knowledge of basic health maintenance, including contraception, and reinforces the role of the female as dominant in family dynamics and planning. Here the female is blamed for procreation and the male for his prowess when neither may have had access to family planning education and material resources. The male is forced into the underground economy, where drugs, petty theft, street crimes, and other income-seeking crimes, become life sustaining.

The same agency that organized the drug awareness group attempted to involve male teens prior to fatherhood in an effort to intervene in this self-family-community cycle of destructive behavior; however well intended and well staffed, this initiative remained an uphill battle. These early-teen groups, effective temporarily, would break up when gang activity became attractive and later became the instrumental foci of the group. Mothers were powerless to offset the gang mentality and influence, although they surely wanted better for their sons. Different initiatives were being planned, including a mothers of teenage boys group, in an effort to help empower the mothers, who were perceived as the stronger positive change agents. Efforts to involve men in an organization of (substitute) father/son activities such as basketball pick-up games and weekend camping trips were also planned.

A corollary for successful work with male clients in this agency depended in large part on successful efforts with mothers, consistent with the focus on community involvement and with the goal of empowering clients to work together toward acquiring needed services and facilitating their ability to offer support to one another. Thus, parents of children who had joined activities groups were invited to participate in these empowerment groups, all of which grew out of needs expressed by the mothers. Mothers often began in a group that met to grocery shop at a discount store or to discuss parenting problems and solutions. As a result of the motivation secured through the group activity, some returned to school, attaining their GED or job training, and went to work. A negative outcome was that when they went to work, their time to continue participation in the group activity through which they received the benefit of social support dropped. Eventually the group, out of member need, would become a therapy group, which by member request and agreement then became a combination support-therapy and action group.

A striking phenomenon identified among the cases was that in the majority of white families, the father was present, while in Latino and African-American families, the fathers were not present. This does not mean that mothers in Latino and African-American families did not have relationships with males. Of note is that the white males tended to be alcoholic, not working, hostile, resistant to agency intervention, and racist. One client told her social worker that "her husband would not come to the agency because some of the workers are black." The relationship in the neighborhood between the white families and families of color was often hostile and combative.

Drug Entrapment

Drug abuse overwhelms clients, practitioners, and the helping system. It has become a widespread problem, yet agencies, like other societal institutions, have underestimated the potency and urgency of it and thus have failed to confront it aggressively.

In continuing to work with families who have addicted members and in offering assistance and services to clients without confrontation about abuse, an agency is colluding in perpetuation of the problem. However, addressing substance abuse is not a simple issue. What should be the parameters? How long should the agency continue to offer service to clients who acknowledge their inability to control their substance abuse habits, but at the same time fail to follow through with planned assistance to address the addiction? What about clients who completely deny their substance abuse problem? Both professional and ethical dilemmas are embodied in this issue. Regardless of theoretical approach and intervention strategy, clinical outcomes are always compromised as long as drugs remain a part of the client's behavioral dynamics, as the following cases show.

A white male in his early twenties sought treatment for depression, stating, "I cut my wrist. I know it was a dumb thing to do." This suicide attempt had followed a breakup of a long-standing romantic relationship. The client had recently left his job and was a heavy abuser of alcohol and drugs.

In treatment his depression abated somewhat, but his denial of his substance abuse and infidelity did not diminish. He refused to enter a detox center for drug and alcohol rehabilitation, insisting that he would detox himself. His denial of addiction compromised the execution of the treatment plan. Raped as a child, this client has been unable to master his maladaptive response to that trauma, seeking relief through drugs.

A twenty-year-old Latino, chronically depressed and with a long history of heavy street drug abuse and arrest for disorderly conduct and assault on police, was referred following hospitalization for suicide risk after a breakup with his girlfriend. His family had a history of multiple suicide, including the client's father. The mother, whose prescription medication was used in the client's suicide attempt, had also attempted suicide earlier, becoming "very sick" afterward.

Medical and social services were heavily utilized in efforts to address these life-threatening problems. Although the suicide impulsivity appeared reduced, the client never resolved the underlying depression related to ongoing mourning of his father's death. Moreover, he was unable to establish a therapeutic relationship that would facilitate work on his drug problem, despite extensive outreach efforts by the agency. It did not matter to him that drug treatment was an expectation of parole. Arrogant, combative, and threatening homicide as well as suicide, he remained an extremely high risk for violent acting out despite intensive efforts by the agency to engage him in the committed delivery of comprehensive inpatient care.

An employed black mother in her mid-fifties with three adult children, one of whom had been seriously injured and is now handicapped, was seen in the medical clinic because of flu symptoms, diabetes, and hypertension. Her depression was identified, and she was referred for psychiatric evaluation.

The clinician's evaluation revealed a woman of many strengths whose depression was connected to relational problems with a boyfriend of twenty *years. The boyfriend manifested disaffection, claiming that the client "had changed after menopause." He had succeeded in creating a sense of worthlessness and self-doubt within this woman while simultaneously exploiting her resources. He continued his addiction to crack cocaine and marijuana, despite couple's therapy.*

As a result of individual intervention, the client was able to give up the relationship with the boyfriend, see her own strengths, and move toward greater self-improvement. The depression lifted, serious anxiety abated, and sleeplessness ceased. The client was able to self-disclose and face the future with confidence, working and not emotionally dependent on the boyfriend, who had not yet faced his drug problem. The client described her change like "a weight was lifted."

In these three cases involving white, Latino, and African-American males, the behaviors manifest extreme denial and manipulation. Treatment of these clients is a challenge. Their behaviors, often characterized by lying, stealing, deception, distortion, and all manner of cunning and streetwise cleverness, test practitioners' ability to remain empathic and, although reduced to powerlessness themselves by the manipulative games of the client, committed to client empowerment. Sometimes dangerous and violent when blocked from gratification of their drug-addicted need, these clients require vigilance on the part of practitioners, and intervention often also requires assistance from law enforcement personnel.

Not to be forgotten, in work with these clients, is that relationship with the practitioner is all too often not enough. The power of the addiction cannot always be overcome by the power of the clinical process. A previous review of successful intervention showed the practitioner's investment and skill and the addicted client's struggle.

In one agency where a large number of clients abused drugs, clinicians were especially reluctant to participate in outcome reviews of their work because of their recognition that drugs undermine the change process. Client self-determination has its high place in social work theory and practice, but at what point does respect for it compromise long-term goals, community welfare, and accountability to the paying public?

One agency confronted the drug problem when workers observed an increase in substance abuse, particularly drugs, by its clients and a discouraging recidivistic pattern. After months of work to help clients gain the strength to become substance-abuse free, clinicians discovered that most clients could not, no matter how motivated they appeared, maintain sobriety. The dynamics of the community were such that they would eventually be pulled back. One major issue to be confronted in a large percentage of the families was the fear that becoming competent, drug free, and successful would bring rejection. Success usually meant isolation, rejection, and abandonment by boyfriends and family members, as well as neighbors and friends. Over and over again the staff saw clients get off drugs and become motivated for school and work, only to fall victim again to the addiction. It was for this reason that a drug awareness group was started.

The agency facilitated the organization of the drug awareness group in response to clients' expressed need. In the meetings, programming and process were completely determined by the members. Some meetings focused exclusively on personal sharing relative to knowledge of the drug scene and struggles to cope with it; others had speakers—physicians, nurses, recovered substance abusers, and others. These community coping strategies had a positive impact on clients; their increased awareness of the dangers and risk of debilitating personal injury carried over into readiness for individual help and the painful process of change.

Agency and Staff Dynamics

One must be mindful of the environment in which much of the therapeutic work occurred. An oasis for clients, all of the agencies were well-kept facilities, attractive but not posh by any stretch of the imagination. Clients seemed comfortable in the environment and well respected by both professional and support staff, as evidenced by the fact that in staff-client exchanges, there was a very high degree of professionalism. Staff were caring individuals who exhibited concern for the plight of clients. They taught by actions and by modeling important roles that may otherwise not be available and would be, in any case, limited. A significant role exhibited by staff was that of being a part of the paid labor force. Being appropriately dressed for work, arriving during regular work hours, often working late into the evenings, weekends, and holidays, and keeping a schedule are all functions many assume that others know, but that may not be the case at all for overwhelmed clients.

The director of professional services in one agency commented on how important appropriate dress is considered by both management and clients, citing a client who stated: "Gee, she [referring to the worker] can't tell me anything when she doesn't even know how to dress. Look, she didn't even have a bra on under that old gauze dress." The director added that staff were expected to "look professional and act professional so that clients and the community are viewed with respect."

Over time, workers serve as models for their clients. Clients were reported as learning how to come into the agency and speak to staff in an appropriate manner. On the initial visit, it is not unusual for some severely depressed clients to arrive at the agency unkempt, angry, and swearing at the receptionist and clinician. In several cases, the anger became more contained after several sessions, and improvement in appearance was noted. This obviously good outcome may not show on an outcome assessment schedule.

In addition to learning how to act and dress and demonstrate acceptable behavior, clients learn how to interact within systems in ways that evoke positive and supportive responses rather then provoking negative ones. There are similarities here to milieu treatment, not a small or insignificant strategy in view of deinstitutionalization and the loss of residential treatment services and education.

In this regard it is critical that helpers in training have guidance regarding appropriate demeanor. A male client behaving in an agitated fashion swore at everyone to such a degree that the receptionist summoned an administrator to help. In the intervening moments before he arrived, a social work student who had heard the commotion had gone to the client and was described as non-professionally confrontative. The administrator ended up rescuing the student from this unprofessional situation, teaching her professional distance and the importance of managing her curiosity.

The energy, intellectual investment, and commitment necessary to work with the multiplicity of problems these clients bring is obvious. Clarity of thinking and a capacity for considering the confluence of all factors impinging on clients' behavior is commendable. This is a clear example of social work's unique person-in-environment perspective.

Working in environments plagued by deprivation of public city services, overwhelmed with needs of citizens who have become withdrawn, hostile, or both, requires not merely commitment but also flexibility. It is one thing to leave a middle-class living environment for work in another attractive, comfortable environment in a neighborhood or downtown. It is quite different to live within, or travel to, and confront daily all of the failures of the American dream: rundown housing, dilapidated and ill-kept neighborhoods, dangerous streets, crack residences, unreliable public transportation, and chronic despair. The psychological strain of knowing that children are abused because of parental exhaustion and economic despair, that children are deprived of enriching experiences and that they are having sexual intercourse starting at preschool ages and gun packing in latency, takes a heavy toll on workers. To the energy, intellectual investment, and commitment on the part of practitioners that are so critical for this work must be added emotional stamina—the capacity to cope with stress, trauma, danger, and societal contradiction.

Consider the strain and drain of working with clients who constantly face danger. A young male social worker in one agency approached the school to meet with his client, a high school student. As he entered the school grounds, a fight between two male students broke out and a crowd gathered. Caught in this unexpected turn of events, he courageously attempted to stop the fight and with assistance from others was successful. Upon his return to the agency, he was visibly upset as he reflected to his supervisor his recognition of the danger that he now might be in if one or both of the students possessed weapons.

Consider a twelve-year-old youngster who was siphoning gas from one car to another in the vicinity of a filling station. Not thinking that the puddle nearby that he thought was water could be gasoline, he carelessly tossed his cigarette there. The immediate explosion left him burned and disfigured. Currently in treatment for unresolved trauma, he was riding in a car with his practitioner when they approached a filling station. Overcome by panic, he jumped out of the car, dashed into ongoing traffic, and sustained serious injuries. Now the client's physical injuries and already unbearable sense of trauma were compounded, a turn of events that drew heavily on the worker's stamina and emotional resources.

A black male social worker discussed the cost of his stressful work in inner-city schools where he conducts youth groups to facilitate coping with violence. Unable to sleep the night after the group processed the members' first experiences with violence, this seasoned social worker could not believe the extent of trauma, abuse, and behavior that had victimized these children. He lay awake trying to manage his own sense of powerlessness in relation to helping his clients transcend the violence endemic to their daily environment. Every child in the group wept as he shared his pain of seeing his mother murdered by a relative watching adults shoot up heroin and then beat up one another and him. So many of these experiences ended in sudden, unexpected, and inexplicable deaths.

Workers who deal with overwhelmed clients on drugs must remain flexible and accessible. The worker and the relationship are the only substitute for submission to the addiction, so whenever the client feels unable to cope with the craving and in danger of submission, it is mandatory that the worker be available by telephone or in person so that the client can talk about the feelings and master them. There is no substitute for the client's recognition that she can develop capacity for this mastery. Telephone calls to the worker in the early morning when loneliness and anxiety appear overwhelming are common. One worker asserted that once contacted, she does not break off with the client until the feelings have abated. She sometimes took a client on walks or helped her engage in an activity such as housework. Once a client called her in the middle of the night hysterical that she had lapsed. This worker emphasized the importance to the client of trying again. After successfully mastering her addiction, the client has been drug free for over three years and has been hired as a coleader of a drug group that the agency organized. The extraordinary effort that marked this successful intervention was manifest whenever drug cases were turned around.

The awesome pressures that are embodied in this work often lead to burnout. Professionals need to find ways to cope with the tremendous demands that confront them daily. Human service providers who work with this population who are highly paid, such as psychiatrists, some psychologists, and even some social workers, can escape to unwind in tranquil, stress-reducing settings. In contrast, many line staff, professionally trained and untrained, do not earn enough to afford such necessary respite. Like the clients, they are trapped in the stressful environment with which they struggle to cope. Some manage the burnout better than others. A positive approach to burnout management was identified in one agency where several workers were encouraged to attend graduate school to earn the M.S.W. degree. Interestingly, one practitioner was clear that although she needed the degree as a credential, she was quite competent, having already trained professionals in social work and in psychology. She matriculated at one of Boston's schools of social work and other than minor problems with writing, which she effectively dealt with, she sailed through the program. Her understanding of human interaction, including knowledge of herself, was unusual. She had benefited from strong and capable clinical supervision, consultation with psychiatrists and social workers, and perhaps above all, life experience. She had turned the negatives of her own life, poverty and stressful family relationships, into a positive force, serving as an excellent role model for clients.

Another well-educated professional, who held an M.S.W. degree plus extensive postgraduate training, did not fare as well. Stressed and burned out, the worker sought relief through inappropriate closeness with clients. This type of response to stress increasingly is being identified and addressed by both clients and practitioners, male and female. The power differential in the clinical encounter offers a context for explaining the vulnerability of clinicians for such abuse of power and exploitation of the helping relationship.

The situations of these two workers are extreme on a continuum; most helpers working with overwhelmed clients find themselves somewhere in the middle, struggling and coping effectively.

In another situation a worker was entrapped in personal, marital, and extended family problems, including a spouse suffering from depression, a sibling who was drug addicted, and parents who depended on their social worker offspring for counseling and support.

Working in an agency where clients came from inner-city census tracts known for serious social pathology, the worker was as overwhelmed as the clients. She sought clinical help and was served as a client at one of the agencies in the study. The helper was able to facilitate some beginning insight on the part of the worker-client concerning the tendency to resist acknowledging the problem and persisting in scapegoating the spouse. At the end of the short-term work in which they engaged, an agreement had been reached whereby the worker-client and the spouse would seek treatment for their marital problem and management of the relationships with the extended family.

Despite the professional competence and investment of energy that could be observed, sometimes the best judgments are not enough to prevent iatrogenic effects on treatment outcome. An Italian father was referred by the juvenile court for alcoholism and sexual abuse of three children. The son was sent to a residential treatment center. The mother, after much support from the worker, separated from the husband and was herself sent to a residential shelter with two daughters. Because the family was broken up and there was no home to which he could return, the son was unable to come home for the visits with his family, which constituted a necessary part of the treatment process planned by the treatment team at the residential center. Situations like this have led to growing interest in family preservation models as alternatives for treatment. In this case, all was well intended, resources were not spared, and expertise and commitment were unquestioned; the outcome was nonetheless a disaster.

In another case, the caregiving systems themselves produced iatrogenic effects. A teenager became pregnant when supervision was not provided because the residential institution failed to coordinate a home visit with the family and the family clinician. The pregnancy aborted naturally after five and a half months, but the teenager and her family had to work through grief and loss of expectations. Once this occurred, the family was back on track.

Iatrogenic effects can sometimes occur when systemic and bureaucratic processes obstruct the best efforts to engage a client. A thirteen-year-old boy suspected of drug and gang activity refused an offer of treatment after assessment of his problems related to truancy, acting out, family dysfunction, and his mother's physical illness. The agency, powerless to intervene, was forced to wait until he committed a robbery and then was sent to residential treatment. Successful management could occur only after the client became more symptomatic, was arrested, and then remanded to a secured, residential treatment center.

Collaboration with Other Helpers

There was considerable interface between teachers and practitioners but not always interaction. A school might make a referral to an agency based on a teacher's recommendation, and there would often be telephone consultations. Practitioners went to the schools regularly to see students who were clients. Their observations were instructive, helping shed light on what the teachers must face daily. One agency's director of professional services stated: "Kids [students] come from stressful households. Parents may be using drugs, unemployed, mentally ill and hostile. They go to school with negative energy which may be personalized by the teacher. Teacher reacts and the student is worse off. Students often seem unmaturated because they are stressed out. Parents are not involved and teacher is reacting. What you have is students out there alone."

Earlier in the discussion of the teenage victim of racism, we noted how critical it is for children from this population to have a good education and many practitioners go to great lengths to ensure such an outcome. But too often the motivating factor for the referral is to get the student to behave in class and protect the teacher from much investment of time and energy on the pupil. This is somewhat understandable, considering the heavy burdens of urban teachers, but more to the point is that many teachers want to avoid working with children of this background. The fact is that the school, the teacher, the practitioners, and the pupil must work together in a partnership, sharing the responsibility for change.

Psychodynamic approach: Posits that the problem is a symptom of underlying unconscious processes set in motion by past traumas about which the client must be made aware. Insight into these processes is believed to allow opportunity consciously to master the disturbing emotions, perceptions, or ideas.

Cognitive-behavioral therapy: Focuses on changing behavior through an alteration of the individual's thinking process. By identifying the negative thinking that maintains the problem behavior and substituting constructive, positive thinking, new behavior is produced.

Family therapy approach: Seeks to change the relationships, boundaries, roles, alliances, and transactions that occur within the family that maintain the problem.

Educational approach: Consists of giving facts, information, and data.

Group therapy: Focuses on changing behavior through the use of group relationships and process. Interactions among members in the context of common goals and purposes bring about new thinking and behavior.

Systems approach: Focuses on changing some aspect of the relationship or interactions among various components of the system and/or the interaction between the system and its environment that is maintaining the problem.

The relationship between practitioners and other cognate service agencies is easier because they understand one another's systems. Policies, administrative regulations, programmatic goals, and service strategies are familiar territory. On the other hand, schools represent a different system and are perceived as a difficult bureaucracy, and they are often reported as harder to access. In some agencies in the study, physicians, nurses, psychiatrists, and other health personnel were part of the same staff and thus sometimes communication hurdles were minimized. Nonetheless, service delivery is complex and especially complicated for these clients, given their dependence on so many services.

Philosophy on Community

Each agency expressed a particular philosophy and mission in relation to the community and its clients. All agencies noted their location and accessibility to the client population. In fact, in over 91 percent of the cases reviewed, some form of utilization occurred. All were situated in desperate neighborhoods. One had a van that transported staff and clients between the neighborhood, a specifically targeted housing project, and the agency. Two agencies are located across the street from housing projects where residents constitute a large proportion of the agency's caseloads. Yet a fourth agency is located in the heart of a business setting. All are in inner-city neighborhoods.

We point again to the quantitative analysis that showed no community change (community building, neighborhood drug-fighting efforts, safer street campaigns) resulting from practitioner intervention with the study population. Nonetheless, as definitive as this finding appears, a look at the agencies' philosophy on community is instructive, possibly shedding light on the interventions used in the funding context that existed when these cases were active.

Although the auspices differ, each agency was proud of its accessibility and the notion that it was "there for the community." One agency espoused a particularly strong sense of identification with the community, which was evidenced in several ways. Although it had not involved community people or clients at the board or policy decision-making level, it fostered client opportunity for staff employment. For example, a recovered substance abuser was the coleader of a drug awareness group. The agency emphasized client change through individual or group therapeutic and educational interventions. However, it also recognizes the need for community change, addressing social change through modifying systems that affect the clients' lives, and sees these efforts as based on a community empowerment model. Serving a smaller clientele, it demonstrates innovation in program design and flexibility in worker roles. The client empowerment philosophy extends also to the community level, whereby groups for clients and nonclients were formed to discuss such issues as substance abuse and educational and school problems. These activities were used as avenues for inviting engagement around intervention for specific family needs and problems. Most of the clients were welfare recipients, and a large number expressed hope of gainful employment, which also was addressed in individual counseling sessions. However, while well intended and successful on the individual and small group level, community change activities were not in evidence.

Since the completion of the case record review, researchers in a second agency, in probing the question of the agency's philosophy toward the community, discovered that groups have since been formed to work with youths around a number of pressing issues. For example, a peer group in a housing project was organized as a gang prevention activity. Similarly a group of ten members with the human immunodeficiency virus (HIV), most of whom live in the housing project, are being trained to understand HIV and to educate other teens about its dynamics, focusing on sexuality, sexually transmitted diseases, and safer sex. Yet a third group, focusing on violence prevention, provides peer leadership training in anger management and the diffusion of explosive situations. A particular feature is a two-day ropes course teaching trust and interdependence in an outdoor environment. At the end of the training a small graduation is held to which parents are invited and do attend.

None of the agencies is involved with a community-wide grassroots, change-oriented effort where adults, who may or may not be clients, meet and plan strategies to help end violence and drug activity or to plan for neighborhood improvements. This type of social change appears to be beyond the agencies' scope. In the absence of major prevention efforts to thwart drugs that spawn unprecedented violence, little is going to change systemically that will help improve the environment, which in turn will help foster positive self-esteem.

CHAPTER 7

Revitalizing Care
Liberation from
Powerlessness and Entrapment

ALTHOUGH SUCCESSFUL CLINICAL OUTCOMES HAVE BEEN CONFIRMED, a forceful undertow exists, and its vorticity, strong enough to compromise the work, has also been confirmed. As helpful as clinical services are to overwhelmed clients, some options for strengthening these services and reinforcing their long-term effect must be explored, and sooner rather than later, given the range of problems, their interlocking, reinforcing nature, and their devastating impact on the lives of fellow human beings.

The larger community must recognize its responsibility for the well-being of all its members. Imperative is the need to understand and share the concept of commonweal and solidarity with others, including those who are of different race, ethnicity, sexual orientation, and socioeconomic class. It is only through this ethos and these values that the work can begin for revitalization of caring at the community level.

Cities have changed and continue to undergo rapid demographic transition. Boston has changed dramatically. The city is no longer inhabited and defined by a small number of ethnic groups around the Brahmin core. Now, in addition to Brahmins, Irish, Italians, African Americans, African Caribbeans, and Jews, there are Latinos (black and white) and Asians of many ethnicities—Chinese, Japanese, Vietnamese, Cambodians, Laotians, Koreans, Pacific Islanders, and East Indians. Agencies and funding bodies must be mindful of new citizens, new racial and ethnic groups, new oppressed groups, and traditional ones, doing much more to anticipate and plan strategically to meet their service needs and to help improve their quality of life. (The groups manifesting greatest need in this discussion are Latino and African Americans.)

People live in communities, an important and central unit between the individual and nation; it is here that they learn rights and responsibilities, to value and respect others, their own property and that of other individuals, as well as that of community institutions—schools, playgrounds, churches, streets, and sidewalks. It is within the community that basic human needs such as production and reproduction, education, consumption, and leisure are met.[1] Where one lives is an important aspect of American life, defining one's status, the caliber of city services such as education, usually dictating the friends and associates one can have. As we know from the cases reviewed, many families are mired in multiple problems—though they also have many strengths. When they experience such heavy burdens, they must turn to other community institutions for help. Agencies and the way they deliver social services are important to the future improvement of individual, family, and community functioning and thus are key components in revitalizing care.

Targeting Services to the Most Needful Groups

Hispanics are a significantly underserved population group, and the data suggest a need for greater outreach to them. That African Americans are using services in higher proportion than Hispanics, though the need for service is greater among the latter, is not to suggest that African Americans do not need further services. Rather, an expansion of programs and services is warranted so that all needful groups can be more adequately served. While much of formulation and implementation of traditional social work practice focused on the disadvantaged, its theories reflected a middle-class orientation. A deficit model that lacked class-related sensitivity invariably defined behavioral life patterns among the disadvantaged as deviant and pathological, thereby minimizing whatever strengths the poor possessed. This arena of practice is now more complete as class and culture become major components in work with the needy.

New groups will have to be involved in social service delivery planning, and in many instances agencies must help them to participate. Culturally relevant services must be developed, which means attending to language differences, cultural value differences and expectations, and ethnic community needs. Language barriers can be addressed when there are agency personnel who are conversant in the language of their clients, while clients themselves are assisted in learning English. No agency should assume that clients can pick up language on their own or that other institutions, churches or schools, are addressing this formidable barrier to full participation in the community. Given budget realities, it would not be feasible for every agency to offer training, but each must make sure that its staff members are connecting and communicating with clients. Language barrier is often cited as a major contributing factor to a high rate of premature termination by clients from Third World countries after the initial contact. The stance of the agency must be such that it supports a philosophy that is not inimical to clients' values and cultural practices. For example, it supports outreach efforts that respect clients' values as such, having a drop-in center for Latina clients who connect more readily when the agency is part of the community family. Or, it does not penalize workers for flexible scheduling with clients whose cultural values do not attach significance to promptness and the fifty-minute hour.

Culturally relevant services lead to policies that strengthen the health of the ethnic community and reinforce action, self-esteem, pride, self-assertion, and mastery among its members, promoting the ability to be fully bicultural, functioning in the American mainstream while remaining connected to the ethnic community. In addition to reinforcing cultural pride by celebrating ethnic holidays and recognizing ethnic values, the culturally relevant agency will make traditional holidays and practices meaningful and enhancing beyond the ethnic community. For example, there will be recognition that Martin Luther King's contributions benefit all people, not only African Americans. However, such a stance would hardly be possible for an agency serving Native Americans, which sought to emphasize the relevance for this population of Columbus Day, connected as it is in the Native American community with the beginning of Indian genocide.

Agencies must also be cognizant and ready to meet the challenges of the newly emerging cultural target groups that have yet to request services. Cultural prohibition may prevent clients from such communities from seeking assistance outside the family unit. Shankar, for example, has shown that at least among Asian Americans, needs exist at a variety of levels. Domestic violence in the Asian community has been hidden in this country for generations and is now being exposed by wives and children. Individuals needing services are still reluctant, however, to go public with their needs.[2] Public disclosures of need are viewed with contempt by the family, and members may come to experience collective guilt, shame, and failure. Agencies must exercise extreme caution and sensitivity when reaching out to reluctant communities. Direct outreach work in such instances is counterproductive and may make clients more resistant. Schools and community organizations, including religious institutions, could function as intermediaries between the client's family and the agency.

Why Not Groups?

Most clients are young, and agencies must gear programs to this population. In all the caseloads single mothers and male children constituted a substantial number. Agencies may need to examine the degree to which their programming is relevant to meeting the needs of these particular client groupings. Programs targeted specifically for mothers and male children should be put in place now that their service needs have been made explicit. Programs that offer mothers support in parenting, relational issues with spouses or boyfriends and children, social skills building, cognitive skills building, and educational and language skills are apparent areas of focus. For children and adolescents, recreation, leisure time activities, educational reinforcements, and character building programs are urgently needed. Preventive programs, not only therapeutic ones, must be encouraged. Early prevention strategies are necessary in many program areas, especially drugs, sex education, aggression and violence management, and negotiation skills.

When parents are functionally absent due to drug abuse or other debilitating circumstances, groups provide a less threatening forum for clients, allowing practitioners through their involvement to pass on the larger society's culture, values, and norms. In one group the practitioner approached the subject of sexual experimentation in a group of latency-aged children with explanations indicating that this was not acceptable activity. Other enrichment programs, games, and site visits were planned for these youngsters, who had little, if any, at-home guidance after the schoolday ended.

Agencies and institutions must put aside their professional affinity for one-on-one intervention, which stems from the individualism so endemic to American culture, and develop the interest in and expertise needed to offer a variety of groups: educational, supportive, recreational, and therapeutic. Natural helping networks, including community groups, could also be mobilized.

One agency used groups as a primary intervention modality. As a means of engagement, they were used initially to approach family need, first via children's activity groups, thus engaging parents in parent-support groups, which usually evolved into problem-solving (including also nonparenting issues) and therapeutic groups. Family therapy and individual work occurred as issues were identified that made such strategies appropriate. This approach could easily be adopted by other agencies. Groups were being planned for grandmothers who had stepped in to provide care for their children's offspring. Practitioners reported that these women's frustrations and depression stemming from a role that had been forced on them because of their grandchildren's drugging parents' inability to provide care seemed awesome. Some grandparents are caring for babies and children who are HIV positive. These women need support, encouragement, and a forum to share stresses unknown to other generations. Their pressing personal family needs are compounded by neighborhood and community deficits.

It is paradoxical that there has not been greater recognition of the value of groups for clinical intervention. Since groups are widely used for training and supervision of staff, the knowledge and skills are already present. In these instances, effectiveness was undisputed. Practitioners were free to learn from one another, to explore new ideas regarding interventions, and to support one another. Group process enhanced the motivation to work with this difficult population and to collaborate in the overall agency effort and neutralize the impact of the stressful work.

University-based professional education programs have not given priority to training for group intervention, leaving practitioners less competent than they otherwise might be in this modality. Change is hard for the academic enterprise, geared as it is for one-on-one or for family intervention. Some greater push for rethinking the use of groups in service delivery may well be warranted. Funding bodies should take heed, knowing the gravity of the need and the effectiveness of this intervention. There would be outcome effectiveness advantages and also those of cost if more groups were organized.

Diversity Within Diversity

Culturally sensitive approaches on the part of clinicians require an understanding of the differential responses to single parenthood and the raising of male children that are manifested by African-American, Latina, and Haitian women. While each ethnic-racial group needs services, assistance must be offered in ways that are relevant to and consistent with cultural values and practices. Jackson, who highlights such a need in her examination of the depression and high role strain in poor African-American working mothers raising male children, cites the need for programs to offer early supportive services.[3] Too often, in practice, these diverse groups who comprise the overwhelmed and whom we earlier identified as undergoing rapid increase, are seen as monolithic.

African Americans, African Canadians, African Caribbeans, and first generation Africans all bring some similarities in background and cultures, but they bring differences also. Likewise there are as many Latina groups: Puerto Rican, Cuban, Chicano, as well as numerous others of South and Central American background. Appropriate work with these clients requires that clinicians recognize how inappropriate, even antagonistic, traditional social work practice may be for their Third World cultural orientation. Social work becomes more complex as practitioners confront diversity within a particular ethnic community. Shankar also pointed out that while South Asians are integrated by a common Indo-Aryan tradition, they exhibit complex diversity and incongruities reflecting regional cultural patterns and practices, languages and religious orientations.[4] Knowledge about the respective groups and specifics of their cultures is important and must be respected. At the same time practitioners must be flexible and knowledgeable enough to work with these varied groups as they present to the agency. Practice today and for the future must be based on attitudinal preparation for work with such differences. This means a way of thinking that involves application of general knowledge about these various cultural groups to a specific client family within the group. A two-level process, it involves a look at the specific within the general and vice versa. For example, to understand Maria and her family (Chapter 6) it is necessary to keep in mind Puerto Rican values that emphasize affiliation, extended family, and investment in children. This information, however, must be applied specifically to Maria to understand that her exaggeration of these values represented dysfunction.

Attitudinal preparation also involves self-knowledge and a sense of responsibility concerning one's biases and beliefs, so that one's behavior with clients, be they culturally different or similar, is not based on these biases. In Chapter 3 we discussed the importance of self awareness in terms of personal power needs so that universal human need for a sense of power would be managed appropriately at the clinical interface. This means managing the power of the clinical role and the clinician's cultural group status (which may be exaggerated by the client) so that this double power differential would not be used for the clinician's benefit. Thus, preparation for managing responses to difference and power is the key.

Other kinds of diversity must also be given attention, such as gay and lesbian identity. In middle- and upper-class communities there have been increasing supports to adolescents in these groups to help sort out identity-related issues, but nothing of this sort was found available in the study cohort.

A caution is that practitioners must not fall into the trap of justi-fying dysfunctional behavior as culturally appropriate. Losing con-trol, striking out, beating children, pimping, or playing dumb, which may be consequences of oppression, cannot be condoned as accept-able within or because of the culture. Nor should these behaviors be automatically used as a basis for diagnosing pathology by clinicians. To do otherwise is to engage in the perpetuation of stereotypes and racist beliefs. Furthermore, cultural sensitivity is only part of the so-lution. Practitioners must be aware that in ethnic-appropriate prac-tice, failure to address the larger system of oppression is no less than helping clients adjust to their oppressors. Oppression must never be viewed as natural or normal. Ethnic-sensitive practice includes a multisystem approach, integrating work at multiple levels.

Principles of Intervention: A Multilevel, Multisystem Approach

The quantitative data show that client progress does occur. Grounds for optimism do exist.[5] The case analysis suggests even more about client change in its focus on the intervention episodes and the use of eclectic interventions. A major problem with effecting change in be-haviors and the norms and values that drive them, however, is the isolated, linear focus of intervention—the approach that works to change only one system at a time. The complexity of the multiple presenting problems requires a multilevel, interactive approach that some of the agencies are not sufficiently funded, structured, or staffed to offer. Clinical interventions can and do make a difference, but that difference is compromised because additional needed systems (e.g., housing, training for men, employment, community supports) are ei-ther unavailable or not available in a timely fashion. Practitioners and other direct service providers are usually good at connecting clients with resources if they are available. When medical attention was needed, a client was helped to gain access. But when a client needed to move to another location because of drugs, physical abuse, and violence in the neighborhood of the housing project, the worker was hard pressed to deliver the needed concrete service. Similarly, when jobs were needed, they were not able to help. Employment training programs were not always available for those who were not work ready. Drug treatment opportunities were not available during the period of attempted job training. Most significant for the clients in question, when has there been serious effort to find or increase the supply of jobs for overwhelmed women even if they were strong, determined, and successful in completing training?

In the service population of one agency in particular, the prevalence of shootings, stabbings, and gang activity was so great that resources were insufficient for coping. When a family member is shot, therapy to help manage grief, loss, anxiety, and fear is available, but to what end? The clients return to violent streets. Young people in gang territories feel they have to join a gang for protection. In the absence of other nurturing opportunities, these powerful affiliations, which appear destructive to the outsider, are essential for survival and development. When family, church, or other institutions are weak or nonexistent, gangs recruit young preadolescents, care for them, and provide food, clothing, and fellowship. In the absence of parental and family guidance or that of traditional institutions, the child may not know that certain activities, such as drug running are even against the norm, let alone illegal. We are mindful here that the poor often cannot depend on positive mutual help and networking because these may not exist in the neighborhood. The poor have smaller, weaker, and less available networks than the nonpoor. Contrary to stereotypes, the poor are not churchgoers to any greater degree than any other group, and they do not participate in voluntary or supportive organizations to the level evident in higher income groups.[6] Low-income neighbors do not have the resources or linkages needed for effective, concrete aid, though their networks are more populous and characterized by strong ties.

Concurrent targeted units of intervention (individual, family, and neighborhood improvement; employment opportunities; drug treatment), rather than a single targeted unit of intervention (individual treatment), are necessary to address the multiple problems faced by overwhelmed clients. This service approach does not guarantee greater upfront client outcome. It does suggest that through a multilevel approach, a particular unit or system of attention has more chance of working if other interventions are available simultaneously as they are needed and when the client is open to learning about and using the potential benefits. This learning moment, critical as it is for client change, means that practitioners must respond when the client is ready and with the needed resources.

Multilevel, multisystem intervention is becoming less and less feasible in this day of managed care, which reinforces the segmenting of problems and the achievement of limited goals. Another major hurdle is the increasing specialization of professionals in some agencies and programs that makes a holistic, blitz approach on many levels unworkable. Interestingly, the agency that had the most holistic approximation of a multilevel, multisystem interventive approach employed nonprofessionally trained staff as first-line workers. Consultation of the highest calibre was provided to these workers by well-educated, experienced professionals from social work, psychiatry, and education. Quality supervision was readily accessible. In this case, consultants and supervisors, while not always on the firing line, provided a strong backup field, always available by telephone and occasionally accompanying the worker in face-to-face meetings with clients in the field and in the agency. The partnership of front-line worker with supervisor-consultant was effective. The auspices of this agency must be noted: small, privately funded for the most part, and not so constrained by rules and directives as are larger agencies, particularly those with some public funding.

The agency that was most successful in implementing the holistic approach had deep roots in the community. Programs had been crafted with needs of the community uppermost. Sometimes services were offered by former clients who had become valued practitioners and even pursued professional education.

Service Coordination

Better coordination may have improved the chances for success with the K family. The following agencies were actively involved or became involved when the K's came to the local service agency for help. For Julian and Vivian: Department of Welfare (AFDC) for Vivian; SSI for Winona, Manny, and Lola and for Ella when she took to her bed. State employment agency for Fred, Sr.; three hospital clinics and a number of separate

services for health problems of Vivian, Winona, Lola, and Ella; psychi-
atric problems for Vivian; a separate program in weight loss for Vivian;
day care center for Oliver and Julian; child guidance clinics for Julian;
local agency for camp and after-school programs and tutoring; alcoholism
program for Winona; job training program for Winona, Manny, Lola—a
total of ten agencies! Except for collaboration between the initial social
service agency and the psychiatric clinic for Vivian and the child guidance
clinic for Julian, some minimal contact with the day care center and the
referrals made by the social service agency for job training, substance
abuse treatment, and weight loss, there was no ongoing monitoring of con-
tact, progress, or follow-up.

It is no wonder that the family's disintegration did not change.

Delivery of needed services, even those that are available, has become very complex, and psychologically and physically taxing for
many overwhelmed clients. Once programs are mandated, they tend
to become categorically isolated entities, each with specific eligibility rules. Needed categorical programs may be located in different
sections of a neighborhood, requiring recipients to travel from point
to point on public transportation that frequently runs off schedule.
Depressed, emotionally drained, poor people do not find it easy to
navigate this kind of service landscape. In an effort to facilitate access to services, it was not unusual for workers to drive or accompany clients to a service facility regularly.

Utilization difficulties can be improved with stronger coordination of services that cross systems and build bridges to clients. For
individuals and families who need counseling or therapy, help in
solving school problems, medical attention, financial aid, access to a
food pantry or clothing bank, drug treatment, job training, housing
services, legal assistance, and others at roughly the same time or in a
short span of time, the overburdening process of becoming engaged
in services can be too much for even motivated clients.

Comprehensive cross-systems approaches increasingly associated
with intensified family preservation services and one-stop service
centers must become the plan for service delivery in the future—
like a service mall. The partnership necessary for driving the development of cross-system intervention or clusters and the mall

concept will not be easy for a plethora of federal, state, and local government agencies that must join a plethora of private agencies, all of which have vested niches in servicing this client group. If they gain any ground, it will be because there is a massive, collective push, recognizing that categorical, specialized, partial efforts are not the best for this client population, which represents with multiple problems that are often inextricably related. Direction of improvements in coordination will need to occur at the national policymaking level, but implementation will have to be local.

Recording and Information Systems

Recording formats and internal monitoring systems are tools that facilitate successful outcomes in that they help keep the practitioner focused on specific targeted goals, anticipated outcomes, and delineated time frames. Helping the worker to synthesize thoughts and actions through use of these tools encourages and directs a reflective, analytic, and accountable practice. Record monitoring also becomes an important supervisory tool in helping workers realize that a certain standard of professionalism is not only expected but demanded.

In this study the agency with the best clinical outcomes was also the one that stated goals with the greatest specificity, consistent with the report by Reid and Hanrahan noted in chapter 4 and the subsequent discussion.[7] Highly structured record keeping was manifested by well-trained, skilled workers. In the agency where less highly trained personnel were practitioners, close supervision provided the needed structure, guidance, and supports that produced successful outcomes despite the absence of professional training and knowledge (theories of intervention, skills in recording, and initial capacity for autonomous practice).

In addition to client-identifying data where standardized forms are in place, the type of record keeping predominantly used was problem oriented[8] with problems identified and treatment services planned and delivered. Time-series records, in which there is often a relation to behavioral interventions, single-system research, and the practitioner-scientist model of practice, were not used.[9] Computers were not used by clinicians to augment record keeping. Records were largely handwritten, sometimes barely legible, and in a few instances had been transcribed by clerical staff. Computers were more likely to be used for management functions, such as billing, budgeting and accounting, and service documentation reports. None of the agencies had used automation as a tool for supporting practice decisions; computers, however, were used to support management decisions. Feedback to practitioners regarding outcome effectiveness came largely through discrete case reviews and suspension but not through management information systems.

In the future, practitioners will need their own personal computers, workstations, and modems by which they can access databases containing information relevant to client problems and needs, as well as agency resources. They will need access to software that helps in important phases of the helping process: assessment, treatment, and recording. Accountability demands have affected practice, largely through managed care and contracting of services, but agencies have not been able to respond with the provision of computers that would help reduce accountability-based pressure on clinicians. To reduce costs, agencies might think more about jointly operated computing facilities (along with continuing education programs and retreat facilities for practitioners as a means of combating stress and burnout).

Expanded Compensation

Many workers carry out their societal and agency missions amid the violence that most Americans see only on the evening news. They are called upon to work in situations and with clients marked by violence (the young boy who was moved to a third placement because of violent gang threats against a sibling of the foster family in the second home), danger in the streets (owing to the proliferation of weapons in the hands of young and old), and trauma (the young boy whose drug-addicted mother's absence from the home had a grave impact on his functioning).

Practitioners' pay and benefits do not adequately reflect the realities and risks embodied in their tasks and workplace. Competitive salaries for online workers are lower than private practice fees and salaries paid to practitioners whose work environment is less stressful and definitely less dangerous. Practitioners who work in these settings should not only be at higher salary levels but should have the support of the area or city-wide stress reduction programs and retreat facilities as well as decent life insurance programs (which are not usually available in agencies' benefit packages).

Education

Education was expected to become the greatest equalizer in the American social system, the process by which the disadvantaged were afforded an opportunity to improve their lot in society. But reports that clearly show African Americans and Hispanics with the same educational attainment as whites receiving lower economic rewards no longer support the assumption of the ratio between earnings and educational attainments, a reflection not only of discrimination but of continuing deficits. Despite the fact that education and job training do not yield the same rewards for this population as for others, they remain important goals in clinical work with overwhelmed clients.

Data show that most of the clients get to the tenth to twelfth grade. With a little more push from the schools and school support systems, clients could complete high school, if not in traditional high schools, then through GED programs. By the year 2000, even the most menial jobs will require a high school diploma. Once they procure the high school diploma, a two-year associate's degree in a community college is not beyond their grasp and/or that of the neighborhoods. In the Boston area, Roxbury Community College and Bunker Hill Community College are geographically available.

Workers have reported lack of confidence in teachers and the school system in any number of settings, not because of teachers' lack of interest in the contact but because of the system's lack of fit with the children's level of readiness. Many of the teachers are caring but are not equipped to teach and prepare for learning children and youths who exhibit multiple problems. Among the approaches under discussion for improving the lot of inner-city children and young adults are integrated service models where a number of services are located in or linked to the school facility.[10] Given their legal mandate, schools are the one institution that affects all children. The facilities are often the only ones that families are linked to.

Public education in America was founded on the principle that a democratic society requires an educated citizenry. Such democratic ideals will ring hollow until a new will is generated and the community wants for all its children what all parents want for their own children. The challenge at all levels of society is to make the education institution live up to its promise by developing a system of education that leads to opportunities for the overwhelmed community. Attitude adjustments must occur so that the child from the inner city is viewed as educable, and the teachers stand and deliver. Reforms in financing of education must reduce the disparity in per pupil expenditures between poor and affluent communities.[11] Innovative programs must be developed, implemented, and made widely available to help provide more equitable learning experiences for poor children.[12]

This means encouraging parents of such children to become active participants in the educational process, not only as policy planners but also as resources in the classroom.[13] Even the most progressive educational experience and quality skills training for the poor will affect their predicament only minimally if the issue of vertical equity remains unresolved. Restructuring of society must inevitably lead to a more equitable reward system for the same level of educational attainment across race or ethnic and gender lines. Equal access for all citizens to political, economic, and social resources must be the collective goal of the community if America is to live up to all its promises. It is only within this context that improving educational opportunities for poor people will make a difference in their lives. Free education must be expanded to include higher education for those who qualify.

Working Toward Justice-Based Clinical Practice

Good, insightful, skilled assessment, treatment, advocacy, and outreach as undertaken by individual workers will help move clinical practice toward justice-based work, which focuses on equity and eliminating inequality and demands a commitment to community building. Research shows practitioners' effectiveness in individual and family systems intervention. There were social group work efforts that proved to be very effective and new groups were being formed. But given the study findings, there is a question whether sufficient attention and resources are directed toward community building with activities focused on improving neighborhoods and on closer collaboration with other social systems, including law enforcement.

Justice-based social work practice is jeopardized by the rapid escalation of managed care. Although managed care projects individualized service plans that incorporate inpatient utilization review, formal after-care planning, and outpatient care (requiring quarterly submission of patient treatment plans), all of which cover both active treatment and maintenance, the basic intent is to control costs by providing effective case management for high-service utilizers. The service changes are driven by dollars—meeting bottom lines, not human needs.

Justice-based clinical work that contributes to community building must develop a bond with males. A good place to start is to help them conquer the social stigma and their own sense of uselessness. When they have fathered children, they have a stake in the child's future and the environment in which the child lives. They can make such a commitment, since they are present and a part of the life of the community. Should such expectations not be demanded of them? Justice-based work demands that there be sufficient jobs and equal opportunity for a job so adults can earn self-respect and be respected by their children. Clinicians will have to advocate for job training and jobs as they advocate for health care, education, and housing. In the interim, since jobs are not a reality, these young fathers should be expected to provide child care or other services to their offspring, as well as to their community or neighborhood, building services.

Prior to World War II, men took an active role in community building in schools and on school grounds and neighborhoods— streets, parks, and other congregate areas. With the war, they had to leave these roles and in large measure never resumed their former level of neighborhood activity and presence. Women filled the vac-uum, but paid work out of the home has recently reduced their time and availability. In overwhelmed areas, men can assume many useful roles: helping in policing and monitoring streets, school hallways, and grounds; cleanup and beautification projects; drug patrols; and structural rehabilitation. Organizing and coordinating these tasks are important and will help provide needed improvements, work ori-entation and skills training, community pride, self-aid, and commu-nity empowerment. The association between a father's employment and the outcome for children is strong. There is also an association between unemployment and child abuse. Youngsters whose parents are not in the work force are faced with problems relative to devel-opmental delay, dysfunctional behavior, reduced social skills, and greater depression.[14]

Developing program initiatives that reduce violence in its many forms must also become a key ingredient of justice-based clinical work, which also reinforces community building. Conflict resolution and anger management must be incorporated broadly in interven-tions. Such activity takes additional time and thought but is essen-tial. One case discussed in chapter 6 showed the practitioner's work with a young male who whitewashed a teacher's car after an experi-ence of racism in the school. In several cases there was focus on helping families to communicate effectively—without hollering, swearing or slapping—and understanding the differences between taking the initiative and being assertive, versus being aggressive and violent. There was emphasis on listening and avoiding both misper-ceptions and heated exchanges, which can escalate to bashing, cut-ting, or shooting. Again, groups proved effective in teaching young people nonviolent street-smart behaviors. Group services in which conflict resolution is addressed should be expanded for all age co-horts, especially adolescent males, who are most at risk for acting-out behavior.[15]

New initiatives are surely needed. Workshops on conflict resolu-tion for community leaders, (some of whom once were overwhelmed clients), parents, clergy, social workers, and teachers would be use-ful. Peer mediation for youths should be tried. Foundations, business, and civic and service organizations can reach out and help by sponsoring projects that focus on violence resolution. Agencies, strapped as they are for funding, may not be in a position to provide this type of service without new resources. Once trained and armed with information about violence, natural leaders and professionals can help develop locality-relevant programs organizing groups to further a violence prevention mission.

Effective community change will also require persistent local community organization efforts, which might include writing to council members, state legislators, and members of the congressional delegation to expose through careful documentation the need for AIDS and drug prevention programs and job opportunities. Clients, many of whom are immigrants, must be helped to become citizens and to understand that full rights are gained through the political process.[16] With improved self-esteem, self-sufficiency, and other indicators of higher functioning, they can take the next step to help change their environment and demand job opportunities. These all constitute steps to empowerment. In the absence of public resources and in the presence of agencies, preoccupation with managed care, private resources must help fill the void in community building and thereby help clients to become shareholders in the community.

CHAPTER 8

National Justice-Based Policies That Support Empowerment of Clients and Communities

POOR PEOPLE OFTEN GET A BAD RAP.[1] MANY FACTORS CONTRIBUTE TO skewed perceptions and limited understanding of their life-styles, ambitions, and interests. They can be dismissed as unambitious, dependent, and uneducated, an undercurrent siphoning resources away from hard-working citizens. Discomforting as it may be, we first must ask whether society has a need for such perceptions. Early on we examined the concept of societal projection process and its application to the overwhelmed client population. It fits here as an explanation for the number of persistent notions held by the public. What we found in many overwhelmed clients was the willingness to work toward a higher level of functioning, competence, and self-sufficiency when their practitioners held them to high expectations. In family after family, the interest in education and acceptance of its role in preparation for employment and a better future was confirmed. Many women had learned something about controlling births (their average 3 children corresponded to the national average of 2.9), were interested in a better future for their children, and understood only too well the precarious position of male children. Mothers were concerned that their sons become linked to programs focused on social learning skills, behavioral improvement and anger

147

management, education, and drug prevention. Despite some of their own serious problems and need for extensive personal work, most were protective of their children—even overprotective—an unfortunately appropriate response to the pathogenic neighborhood conditions and drugs.

Paramount to any solution for improving conditions for overwhelmed people but ignored thus far in programs or public consideration is concern for the men. Although they did not show up significantly as clients, they most definitely are involved. Much of their individual behavior cannot be excused. Drug use, stud behavior, and financial exploitation of women, sometimes even daughters and mothers, all appeared in the study's randomly selected cases. Yet society's response to these men cannot be excused either. Its failure to provide opportunity and access to resources so that males in the overwhelmed client population can live up to a major symbol of manhood—capacity to support self and family—is a major factor in their problematic lives. The resulting conviction of uselessness is a nonsolution for them, their families, and their communities. Lack of meaning is the axis in a cycle of idleness, demoralization, and abandonment that is also debilitating to the commonweal. Critical to a breakthrough are new steps to help them assert their manhood in socially acceptable ways. Uselessness can and must be overcome through a revitalization of caring approaches on the interpersonal level and the implementation of justice-based policies on the national level, both of which will require major redistribution of resources for human capital investments in disadvantaged populations. National policies must support clients' efforts and workers' assistance of clients' efforts to move out of personal and community entrapment and into the mainstream.

In justice-based work, intervention is multilevel, focused on the individual, family, group, and community. Eclectic interventions by flexible and caring workers are the components of empowerment on individual, family, and group levels. Increased opportunity for personal and community growth can become available when practitioners, agencies, clients, and community push for a more equitable share of national resources whereby clients can continue to improve their capacities and embrace more self-help initiatives. If work, new opportunities, and resources for community building were available, these practitioners would have a basis for outreach, especially in engaging men, becoming able to hold them to the same high expectations that they have held for overwhelmed women and which they are growing accustomed to utilizing in their practice. With new opportunities made possible by justice-based policies, a serious effort can be made to restore and rebuild communities, address individual pathology, and at the same time conquer the uselessness syndrome.

Conquering Uselessness:
Work and Investment in Human Capital

Work, employment per se, was not usually a primary focus in the cases, although work preparation was often a unit of attention and served as a treatment goal, a path to self-sufficiency. When asked why employment was not a focus in cases, a director of clinical services queried, "Where are the jobs?"

B stated:

> While I was on welfare, my social worker told me I had to go for training. So, I went to this program and they taught me clerical and office work. I could not find a job. Then, they sent me to another training program. Same old story. Then, they told me I had to get more training but after this [third] program, I learned something there. I was able to get a job. It's a good job, processing medical records data.

Another client said, "I want to work but I need Medicare and I don't have any place to leave my child."

Work opportunity is a particularly critical motivating factor for engaging males in clinical work. Without a societally accepted way of contributing to families through earnings, many males will not sit through sessions in which their role is reviewed, subjecting themselves to additional humiliation, which can only compound feelings of uselessness. Yet work is an organizer and self-esteem builder. From childhood when, according to Erikson's notion of the significance of industry, chores become an important source of mastery and sense of well-being, through adolescence when the responsibility contributes fundamentally to a sense of competence, into old age when it constitutes a part of the total life experience, work enhances a sense of integrity.[2] Work opportunity, along with fair wages and benefits, must become a birthright just as education is, and health is becoming, although no one would argue that these two systems are adequate yet.

This country has not promulgated or supported a full-employment policy. In fact, we seem comfortable as a nation with 6 percent unemployment as a mechanism to chill inflation and keep the economy going. But certain individuals and communities suffer most under government-sanctioned unemployment. The 6 percent rate translates to at least double that for people of color and even more for teenagers of color. Feagin and Feagin argue that unemployment and underemployment are endemic to a capitalist economy, because of the need to have on hand an accessible pool of workers who could supply labor in changing economic winds.[3] Historically, some groups—the physically and mentally disabled, the frail and ill, mothers and children—have not been expected to participate in the paid labor force. Able-bodied men were expected to work and to receive personal status and standing in the community based on what they earned (or inherited from forebears' work).[4]

Equal work opportunity and pay has always been a postslavery issue for African Americans and is still a concern for this population, as well as for other people of color, despite civil rights and fair employment legislation.[5] With the loss over the past two decades of the heavy industrial and rust belt jobs, which had attracted many to the cities from the rural South during and after World War II, work options for this group have become further constrained.[6] African Americans, many of whom used World War II veteran status as both a philosophical and political base to demand equal access and equal pay, had become the leaders, providers, and supporters in inner-city neighborhoods.[7] As they and their often better educated offspring moved out to suburbs or to enclaves in which people of color form large pluralities, the inner cities were left to the less advantaged, increasingly younger, and less educated. Although the men in this group have fathered children, they are poorly equipped—if not unable—to give to their children or to the community. However, they consume resources through heavy participation in crime, undermining their own communities and holding wide areas of the city hostage. Many can only secure funds illegally, often just enough to support drugs, a form of escape from their plight of uselessness and depression. Were they in rural communities, there might be financial and/or morale outlets through small cash crops (although there is also the temptation of illegal ones), but in the city, when there are no jobs or barter, they often feel pushed to illegal activities.

Trying to show how pivotal full employment is to other societal goals, William Beveridge wrote nearly fifty years ago, "Idleness is not the same as Want; it is a positive, a separate evil . . . idleness even on an income corrupts; the feeling of not being wanted demoralizes."[8] As the client J. J. commented about his uselessness: "I had nothin', nothin' to do, and nothin' to lose."

The availability of skill building and sustainable jobs would mean that feelings of idleness and uselessness could be attacked. In such a climate, a job even at the minimum wage (which if full time would yield a salary of $8,500) would help nurture self-respect, self-esteem, and hope. It would be a beginning, and in an expansionist economy, new workers could move up the occupational ladder. The recently expanded earned income tax credit would offer potential for supplementing the wages of these workers.[9] (Income supplement to low-earning workers seems more desirable as a wage standard than increasing the minimum wage because the latter could actually reduce jobs.) Long-deferred physical improvements in the community and schools; care for the elderly, children, AIDS patients, drug addicts in institutions; and constructing and staffing shelters and other housing for the homeless are areas where many hands are essential. They can provide the needs base for community jobs that are not being performed and make moot the argument that jobs would be taken from other workers. Granted that many have little, if any, work history, they will never get it if they are not provided the opportunity. This also makes the case for investment in training, however, for spurious "opportunities" that do not strengthen qualifications are as much a betrayal of hope and progress as are social promotions in the schools, dooming victims to failure.

This emphasis would foster stronger hope for family development and stability. Young mothers might marry their infants' fathers if some money and benefits were available to them that would accrue to the family. If education, training, and opportunity for employment were also available to mothers, the earnings for a couple employed full time would be above the poverty line. (If universal health care reform initiatives are enacted, the concern about losing medical coverage would be removed.) Day care would be essential, and would also be a source of locality-based jobs. Children would be exposed to work-oriented behaviors: understanding and organizing time, getting up and getting dressed, meeting a public transportation schedule, talking about work problems at home and thinking through their resolution, taking pride in accomplished tasks, building bridges to other workers and worker networks, and learning the difference between a pay check and a welfare check. These small steps would help socialize children who have experienced little concept of time, seriation, or constructive cause and effect.[10] There would be greater at-home reinforcement of the connection between education and skills training and earnings. There would also be a strengthening of the father image and role in communities of color, as well as healthier relationships for fathers with their partners and children. Most important, new attitudes and behavioral expectations would flow to the next generation.

In addition to more job options in the cities, we must facilitate opportunities for overwhelmed people to move to suburban areas where jobs are more readily available, should it be their personal choice to do so.[11] But there is a caveat. With the African-American movement to older suburbs, there is some indication that businesses then avoid these areas because of this group's presence.[12] Thus, a traditional route to upward mobility seems to be blocked; suburbanization is not providing them the entry to solid wages that it provided for whites. Good incomes for these families who do move out come from combining the low wages of several family members.[13] The dilemma is that there are no jobs in the cities, suburban movement does not provide access to jobs, and there is little access to capital given discrimination in banking. Individuals and communities are entrapped. The lack of access to capital inhibits—if it does not stifle—the development of small family operations, cottage industries, a variety of self-help initiatives, and other small-scale operations that are major sources of job creation in the wider economy.

It is beyond the scope of this book to outline the tenets of a national jobs and community development program. What has been demonstrated is the place of and need for work in individual, family, and community functioning, suggesting that since the need is national, the response must be just as broadscale. This country has a history of government's intervening and making a difference in people's lives through the provision of opportunity. The Homestead Act and other early policies gave countless numbers a start. In response to the Great Depression and circumstances of the "deserving and worthy" poor, the Social Security Act of 1935 was enacted and provided a vehicle to bring an end to massive hunger and human devastation. There was indeed a New Deal, delivered by President Franklin Delano Roosevelt. Capstone programs to get people working and the economy moving were the Works Progress Administration and the Civilian Conservation Corp. Later, the GI Bill of Rights helped veterans to gain education and thus better jobs. There is evidence, too, that government employment in the 1960s and 1970s beginning with the Great Society's War on Poverty and programs targeted to youth, such as the 1964 Economic Opportunity Act, helped uplift many by providing paid work.[14] The Comprehensive Employment Training Act, enacted in 1973, provided jobs to several hundred thousand its first year and by fiscal year 1995 exceeded 1 million.[15] With the Marshall Plan, the government also played a big role in rebuilding Europe after World War II.[16] Surely, troubled and poor Americans as well as the communities in which they live are as deserving of similar concentrated help.

Today the government must again be the intervenor and the provider of jobs as a first or last resort. It is especially important to target young people, so that if they are not in school they are enrolled in a work training program. Skills development and job readiness can be implemented on the school site. Adolescents are at great risk, often idle in neighborhoods that cannot give them necessary nurturance, and they see little hope of a constructive future. Unlike workers in the New Deal's Works Progress Administration, a substantial number of this client group do not have work-oriented attitudes or skills. Work readiness programs and supportive clinical services will be mandatory for many if work is to become a viable option. Problems of access will need to be addressed and services coordinated.

Eclectic interventions and caring, flexible workers will need to be available not just to help initially but to provide support to clients until they have adjusted to the world of work. These interventions and the tasks required of clinicians constitute a combination of old-fashioned casework and the latest clinical techniques. Three decades ago, the 1962 amendments to the Social Security Act expanded social case work to welfare (AFDC) recipients as a way to address lack of motivation, lack of self-sufficiency, and dependency.[17] But counseling services were oversold, and clients were overtherapized. In those days, the profession did not address outcome effectiveness, nor had it been forced to do so.

Now, by joining macrointerventions—jobs and community building—with microinterventions—eclectic clinical work with full recognition of the value and place of each—there is a chance to avoid the perennial problem of mistargeting interventions, that is, using microtechniques for macroproblems (and vice versa).[18] With both the individual and the environment as units of attention, the likelihood of outcome effectiveness would be enhanced. Given the strong belief in individualism in this country, it has been easy for the comfortable to define the poor's problems solely as products of individual weakness, often minimizing and even excluding the environmental or socioeconomic and political context. This distorted emphasis even gives a religious rationale, defying the insights of churches' spokesmen as diverse as John Winthrop, governor in 1630, and 1980 American bishops about the need and value of commonweal and the consequences of unbridled individualism and competitiveness.[19] Winthrop, puritan par excellence and extoller of the work ethic, nevertheless warned in his City on a Hill homily that "for this end, we must be knit together. . . . We must be willing to abridge ourselves of our superfluities for the supply of others' necessities, and he predicted the disintegration that would result if that balance was ignored.[20]

In 1981, George Gilder asserted that the conditions of broken families and lives of African Americans that he decried as worse at that time than those that resulted from slavery were attributable to

welfare programs. He was among the first to point out and was especially critical of welfare's impact on the roles of men whose contributions to family are devalued; suggesting that as roles changed,
so did behavior. Family break-up becomes an expectable outcome
when cash and in-kind benefits are larger than the man's earnings.[21]
Charles Murray followed with the belief that social welfare programs
are disincentives for the work ethic.[22] Like Gilder, he noted how the
family structure and stability of African Americans suffered despite
a period of national attention and great welfare expenditure in the
1960s and 1970s. Expansion in welfare benefits, however, ended two
decades ago owing to inflation, program cuts, and tightening of program eligibility. If expansion of welfare was the source of a negative
impact on families, why has the alternative style of single-parent
families continued to grow since the erosion of those benefits in the
1970s?[23] In fact, social welfare program benefits for the poor continued to decline while those for the middle class increased, largely
via tax exclusion policies such as retirement and mortgage interest
write-offs.

Early on, we questioned whether new light could be shed on observations regarding the family structure of overwhelmed clients. It
was noted that men among the overwhelmed client population are
present, in many instances, retreating from girlfriend to mother, to
another girlfriend, servicing women sexually, but seen increasingly as
unattractive marriage partners because they have nothing to contribute substantively to family life and are even seen as a drain on it.
MacAdoo's research underscores the dismal picture of employment
for minority males (both poor and middle class) and the serious consequences for family solidarity.[24] She has stated that instances where
parents block the marriage of a pregnant daughter to the unborn infant's father can be understood in the context of their expectation
that marriage would require them to support the father as well as
their daughter and her baby. This is borne out in our sample of overwhelmed clients. For example, a teenager was referred for service
after becoming pregnant. A plan was made that the family would
keep the baby, who would be with the grandmother in her small day
care operation while the baby's mother would attend high school and

hopefully go on to the nearby community college. Marriage to the baby's father was not a viable option because he had nothing to contribute to the economics of the family unit. We forget that during and shortly after slavery, African Americans were among the most skilled artisans, craftspersons, and workers.[25] There was a strong tradition of work and support of families among males of color. That tradition of work as an expectation and necessary societal role was dangerously weakened by rejection of free black competition, enforced discrimination, and the changing economy long before access to welfare programs was a possibility.

The fragile structure of families, perceived as more a problem for the poor than for the middle class, is not likely to change without attention to education, training, and jobs, as well as clinical intervention when appropriate. A national jobs program, supportive social services, and education would carry a high price tag for a time, but the cost of programs now in place is both high and self-perpetuating, with consequences that can be destructive. Yet had the programs not existed, hunger, poor health, and criminalization would be even more widespread. The dilemma calls out for new direction, but the response is abandonment. Society's investment in cities is eroding while fewer and fewer citizens are able to move about in reasonably decent and safe surroundings. Public safety in cities is now a preoccupation. Ironically, it is concern about safety of the better off rather than the suffering of those enmeshed in the overwhelmed pattern that is forcing the country to look at joblessness, poverty, and personal insecurity as primary causes of violence.

Resistance to government-supported work will be strong from those, including some politicians, who are opposed because of philosophy or cost. For other reasons unions have resisted such programs, fearing that government could gain a measure of control over yet another group of workers and siphon off jobs that could otherwise strengthen unions.[26]

Jobs, Welfare Reform, and Overwhelmed Clients

Current Clinton administration proposals on welfare reform are still evolving, having been subordinated to the resolution of health care as a prerequisite. As a candidate, Clinton espoused the position that he would "end welfare as we know it," calling for two years' support to get people over hard times and then into the labor force. His tentative plan would provide recipients with education, skills training, child care, and health coverage during the first two years of public assistance. Thus prepared for work, recipients would move to private sector jobs or, should these be unavailable, to community service jobs.

Such a plan might constitute appealing political rhetoric but is not realistic as a reform for welfare policy. Given what we know about this clientele, their range of problems, ambitions, and capacity for change, it is good sense to establish expectations, but non-sense to cut off help arbitrarily after two years. Many clients could not be work ready on a time basis alone. Individuals have different problems. Some, after long-term dependency, need more than two years, while some need less than two years to engage in clinical work, job training, and other steps to self-sufficiency. A thirty-year-old mother, alone, with three young children may not be able to achieve her goals as quickly as a twenty year old with one child and some family supports. A twenty-five-year-old male with children may be more motivated to get some schooling and work readiness skills if he knows that he is expected to work and provide for his family and that he can get a job. In each case, differential assessment, clear expectations, specific goals, and reasonable time frames for achieving them are necessary. Although most of our study cases were closed within two years or less, more time can be needed for successful job placement and should not be axed arbitrarily.

Realistically and foremost, the president must discover or develop jobs and must have popular support to do so, especially since the beneficiaries are considered unworthy by society. Neither he nor any subordinate can succeed in a vacuum. He must provide an answer for the social agency executive who asked, "Where are the jobs?" He must provide a solution for B, who as a welfare recipient had to take three training programs before she could find a job. He must provide hope and expectations to J. J., who "had nothin'—nothin' to do, and nothin' to lose." Further, what options and time frame would have been realistic for the K's to move to self-sufficiency (even if the practitioners had not colluded with that family)? Would it have been ethical to provide no financial and supportive services to the children? To aging adults? The K men?

It is one thing to provide job training and address structural problems in the labor supply, but it seems harder to address structural problems in the economy, confronting downsizing of corporations and the military, restructuring of jobs, globalization, and racial as well as gender-based discrimination. The country is facing massive technological change on a plane not unlike that following the invention of the printing press in the mid-fifteenth century or the industrial revolution in the late eighteenth century. In his 1993 book, *Post-Capitalist Society*, Peter Drucker argues that information, not machines, is what drives this new revolution. The basic resource *"is and will be knowledge."* Further: knowledge is now fast becoming the sole factor of production, sidelining both capital and labor."[27]

If this scenario is even partly predictive of the future, the movement of society toward ever greater stratification is likely, with the highly educated and knowledgeable scientists, professionals, and managers at the top, and service workers such as part-time restaurant and shop employees at the bottom. If overwhelmed clients are to be active, productive members of society, much effort is needed to address basic academic deficits and will include seeing whole communities of people at least through high school. High school equivalency is a reachable goal since the majority of overwhelmed clients get to the tenth to twelveth grades and share a strong belief in and support for education as a pathway to a better future. However, too many get stuck without sufficient freedom to move ahead. They are forced to settle for much less than they want, and welfare becomes an anchor.

A single mother in Massachusetts can receive roughly $440 per month in AFDC, $150 in food stamps, and $600 from rent supplement, plus Medicare. Work must be at least as attractive and would require that benefits (health and day care) be in place. No work opportunity program can succeed without jobs, good jobs. No jobs program can succeed without motivated, trained workers. (It has been demonstrated that welfare jobs programs yielded savings for AFDC; however, neither jobs for recipients and the employment opportunities nor savings were great.[28] The long-debated question of vertical equity is applicable since benefits cannot be reduced without risking recidivism, and, if enacted, health care reform will handle a major obstacle to work incentive among this clientele.)

The 1988 Family Support Act was the latest national attempt to reform welfare. That legislation made the Job Opportunities and Basic Skills Training Programs (JOBS) a cornerstone of the reform package. The act also clarified the expectation that parents are responsible for the care and maintenance of their offspring. Self-sufficiency, not income maintenance, was the basic philosophy driving the 1988 legislation. Reciprocity between states and recipients was acknowledged; states have an obligation to provide financial aid and supportive services, and recipients have an obligation to take steps to prepare for employability. The Family Support Act also attempted to deal with the prospect of states' targeting services largely to the most attractive clients by requiring that 55 percent of the funding allocated for JOBS be used to assist clients who are or just possibly will become long-term dependent clients. (Long-term dependents, though only 17 percent of the AFDC case load, account for the bulk of the expenditures.)[29] Unfortunately, the Family Support Act has not produced the results expected, and only 60 percent of the $1 billion available in federal funding in 1991 for operating a JOBS program was drawn by the states (which have to match some state dollars in order to get the federal funds).[30] Only twelve states used 95 percent of their allocation, and five used less than 30 percent.

States take varied approaches to welfare reform. What is becoming clearer is that they are assuming the initiative, reflecting growing impatience with Washington and not waiting for its leadership. Governors and legislators are responding to public pressure that welfare needs revamping, and the reforms proffered by states are emphasizing job training and day care.[31] Some states are discussing strict time limits on AFDC, from the sixty-day limit proposed by the governor of Massachusetts (and defeated in the Massachusetts House in May, 1994), to various programs emphasizing a two-year limit on support, as proposed by Florida, Wisconsin, and Vermont. Other states, such as New Jersey, Arkansas, and Georgia, are refusing additional benefits to clients who bear additional offspring. Expectations that children of recipients attend school (or the benefits will be cut) have been implemented in Ohio and Wisconsin.[32]

Whether driven by punitiveness, intolerance, lack of knowledge, or lack of compassion, some of these responses are ill founded and based on misperceptions. First, there is no proof that AFDC mothers bear additional children to get additional funds. The state that gives the largest AFDC grant has the lowest percentage of AFDC recipients, while several states granting the lowest payments have the highest number of participants.[33] In Massachusetts, the increase would amount to slightly more than $3 per day. Second, there is little justification for the view that overwhelmed or poor women want to sit at home. They want to work. Many of the clients in this study worked, facing great obstacles, including having their small earnings taken from them by men. In family after family there was preparation for a brighter future through emphasis on school and job training. Clients have realistic problems: health, day care, unreliable transportation, and most important, lack of good jobs. Most poor women want the option of joining other women in America's work force.

Clients' interest in education or training should be supported even in the absence of jobs. A sure way to help buoy the next generation is for their parents to be able to participate intelligently as citizens of a democracy and to register and vote. They would have a better appreciation of the value for their children to stay in school, and they and their families would be at a level where they could partake of rich public libraries, museums, and historical sites.

Third, there is not going to be a major reversal of crime, drugs, and new life-style in overwhelmed communities unless the problems of men are addressed. They too need education, training, supportive services, and paid work. They are a major part of and contribution to the pathogenic situation, caught up in unrelenting entrapment and social emasculation.

The purpose of AFDC is to help children. Welfare policy should not attack them; rather, it should help by strengthening their families through provision of education, supportive clinical intervention when needed, and job opportunity, thereby attacking dependency. Because of the structure of AFDC, it has been difficult for that program to function as an antipoverty effort that helps children and simultaneously functions as a control agent on the behavior of their parents, most particularly, mothers.

Realistic Approaches to Drug Abuse

A drug prevention initiative must accompany any work program if clients are to have a chance of success. Drug-treating and -fighting efforts in agencies are client centered and hardly broad enough to make a dent in the neighborhood drug supply. Prevention must become the cornerstone of the national campaign against drugs, which should be treated as a public health issue. Currently, the nation targets 70 percent of resources allocated for drug abuse to law enforcement.[34] This approach has not worked, evidenced by ongoing high rates of drug abuse, drug-related acting out, and violence.

A preventive public health approach could be based on the anti-smoking model, which has been effective in producing significant changes in attitude and behavior in less than three decades. There is growing public intolerance of smoking in public spaces. Similarly, alcohol abuse has been targeted as a public menace, and campaigns aimed at prevention are in place. The designated driver concept was unheard of even a decade ago but now is widely accepted and increasingly used. More to the point, there has been a significant reduction in alcohol-related accidents and fatalities.[35] Drinking and smoking are no longer cool, chic, or in vogue. Marijuana, crack cocaine, mushrooms, and other narcotics can also be addressed via education on the public's health.

The inappropriate use of prescription drugs must also be targeted. Psychiatrists may not even be aware of how medications are misused by the overwhelmed clientele as well as others. It is in easy reach, taken by those who are seriously depressed and have little experience with self-directed limit setting.

Any national approach, to be effective, needs to rely heavily on local neighborhoods for implementation. The "Think globally, act locally" slogan has never before been more apt. Overwhelmed clients should be participants in these neighborhood efforts—in the agencies, community-based groups, churches, and school-based forums. A public sensitized to the hazards of drugs is key in developing the local consensus necessary if drug abuse is to be attacked at the grass-roots level, where the impact can be most effective. This kind of involvement will also aid in the empowerment of clients and communities.

Integration, Clusters, and Partnerships: New Organizational Principles and Structures

Organization of services stems from the manner in which programs are legislated and funded in the national policy arena. Historically, services are developed and mandated in an incremental, fragmented fashion. The shaping of policy is not a tidy, rational, step-by-step process but a political one.[36] Congress, in response to interest groups and increasingly to politically savvy lobbyists,[37] has nonetheless created policies that define eligibility and implementation of services in a fragmented, sometimes counterproductive, way.

Holistic views of human need are ignored in the piecemeal construction of policy, and thus holistic service systems to meet these needs are nonexistent. Vital are policies at the national level that facilitate community development and the building of community programs and activities to support all the instrumental tasks of families and communities.

Programs affecting this multiple-need clientele are located in many different federal departments: Health and Human Services, Labor, Housing and Urban Development, Education, Transportation, and Drugs. (Though not a cabinet-level department, the drug czar does sit with the cabinet.) Because of the way they are constructed and housed, each with different categorical requirements and specific problems to address, they fail to take into account how a focus on problem specificity can address the needs of the whole person and may in fact compound people's misery. Acting separately, each is a poor fit with the multiproblem aspect of overwhelmed client families and communities. This is particularly so with the population studied, in which 71 percent presented with multiple problems and most of the remainder ended up with multiple diagnoses.

Comprehensive cross-system approaches whereby agencies and practitioners can span boundaries and engage in necessary exchanges with each other in an arrangement that transcends traditional systems are urgently needed. Bureaucracies being what they are, however, there will need to be mandated integration of services and partnerships, or the appointment of an overall director to give focus and coordination to their work. Overall, there is a great need for reformation of existing programs, whereby structures are decentralized, turf is less protected, and competition among professional groups is reduced.[38]

Humanizing bureaucracies is another initiative that must be undertaken. Too often bureaucrats see their roles as very limited and prescribed by specific policies. Removed from the realities of clients' lives and from the context of local practice, they may not see the need for holistic approaches, which would require them to move beyond their turf. This is perhaps especially true for higher-level career bureaucrats who are insulated from changes that executive offices face through elections. Humanistic innovation is hard for bureaucracies, but is mandatory if new opportunities for services to the overwhelmed are to be created.

New integrated services or clusters will be delivered at the local level. Inclusive service agencies or malls need to be developed to complement school-based services. The critical point, however, is that structures and ethos supporting partnerships and collaboration are means and not ends to facilitating quality, holistic approaches to services, which ought to be delivered by flexible and caring practitioners who hold clients to high expectations.

Training of Professionals and Challenges to Social Work and Allied Professions

What lessons are there for educators preparing professional helpers for the important task of working with those who have traits and characteristics similar to the overwhelmed clients described in this book?

First, we must acknowledge the role of clinical practice knowledge in work with this client group. The two agencies in the study demonstrating the greatest success approached service delivery differently. One used untrained but empathic line workers indigenous to and familiar with the community, and provided them with extensive backup from highly educated, seasoned practitioners—social workers, psychiatrists, and family therapists. The other agency employed professional staff, primarily those with the M.S.W., who collaborated extensively with other professionals—psychiatrists, nurses, psychologists, and physical therapists. In another agency the value of professional education could be seen in the quality of the assessments of clients' predicaments. In the fourth, there was no question of educational level and expertise of workers, but rather, less sensitivity toward clients and community. Ironically, the agency with the most credentialed staff produced the least successful outcomes. What was at question was not education but rather philosophy toward clients and community. While clinical knowledge is critical, helpers need greater orientation to culture and respect for clients' backgrounds and nuances in order to establish effective interaction.

Clinicians in training must be able to demonstrate throughout the formal education period a capacity to relate to poor, disadvantaged people; to respect them and share a strong belief that they can change, and to hold themselves as well as clients to high professional standards and highly improved levels of functioning. To maintain a vision for the future and hold out for high standards is a goal within reach when practitioners are helped to challenge rather than buy into the notion of a monolithic poverty or a subculture. Professors must reexamine their own stereotypes about poor people, which can be passed on to practitioners in training.

Educators of practitioners can feel justifiably proud of the contributions of their trainees, those with advanced degrees. There is a thought-provoking issue, though, that should concern social work education as well as graduate psychology and counseling programs: the effectiveness of untrained helpers. Granted, those in this study were supervised by master clinicians, but the direct service workers in many instances demonstrated unquestionable effectiveness. Two attributes associated with success, caring and flexibility, do not require training, although such programs can—and have an obligation to—enhance them. If the goal is optimal service to clients, caring and knowledge must complement, not compete with, each other.

In many ways, given resource constraints in funding and nonavailability of graduate-educated personnel, the use of such practitioners has some advantages. In a resource-tight economy, some may see this as a potential threat to highly educated practitioners. On the other hand, the availability of nonprofessionally trained helpers offers an employment source and a means of participation in the community for people who are motivated to move out of poverty. This is a valuable recruitment base for professional programs, which are challenged to increase diversity among their ranks. Social work has probably given greater voice to recruiting people of color than has psychology and psychiatry but is actually losing ground. Social work needs to recruit men, where it is also losing ground, to help serve this population and to become role models.[39]

Group Work

The education establishment—professional schools of social work, graduate psychology, and counseling programs and psychiatry—must realize that group work offers strong potential for changing behaviors and norms of overwhelmed clients, particularly youths and young adults. The successes noted in this discussion—improved overall functioning as demonstrated by movements in self-esteem, self-mastery, competence, enhanced differentiation—were encouraging. There is also positive review of group intervention.[40] Groups were effective in engaging overwhelmed clients and in helping them focus action on urgent and pressing problems, such as drugs and violence in their neighborhoods.

We noted also that agencies use group work for supervision of staff and report great success, but when they work with overwhelmed clients, they fall back on the preferred clinical (individual or family) intervention. This contradiction is not easily explained. Many of the professional social workers received their training at the Boston area schools of social work. Although social work with group content is offered and some faculty contribute to the profession's literature on groups, these highly regarded schools should nonetheless examine the value accorded this practice method. A possible explanation lies in the individualism mystique and social work's strong identification with and embracing of psychiatry.[41]

———

To make us all a caring community will require a new dedication to our common purpose of promoting the general welfare, not just providing for the common defense. Ultimate security lies not in locks and electronics, retreating to private communities and guns, but in mutual trust.

Schools of social work and other helping professions will have to teach eclectic interventions as well as functional understanding of diversity, the place and value of groups, and community building. Government and the private sector will have to fund differently to foster holistic human development rather than categorical problems and imperatives. The neglected will have to be given credible reason to trust (despite their lived realities) and to assume more responsibility. Practitioners will truly have to believe in and know how to facilitate their clients' ability to grow and to exchange isolation or dependence for the productive interdependence that marks a mature society. And as a nation, we will have to acknowledge our collective indifference to this segment of society.

Most important, those Americans who have raised individualism to the level of ideology finally have to recognize that like all other -isms, it has entrapped us with some false gods to whom we have begun sacrificing our children and our communities. We have a common origin and destiny and must find new, communal ways to resolve the destructive inequities that have undercut justice and threaten to fragment us. We are all trustees of the public welfare, who have the power to care.

Investigative Procedures and Study Implementation of Clinical Practice Effectiveness

The investigation of clinical practice effectiveness with overwhelmed clients can appropriately be characterized as *evaluative* research of models used to determine program or organization effectiveness.[1] The effectiveness of intervention strategies in work with overwhelmed clients is the focus of this analysis, which has the following objectives:

1. To determine and describe the intervention strategies that hold promise in work with overwhelmed clients.
2. To identify and describe successful outcomes associated with effective intervention strategies.
3. To determine and describe which intervention strategies show the most promise in work with overwhelmed clients.
4. To determine and describe the combinations of strategies and the conditions under which they would be more likely to produce the largest frequency of success outcomes.
5. To generate empirical evidence for further testing with other samples.

Implicit in this research is a definitive judgment of the effectiveness of intervention strategies that show promise in work with overwhelmed clients. Thus, the objectives of the study are to examine intervention strategies, utility, and outcomes in terms of what they accomplished, which means asking and answering basic questions about efforts and results.

Study Design

The scope of evaluation research is varied, but Rossi and Freeman distinguish three major classifications of evaluation research: (1) analysis related to the conceptualization and design of interventions (2) monitoring of program implementation, and (3) assessment of program effectiveness and efficiency.[2] The major focus of this study is the assessment of effectiveness in work with overwhelmed clients.

Assessment of effectiveness has veen variously referred to as *impact assessment* or *outcome evaluation*.[3] A critical concern for the investigator is to demonstrate persuasively that observed changes are a function of the intervention and cannot be accounted for in other ways.

In clinical research, experimental design is not always feasible or preferred, for several reasons. Monette, Sullivan, and DeJong, for example, have argued that experimental results often constitute an average of the whole group, obscuring the individual reactions.[4] Because experimental research is unable to capture the processes by which change occurs, causality in such research is always inferred rather than firmly established. The use of control groups, from which treatment is withheld, has been a source of ethical concern to practitioners.[5] The limited findings produced by any one experiment alone means that even when experiments are undertaken, the knowledge derived can easily be fragmented. Unless there is some way of coordinating experiments into a unified program of research, much of the potential for this design can go unrealized.

In this study no preintervention measures existed, and all clients had been exposed to a set of uniform treatment conditions over time. Therefore, preexperimental design or judgmental design provided a more feasible alternative to an experimental study.[6]

Underlying all preexperimental designs is a common frame of reference: that presumed experts, program administrators, and/or participants play the major roles in assessing the impact or outcomes. In this study, the task was one of estimating the net effect of the intervention, that is, the effect of outcomes with limited influence from other variables. In designing this study, caution was exercised in distinguishing between gross outcomes (all changes in an outcome measure) and net outcomes (effects attributed to intervention since factors other than the intervention may account for outcomes). Service record files were examined and judgments were made about the estimated net outcomes of intervention strategies in work with overwhelmed clients, and these were derived from a critical analysis of the *explanatory variables.*[7] Correlation and regression analysis were employed to isolate gross and net outcomes.

Population and Sampling Procedure

Operationally defined, an overwhelmed client is one who suffers from such problems as emotional and psychological problems, spotty (if any) employment, family violence, substance and child abuse, truancy and teenage pregnancy, unhealthy living conditions, complex developmental problems, physical illness, minimal coping capacity, poverty, and/or a sense of extreme powerlessness.

In order to obtain a sample, five Boston area inner-city agencies providing services to overwhelmed clients were contacted. A research prospectus with an invitation to participate in the study was submitted to each agency director. Subsequently the researchers made a presentation to each agency, including the director and selected clinical staff, that introduced the research team, made researchers available to discuss and interpret the research prospectus, and to answer questions regarding the project. In all cases, the agency directors sought approval from their respective boards to participate in the study. Approvals were granted by four agencies who informed the researchers of their willingness to participate and cooperate in completing the project. The four agencies were private and nonprofit (although three had extensive contracts from governmental sources); two were medical or health centers with mental health and social service components. All provided one or more of the following services:

Family based, community, and home based

Prevention and outreach

Early intervention

Neighborhood and family services for mentally disabled and retarded

Residential services for mentally retarded

Respite care

Supported employment program

Health and dental

Nutrition

Eye care

Speech, language, and hearing

Mental health

Social services

Young parents' program

Recreational

Social and vocational for all ages

GED and English as a second language

Day care

Hot lines (teen, parental stress, battered women, alcohol and drug, AIDS)

Each agency was requested to extract from its total mental health and social service client population a sampling frame consisting of all terminated and/or closed client service case files covering interventions over a three- to five-year period during the late 1980s and early 1990s. A total of 2,369 case files meeting all the criteria for inclusion in the study constituted the population size from the four agencies.[8]

The sample size was established based on a literature review that suggested sample sizes between 50 to 100 cases (see tables in appendix C) in most clinical research. It was determined that a sample size of 200 (50 from each of the four agencies) would be appropriate for this study.

The four agencies furnished 2,369 client service files. Each client service file from three of the agencies was assigned a number equal to the total in each sampling frame. From each of these three clusters, an equal-sized random sample of 50 client service files were selected using a table of *A Million Random Digits with 100,000 Normal Deviates* generated by RAND Corporation.[9] Since the fourth agency provided a sampling frame of fewer than 50 case files, 187 case files constituted the total sample size for this study. Sample size was further reduced due to insufficient entries in files and duplication of records. When these service records were excluded from the analysis, the final sample size, 178, was still well above the mean for most clinical research.

Instrument Development

Several instruments were developed to accomplish the research objectives. An instrument for extracting necessary data from agency files was developed from a pretest using a sample of closed client case files. Two researchers, both educators and licensed social workers, identified from these sample case files the presenting problem(s) and intervention strategies. From a composite list of intervention strategies, which was established and operationally defined, success outcomes for each strategy were determined and theoretical underpinnings of each intervention were identified. Ten randomly selected case files were evaluated independently by the two investigators; they identified the interventions implemented in each case, synthesizing and integrating the findings of each into a composite. The instrument developed to collect data on intervention outcomes identified the following intervention strategies:

1. Assessment: To determine the dynamics of individual and family functioning, including all significant relationships in the context of environmental support or lack of support; to assess needs and identify relevant resources.
2. Advocacy: To get all resources for the client, explain entitlements, help to teach the client to speak for self, differentiate, and become stronger.
3. Empowerment: To enhance the client's self-esteem; to help clients to take charge, achieve greater self-differentiation, develop personal power for positive use.
4. Individual work: To provide the clients with counseling and support, enhancing the client's self-esteem, increasing communications in the family; to teach budgeting of money and time, parent skills, health and hygiene.

5. Group work: Same definition as individual/family work.
6. Community change: To teach the clients advocacy; to help the clients institute change and work to change policy to benefit groups of residents and the community.

Successful outcomes for each intervention strategy were operationalized and behavioral and attitudinal patterns found when the intervention was successful in accomplishing its goal. The outcomes were categorized as *proximal* (closely linked to the goals of service/intervention, including achievement of those goals: improved self-esteem, exhibiting improved differentiation, and competence) and *distal* (outcomes of a more global nature, which include getting own resources, making decisions and pursuing personal goals, making connections with external resources, and manifesting a reduction in complex social problems that produce a sense of being overwhelmed).

The following success outcomes were identified as congruent with the intervention and exhibiting proximal and distal changes:

1. Assessment:
   a. Exhibits improved coping, improved ability to be self-sufficient, more independent and at the same time interdependent
   b. Exhibits reduced scapegoating, accepts responsibility for own behavior
2. Advocacy:
   a. Effective coping:
   b. Seeks needed resources from community institutions
3. Empowering:
   a. Uses personal power for positive use
   b. Takes charge of personal problems; sets and pursues personal goals
   c. Exhibits positive self-esteem, sees self as worthwhile and valued
4. Individual/family work:
   a. Exhibits positive self-esteem: same as 3c.
   b. Exhibits differentiation—a clear sense of self as a separate person, capable of intimacy with others, able to set goals to maintain behavioral intent; interacts positively and productively with others; is independent and interdependent

    c. Exhibits competence, has a sense of mastery, of being able to function adequately

    d. Able to manage and budget money resources and time

    e. Exhibits effective communications and improved parenting skills, which improve family functioning

    f. Exhibits health and personal hygiene; works to maintain good physical and mental health

6. Group work:

    a. Exhibits positive self-esteem: same as 4c

    b. Exhibits differentiation: same as 5b

    c. Exhibits competence: same as 5c

    d. Able to manage and budget money resources and time: same as 5d

    e. Exhibits effective communications skills: same as 5e

    f. Exhibits health and personal hygiene: same as 5f

7. Community change:

    a. Demonstrates advocacy for community improvement

    b. Institutes change in policy to benefit groups of residents, involvement with community-wide, grass-roots social change

Noninterventive variables were identified as well. They are not considered clinical in nature but had an impact on success outcomes. The following noninterventive, explanatory variables were included in the instrument:

1. Worker time investment: Total contacts per family (per case), time investment (total contacts per week, individual contacts, collateral contacts).

2. Worker flexibility: Individualizing client's situation, being flexible and responsive to individual needs, rolling with the punches and readiness to respond quickly.

3. Worker caring: Attending to needs of individuals and families; going out of way to visit and to refer.

4. Worker positive reinforcement for education: Serving as a role model and providing positive reinforcement for education.

5. Worker acceptance of race: Serving as a role model for tolerance and acceptance of race, ethnicity, and gender.

6. Worker race: Racial and ethnic identification.

7. Worker education: High school, B.A., M.A., M.S.W., Ph.D., Psy.D., M.D., and other.
8. Program accessibility: Availability and utilization of services, offers home visits and neighborhood activities.

The following success indexes were associated with the noninterventive, explanatory variables:

1. Worker flexibility: Worker is flexible in thinking and behavior; client may model this behavior, remain engaged in service relationship, and work toward change.
2. Worker caring: Worker exhibits caring and supportive behavior. Client may exhibit role imitation or model caring behavior.
3. Worker positive reinforcement for education: Worker exhibits positive interest in education; client may exhibit positive interest in education, may set, pursue, and/or complete educational goals.
4. Worker acceptance for race and gender: Worker exhibits tolerance/acceptance and respect for diversity, and client models same.
5. Worker time investment: Relationship formed, goals set, strategies implemented; no premature termination.
6. Program accessibility: Demonstrates responsiveness and utilization.

(Worker characteristics of race and education were primarily included here to determine if they had any impact on the direction of client change.)

In addition, data on the following sociodemographic characteristics and conditions, systemic influences, and client characteristics were included in the instrument:

1. Sex
2. Race and ethnicity
3. Age
4. Marital status
5. Number of children
6. Employment status of client
7. Number of years of education completed
8. Composition of household

9. Length of time serviced by the agency
10. Presenting problem

Figure A-1 shows the instrument developed. Additionally, a second instrument, an unstructured interview schedule, was developed to be administered to prospective client interviewees in each agency (figure A-2).

Interviews and focus group discussions were conducted with clients, and staff; agency directors were similarly interviewed regarding programs and services, agency mission, goals and objectives, fund allocation and its impact on the programs and services provided, client cost expenditure, and staffing needs.

Study Implementation

Two researchers critically assessed a random sample of 178 client case files provided by the participating agencies. For each case file examined, the researchers utilized the Client Service/Record Data Instrument (figure A-1) to determine sociodemographic characteristics; whether there was sufficient evidence of change in client functioning connected to a particular intervention strategy employed by the attending clinician; and whether there was sufficient evidence of change in client functioning connected to a particular noninterventive or explanatory variable. For each case file evaluated, the researchers also made additional and extensive qualitative observations related to assessment plan, treatment plan, treatment process, and outcome.

The planned interviews and focus groups with selected clients, workers, and agency directors provided additional essential data for the qualitative analysis component of the investigation.

Data Analysis

The following quantitative analyses were conducted using SPSS-X:

1. Frequency runs of all research variables to summarize information about them.
2. Cross-tabulations developed to quantify the association between agencies and success outcomes.

3. Pearson's correlation coefficient computed to examine the correlation between background characteristics of workers and intervention strategies.
4. Application of factor analysis to determine the dimensions of the overall improved well-being and functioning of the overwhelmed client.
5. Computation of regression analysis to identify the worker characteristics most effective in predicting the overall improved well-being and functioning of the overwhelmed client.

Reliability and Validity

Threats to internal validity are reduced when archival program records and service files are used because subject bias, which can minimize the reliability and validity of outcome measures, is limited and participant loss due to refusal or inability to participate in the study is nonexistent. In this study, confidentiality in the use of records was dealt with by an agency staff member blocking out any entries that would identify the subject.

A pretest was done to evaluate outcome measures. Since the operational definition of each outcome measure was derived from the theoretical approaches used to inform that intervention, the instrument was deemed to possess content validity. Overall well-being and functioning of a client reflect a set of behavioral and additional patterns, and to the extent that all outcome measures are linked to the overall well-being and functioning, the instrument had construct validity.

Since outcome measures dealt with concrete data and manifest behavior items, including worker characteristics and sociodemographic characteristics of clients, and there was little scope for variation in responses that could have been due to the observer or the recording instrument, the problems of reliability were minimal.

Reliability of the entire set of success outcomes as measures of improved overall client well-being and functioning, the Kaiser-Meyer-Olkin (KMO) measure of sampling adequacy, was computed for all pairs of success outcomes listed in a correlation matrix.[10] The obtained KMO value for the correlation matrix was .92, indicating that a factor analysis of success outcomes was appropriate. Two factors were isolated, and Cronbach's alpha was computed to test the reliability of these factors. Reliability for Factor 1, self-efficacy–personal mastery, was .847 and for Factor 2, competence–behavior for action, .621.

Worker characteristic links to improved overall client well-being and functioning were measured by regression analysis. Adjusted R value of .86259 indicated that certain client characteristics have strong predictive validity of improved overall client well-being and functioning.

Finally, the random sample of cases from a sampling frame of over 2,000 examined in this study would be reflective of larger populations of overwhelmed clients. Therefore, the results and findings lend themselves to generalizations about clients with profiles similar to those in this discussion.

Figure A-1

CLIENT SERVICE/RECORD DATA INSTRUMENT

Please check the appropriate category for each question.

PART A: CLIENT PROFILE

1. Client Identification Number: _____   ___
                                                                 1–3

2. Agency Identification: *[Name]* __ *[Name]* __ *[Name]* __
   [Name] __   ___
                                                                 5

3. Sex of Client: Male __ Female __   ___
                                                                 7

4. Race/Ethnicity of Client: African American __ Latino __
   Asian __ Caribbean __ White __ Other (specify) __   ___
                                                                 9

5. Age of Client: Under 19 yrs. __ 20–29 __ 30–39 __ 40–49 __
   50–59 __ 60–69 __ 70 yrs. and Older __ Entire Family__   ___
                                                                 11

6. Marital Status of Client: Married __ Legally Divorced __
   Separated __ Never Married __ Widow/Widower __
   Other (specify) __ Child __   ___
                                                                 13

7. Number of Children: None __ 1–2 __ 3–4 __ 5–6 __ 7–8 __
   9 or more __   ___
                                                                 15

8. Employment Status: Employed __ Unemployed Job Search __
   Unemployed, No Job Search __
   Unemployed with Dependent Child __
   Unemployed, Disabled/Health Problems __
   Other (specify) __ AFDC __   ___
                                                                 17

9. Number of Yrs. of Education: Zero __ 1–6 __ 7–9 __
   10–12 __ 13–14 __ 15–16 __ 17 and More __   ___
                                                                 19

10. Composition of Household: Alone __ Husband and Wife __
    Husband/Wife/Child __

    Husband/Wife/Child/Other Releatives __
    Single Parent __ Other (specify) __ __

11. Length of Time Client Serviced by the Agency:
    Less Than 1 yr. __ 1–2 yrs. __ 2–3 yrs. __

    3–4 yrs. __ 4–5 yrs. __ More Than 5 yrs. __

    Closed Case __ __

12. Presenting Problem: Psychological __ Behavioral __

    Environmental __ Medical __ Physical __

    Substance Abuse __ Multiple __ Other __ __

PART B: INTERVENTIONS AND SUCCESS INDICES

13. Advocacy—Differentiating? Definitely No __ Probably No __
    Probably Yes __ Definitely Yes __ __

14. Advocacy—Getting Own Resources? Definitely No __
    Probably No __ Probably Yes __ Definitely Yes __ __

15. Assessment—Differentiating? Definitely No __ Probably No __
    Probably Yes __ Definitely Yes __ __

16. Assessment—Exhibiting Reduced Scapegoating?
    Definitely No __ Probably No __ Probably Yes __
    Definitely Yes __ __

17. Empowering—Use of Personal Power? Definitely No __
    Probably No __ Probably Yes __ Definitely Yes __ __

18. Empowering—Makes Decisions and Pursues Personal Goals?
    Definitely No __ Probably No __ Probably Yes __
    Definitely Yes __ __

19. Empowering—Exhibits Self-Esteem? Definitely No __
    Probably No __ Probably Yes __ Definitely Yes __ __

20. Teaching—Able to Budget Time/Money? Definitely No $\underset{1}{\_\_}$ Probably No $\underset{2}{\_\_}$ Probably Yes $\underset{3}{\_\_}$ Definitely Yes $\underset{4}{\_\_}$ $\overline{41}$

21. Teaching—Exhibits Communications Skills? Definitely No $\underset{1}{\_\_}$ Probably No $\underset{2}{\_\_}$ Probably Yes $\underset{3}{\_\_}$ Definitely Yes $\underset{4}{\_\_}$ $\overline{43}$

22. Teaching—Exhibits Health/Personal Hygiene? Definitely No $\underset{1}{\_\_}$ Probably No $\underset{2}{\_\_}$ Probably Yes $\underset{3}{\_\_}$ Definitely Yes $\underset{4}{\_\_}$ $\overline{45}$

23. Individual Work—Exhibits Self-Esteem? Definitely No $\underset{1}{\_\_}$ Probably No $\underset{2}{\_\_}$ Probably Yes $\underset{3}{\_\_}$ Definitely Yes $\underset{4}{\_\_}$ $\overline{47}$

24. Individual Work—Exhibits Differentiation? Definitely No $\underset{1}{\_\_}$ Probably No $\underset{2}{\_\_}$ Probably Yes $\underset{3}{\_\_}$ Definitely Yes $\underset{4}{\_\_}$ $\overline{49}$

25. Individual Work—Exhibits Competence? Definitely No $\underset{1}{\_\_}$ Probably No $\underset{2}{\_\_}$ Probably Yes $\underset{3}{\_\_}$ Definitely Yes $\underset{4}{\_\_}$ $\overline{51}$

26. Group Work—Exhibits Self-Esteem? Definitely No $\underset{1}{\_\_}$ Probably No $\underset{2}{\_\_}$ Probably Yes $\underset{3}{\_\_}$ Definitely Yes $\underset{4}{\_\_}$ $\overline{53}$

27. Group Work—Exhibits Differentiation? Definitely No $\underset{1}{\_\_}$ Probably No $\underset{2}{\_\_}$ Probably Yes $\underset{3}{\_\_}$ Definitely Yes $\underset{4}{\_\_}$ $\overline{55}$

28. Group Work—Exhibits Competence? Definitely No $\underset{1}{\_\_}$ Probably No $\underset{2}{\_\_}$ Probably Yes $\underset{3}{\_\_}$ Definitely Yes $\underset{4}{\_\_}$ $\overline{57}$

29. Community Change—Demonstrates Advocacy? Definitely No $\underset{1}{\_\_}$ Probably No $\underset{2}{\_\_}$ Probably Yes $\underset{3}{\_\_}$ Definitely Yes $\underset{4}{\_\_}$ $\overline{59}$

30. Community Change—Institutes Change? Definitely No $\underset{1}{\_\_}$ Probably No $\underset{2}{\_\_}$ Probably Yes $\underset{3}{\_\_}$ Definitely Yes $\underset{4}{\_\_}$ $\overline{61}$

PART C: WORKER CHARACTERISTICS

31. Worker Characteristic Flexibility—Exhibits Role Imitation or Modeling? Definitely No $\underset{1}{\_\_}$ Probably No $\underset{2}{\_\_}$ Probably Yes $\underset{3}{\_\_}$ Definitely Yes $\underset{4}{\_\_}$ $\overline{63}$

32. Worker Characteristic Caring—Exhibits Role Imitation or Modeling? Definitely No __ Probably No __ Probably Yes __
    $\overline{}_1$ $\overline{}_2$ $\overline{}_3$
    Definitely Yes __
    $\overline{}_4$ $\overline{}_{65}$

33. Worker Characteristic Race—Exhibits Tolerance/Acceptance of Race and Gender? Definitely No __ Probably No __
    $\overline{}_1$ $\overline{}_2$
    Probably Yes __ Definitely Yes __
    $\overline{}_3$ $\overline{}_4$ $\overline{}_{67}$

34. Worker Characteristic Education—Exhibits Positive Reinforcement for Education? Definitely No __ Probably No __
    $\overline{}_1$ $\overline{}_2$
    Probably Yes __ Definitely Yes __
    $\overline{}_3$ $\overline{}_4$ $\overline{}_{69}$

35. Total Contact Hours per Week: 1–2 __ 3–4 __ 5–6 __ 7–8 __
    $\overline{}_1$ $\overline{}_2$ $\overline{}_3$ $\overline{}_4$
    9–10 __ 11 and More __
    $\overline{}_5$ $\overline{}_6$ $\overline{}_{71}$

36. Race/Ethnicity: African American __ Latino __ Asian __
    $\overline{}_1$ $\overline{}_2$ $\overline{}_3$
    Caribbean __ White __ Multiple __ Other (Specify) __
    $\overline{}_4$ $\overline{}_5$ $\overline{}_6$ $\overline{}_7$ $\overline{}_{73}$

37. Education: Less Than High School __ High School __ A.A. __
    $\overline{}_1$ $\overline{}_2$ $\overline{}_3$
    B.A. __ M.A. __ M.S.W. __ Other (Specify) __
    $\overline{}_4$ $\overline{}_5$ $\overline{}_6$ $\overline{}_7$ $\overline{}_{75}$

PART D: PROGRAM

38. Program Accessibility—Client Exhibits:
    Only Responsiveness __ Only Utilization __
    $\overline{}_1$ $\overline{}_2$
    Both __ Neither __
    $\overline{}_3$ $\overline{}_4$ $\overline{}_{77}$

Notes From Client Record

Assessment Plan:

Treatment Plan:

Treatment Processes (strategies):

Treatment Outcomes:

Other Comments:

Figure A-2

CLIENT INTERVIEW SCHEDULE

1. How long have you been off-services from this agency?
2. Since you have been off-services from this agency, have you received services at any other agency? Yes ___ No ___
3. If yes, can you describe the nature of such services?
4. Would you tell me about the conditions leading to your decision to seek help from the previous service provider? Present service provider?
5. Would you tell me about your experiences of getting help from this agency?
6. What were your most helpful experiences? Least helpful experiences?
7. Can you describe your life before you got help from this agency?
8. Can you describe your life after you got help from this agency? Any involvement in community change? Pursuing education? Employment?
9. How, do you believe, has this agency helped you to make the transition into the larger community?
10. Did you maintain any type of contact with your worker or the agency after you were terminated? Yes ___ No ___
11. Would you tell me about the purpose and the nature of such contacts?
12. How often and for what period of time did you maintain these contacts?
13. If something could have been done differently, either with your worker or with your experiences at the agency, what would these be?
14. Please feel free to provide additional information on any area of the interview completed and/or comment on an area neglected in the interview.
15. Race/Ethnicity? African American ___ Latino ___ Asian ___ Caribbean ___ Anglo ___ Other (Specify) ___

APPENDIX B

Summary of Studies
Cited in Chapter 4

Table B-1: Summary of Controlled Studies Reviewed by Mullen and Dumpson (1972)

Table B-2: Summary of Evaluative Studies Reviewed by Geismar (1972)

Table B-3: Summary of Research on Social Work Intervention Reviewed by Segal (1972)

Table B-4: Summary of Delinquency Prevention Studies Reviewed by Segal (1972)

Table B-5: Summary of Delinquency Ameliorative Studies Reviewed by Segal (1972)

Table B-6: Summary of Controlled Studies of the Effectiveness of Casework Reviewed by Fischer (1973)

Table B-7: Summary of Other Treated Controlled Studies of the Effectiveness of Casework Reviewed by Fischer (1973)

Table B-8: Summary of Controlled Studies of Delinquency Reviewed by Wood (1978)

Table B-9:   Summary of Controlled Studies of Intervention with Preadolescent Children Reviewed by Wood (1978)

Table B-10:   Summary of Controlled Studies of the Poor Reviewed by Wood (1978)

Table B-11:   Summary of Controlled Studies Reviewed by Reid and Hanrahan (1982)

Table B-12:   Summary of Controlled Studies Reviewed by Rubin (1985)

The following studies are tabulated in this appendix:

Fisher, J. 1973. "Is Casework Effective?" *Social Work* 18:5–21.

Geismar, Ludwig. 1972. "Thirteen Evaluative Studies," in Edward F. Mullen and James R. Dumpson, eds., *Evaluation of Social Work Interventions* (San Francisco: Jossey-Bass).

Reid, W. J., and P. Hanrahan. 1982. "Recent Evaluations of Social Work: Grounds for Optimism," *Social Work* 27:328–340.

Rubin, Allen. 1985. "Practice Effectiveness: More Grounds for Optimism," *Social Work* (November–December): 469–476.

Segal, Steven Paul. 1972. "Research on the Outcome of Social Work Therapeutic Interventions: A Review of the Literature," *Journal of Health and Social Behavior* 13 (March): 3–17.

Wood, K. M. 1978. "Casework Effectiveness: A New Look at the Research Evidence," *Social Work* 23:437–458.

For full documentation of each study tabulated the reader may consult the original research.

Table B-1
Summary of Controlled Studies Reviewed by Mullen and Dumpson (1972)

Author/Date	Clients/ Subjects (N)	Presenting Problem	Study Design	Intervenor	Intervention	Dependent Variable	Assessment	Outcome
Powers and Witmer (1951)	Predelinquent and delinquent males ages 6–10 (N=35)	Delinquency	Randomized/ controlled experiment	Social worker	Big Brother Psychoanalytical oriented interviews	Delinquency rates	Court records	Lack of difference between experimental and control groups
Meyer et al. (1965)	Vocational high school girls (N=381: experimental group, 189; control group, 192)	Predelinquency	Controlled experiment	Social worker	Individual/group counseling services	Behavioral and school problems	Completion Out-of-school behavior Academic performance School-related behavior Self-reports	Minimal effects; no statistical difference between control and experimental groups
Brown (1968)	Multiproblem families receiving public assistance (N=100: experimental group, 50; control group, 50)	Multiproblems	Controlled experiment	M.S.W. social workers, public assistance workers	Intensive casework Public assistance	Family functioning	Interviews Self-reports	No significant difference between control and experimental groups

Table B-2
Summary of Evaluative Studies Reviewed by Geismar (1972)

Author/Date	Clients/ Subjects (N)	Presenting Problem	Study Design	Intervenor	Intervention	Dependent Variable	Assessment	Outcome
United Services of the Greater Vancouver Area (1968–1969)	Multiproblem families (N=214: experimental group, 92; control group, 122)	Socioeconomic deprivation Human distress	Randomized controlled experiment	Social workers	Casework Group work Neighborhood/ community services	Family functioning	St. Paul Scale of Family Functioning	Positive effect in five out of eight areas of social functioning for experimental group
Reid and Shyne (1969)	Intact families (N=120: random assignment to treatment groups)	Psychosocial	Preexperimental without control	Unspecified	Interpersonal treatment: open-ended versus planned short-term service	Client functioning	Analysis of tape-recorded interviews	Favorable outcomes for short-term group, some statistical differences
Brown (1968)	Families on welfare assistance (N=150)[a]	Multiproblem	Randomized controlled experiment	Trained caseworkers Public workers	Intensive casework services	Social family functioning	St. Paul Scale of Family Functioning CSS Movement Scale	Small but statistically non-significant

Mullen et al. (1970)	Families first time on public assistance (N=173: experimental group, 105; control group, 68)	Individual and family disorganization	Randomized controlled experiment	Trained caseworkers Public assistance workers	Professional casework counseling	Psychological functioning Economic independence Individual/family organization	Interviews Economic changes Clients assessment of their changes	Some changes in experimental group General lack of support for positive outcomes for experimental group
Martin (1969)	Multiproblem families in Puerto Rico (N=240: experimental group, 120; control group, 120)	Multiproblem	Randomized controlled experiment	Unspecified social workers	Casework Group work Community organ	Social functioning	Before-after Tests Attitude scales Projective tests	Nonsignificant differences between experimental and control groups
Behling (1961)	Individuals and families on relief (N=400: experimental group, 200; control group, 200)	Social and psychological well-being	Matched/ controlled experiment	Public assistance workers	Intensive casework	Social and psychological functioning	CSS Movement Scale	Statistically significant positive outcomes
Geismar et al. (1970)	Young urban families (N=352: experimental group, 177; control group, 175)	Developmental Difficulties of urban living	Randomized controlled experiment	Unspecified social worker	Giving information Vocational guidance Advocacy Counseling Finding housing and jobs	Family functioning	St. Paul Scale of Family Functioning	Some improvement, not statistically significant

(continues)

Author/Date	Clients/Subjects (N)	Presenting Problem	Study Design	Intervenor	Intervention	Dependent Variable	Assessment	Outcome
Kuhl (1969)	Multiproblem families in Copenhagen (N=140: experimental group, 70; control group, 70)	Multiproblem	Randomized controlled experiment	Social workers under a psychologist	Giving advice and support Outreach and advocacy Alleviate problems Modify client attitudes	Social rehabilitation (multiproblems)	Before-and-after test	Moderate improvement Statistically significant improvement for experimental group (p<.10)
Meyers et al. (1965)	Adolescent girls (N=381: experimental group, 189; control group, 192)	School problems Psychological Unmanageable at home Prone to deviant behavior	Randomized controlled experiment	Unspecified workers	Casework Group work	Deviant behavior	Academic performance In- and out-of-school behavior Health records Number of pregnancies Attitude scales Personality tests Sociometric data Client rating CSS Movement Scale	Service provided had little impact
Schwartz and Sample (1970)	Clients on public assistance (N=135: nonrandom assignment to patterns of service delivery)	Individual and family functioning	Nonexperimental	Unspecified workers	Patterns of service Financial assistance Crisis counseling and rehabilitation Needed service	Client functioning Utilization	Work statistics Attitude scales	Positive results for experimental group

Study	Sample	Focus	Design	Workers	Services	Outcome focus	Measures	Results
Geismar and Krisberg (1967)	Low-class multi-problem families in low-income housing project (N=80: experimental group, 30; control group, 50)	Social functioning	Nonrandom matched experimental	Unspecified workers	Open-door casework Intense casework Nursery school Community center activities Social and educational activities	Social functioning	St. Paul Scale of Family Functioning Delinquency rates	Mixed results
McCabe et al. (1967)	Intellectually superior disadvantaged black and Puerto Rican children (N=67: experimental group, 42; control group, 25)	Scholastic and social functioning	Randomized controlled experiment	Unspecified workers	Group activities Role modeling Engagement of parents Casework Open house for parents	Intellectual, academic, and ego functioning	Twenty-eight measures reflecting intellectual, academic, and ego functions Twenty-two measures reflecting parent functioning Eight measures reflecting family functioning	Mixed results for both races
Blenkner et al. (1964)	Noninstitutionalized aged (N=323); assignment to three service modes; nonparticipant comparison group.	Services for aged	Randomized controlled experiment	Caseworker nurse	Modes of services Ongoing versus short term	Benefits of services	CSS Scale	No significant differences

[a]*Note:* Sizes of samples differ as reported by Dumpson and Geismar.

Table B-3

Summary of Research on Social Work Intervention Reviewed by Segal (1972)

Author/Date	Clients/Subjects (N)	Presenting Problem	Study Design	Intervenor	Intervention	Dependent Variable	Assessment	Outcome
Barron and Leary (1955)	Psychoneurotic patients (N=150: treatment groups, N=127; nonrandom/nontreatment group, N=23)	Psychological	Nonrandomized controlled experiment	Social workers Psychiatrists Psychologists	Individual and group therapy	Minnesota Multiphasic Personality Inventory profiles	Pre- and Post- MMPI scores	No significant difference between therapy and nontreatment group
Cartwright and Vogel (1960)	Self-referred psychoneurotic patients (N=22)	Psychological	Time-series	Nonsocial workers	Psychotherapy	Psychoneurosis	Q-Sort Thematic Apperception Test	Significant changes for therapy period, attributed to experiences of therapists

Table B-4
Summary of Delinquency Prevention Studies Reviewed by Segal (1972)

Author/Date	Clients/ Subjects (N)	Presenting Problem	Study Design	Intervenor	Intervention	Dependent Variable	Assessment	Outcome
Powers (1949), Powers and Witmer (1951)	Predelinquent boys ages 6–10 (N=650: experimental group, 325; control group, 325)	Delinquency	Randomized controlled experiment	Mostly professionally trained social workers	Varied— friendly informal relationship to formal intensive psychotherapy	Delinquency rate	Court records	No difference between the control and experimental groups
Meyer et al. (1965)	Predelinquent girls (N=400: Data only from experimental group, 189; control group, 192)	Delinquency	Randomized controlled experiment	Unspecified professional staff	Individual casework Group therapy	Delinquency rate	Completion of school/ highest grade completed Junior Personality Quiz and Make a Sentence Test Attitude and sociometric questionnaires Workers' clinical judgment	No difference between the experimental and control populations

(continues)

Author/Date	Clients/ Subjects (N)	Presenting Problem	Study Design	Intervenor	Intervention	Dependent Variable	Assessment	Outcome
Tait and Hodges (1962)	Elementary school children ages 5–12 (N=179) Parents (usually mothers)	Predelinquency	Nonrandomized/ controlled experiment	Unspecified interviewers	Interviews	Delinquency rate	Police and/or court experiences	Minimal (10%) difference between the groups
Craig and Furst (1965)	Six-year-old first-grade students (N=58: treatment group, 29; non-treatment group, 29)	Predelinquency	Nonrandomized experiment	Social workers Psychologists Psychiatrists	Unspecified treatment	Delinquency rate	Police records	No difference in delinquency rates between the two groups

Table B-5

Summary of Delinquency Ameliorative Studies Reviewed by Segal (1972)

Author/Date	Clients/ Subjects (N)	Presenting Problem	Study Design	Intervenor	Intervention	Dependent Variable	Assessment	Outcome
Massimo and Shore (1963)	Adolescent boys, ages 15–17 (N=20: experimental group, 10; control group, 10)	Antisocial activities	Randomized/ controlled experiment	Unspecified workers	Intensive psychotherapy Remedial education Employment	Delinquency rate	Academic achievement (Metropolitan Achievement Test) Attitudinal change (TAT) Behavioral change	Positive-sign difference between treatment and nontreatment groups
Miller (1964)	Gang members ages 12–21 (N= 400: treatment group, 205)	Antisocial behaviors	Nonrandomized/controlled experiment	Unspecified workers	Intensive group work	Delinquency rate	Observed behavior Court records	Negligible impact
Wiltse (1954)	Families on ADC	Economic dependency	One-group pretest-posttest, preexperimental	Unspecified workers	Social casework	Social independence	Employment	Inconclusive

(continues)

Author/Date	Clients/Subjects (N)	Presenting Problem	Study Design	Intervenor	Intervention	Dependent Variable	Assessment	Outcome
Geismar (1967)	Project families (N = 81: treatment group, 30; control group, 51)	Multiproblem	Nonrandomized/matched control treatment groups	Unspecified workers	Social casework	Family functioning	Geismar Scale of Family Functioning	Positive for treatment group
Brown (1968)	Dependent families (N = 195: treatment group, 50; control group 1, 50; control group 2, 50)	Multiproblem	Randomized controlled experiment	Unspecified workers	Casework	Family functioning	Geismer Scale of Family Functioning Hunt-Kogan Movement Scale	No difference between treatment and control groups

Table B-6

Summary of Controlled Studies of the Effectiveness of Casework Reviewed by Fischer (1973)

Author/Date	Clients/ Subjects (N)	Presenting Problem	Study Design	Intervenor	Intervention	Dependent Variable	Assessment	Outcome
Berleman and Steiner (1967)	Black seventh-grade boys (N=47: experimental group, 21; control group, 26)	School disciplinary problems Police records	Matched randomized/ controlled experiment	Trained social workers	Intensive, direct, individualized and group services	Acting-out behavior	School disciplinary records Police records	No significant difference between experimental and control groups
Craig and Furst (1965)	First-grade boys (N=58: experimental group, 29; control group, 29)	Predelinquency	Matched/ controlled experiment	Psychiatric social workers Clinical professionals	Intensive child guidance therapy	Delinquency rates	Teacher's behavior reports and delinquency records	No significant difference between experimental and control groups
McCabe (1967)	Intellectually superior, socially disadvantaged black and Puerto Rican children (N=67: experimental group, 42; control group, 25)	Deterioration of scholastic and social functioning	Matched randomized/ controlled experiment	Social workers	Group and individual services	Intellectual functioning of children Parental functioning Family functioning	Intelligence tests School achievement Behavior rating scale Ego functioning scale Ratings of parental and family scales	No significant difference between experimental and control groups

(continues)

Author/Date	Clients/ Subjects (N)	Presenting Problem	Study Design	Intervenor	Intervention	Dependent Variable	Assessment	Outcome
Meyer, Borgatta, and Jones (1965)	High school girls (N=381: experimental group, 189; control group, 192)	"Potential problem"	Randomized/ controlled experiment	Trained social workers	Group and individualized services	School behavior Social functioning	Client and worker ratings School grades and school-related behavior Teacher ratings Personality and attitude inventories	No significant difference between experimental and control groups
Miller (1962)	Lower socioeconomic status gang members (N=377: experimental group, 205; control group, 172)	Predelinquency	Matched/ controlled experiment	Unspecified workers	Group and individualized services	Delinquency rates	Number of court appearances	No significant difference between experimental and control groups
Powers and Witmer (1951)	Predelinquent boys ages 10–17 (N=650: experimental group, 325; control group, 325)	Predelinquency	Matched randomized/ controlled experiment	Caseworker-counselor	Direct individualized services	Frequency and seriousness of delinquency	Court records Police statistics Ratings of seriousness of offenses Ratings of social adjustment Psychological inventories	No significant difference between experimental and control groups

Table B-7

Summary of Other Treated Controlled Studies of the Effectiveness of Casework Reviewed by Fischer (1973)

Author/Date	Clients/ Subjects (N)	Presenting Problem	Study Design	Intervenor	Intervention	Dependent Variable	Assessment	Outcome
Blenkner, Bloom, and Nielson (1971)	Mentally impaired age (N=164: experimental group, 76; control group, 88)	Difficulty in caring for themselves	Randomized/ controlled experiment	Experienced caseworkers	Intensive direct services use of environmental resources	Competence Environmental protection Effects on others	Ratings from interviews Observer ratings Clinical ratings Death and institutionalization rates	Higher death and institutional rate for experimental group Intervention favored control group
Brown (1968)	Families on AFDC (N=100: experimental group, 50; control group, 50)	Multiproblem	Randomized/ controlled experiment	Professional caseworkers	Intensive direct services Use of environmental resources	Family functioning	Geismar Scale of Family Functioning Hunt-Kogan Movement Scale	No significant difference between experimental and control groups
Geismar and Krisberg (1967)	Low-income families (N=81: experimental group, 30; control group, 51)	Multiproblem	Nonrandomized/quasi-controlled experiment	Unspecified caseworkers	Intensive direct services Use of environmental resources	Family functioning	Geismar Scale of Family Functioning	Improvement for experimental; however, inconclusive (outcome results due to unequal comparison groups)

(continues)

Author/Date	*Clients/ Subjects (N)*	*Presenting Problem*	*Study Design*	*Intervenor*	*Intervention*	*Dependent Variable*	*Assessment*	*Outcome*
Mullen, Chazin, and Feldstein (1979)	Public assistance families (N=156: experimental group, 88; control group, 68)	Family disorganization	Randomized/ controlled experiment	Professional caseworkers	Direct individualized services	Individual and family functioning	Ratings of structured with clients	No significant difference in family functioning between experimental and control groups
Webb and Riley (1970)	Female probationers ages 18–25 (N=58: experimental group, 26; control group, 32)	Life adjustment	Randomized/ controlled experiment	Caseworkers	Direct individualized services	Life adjustment	MMPI Semantic differential Behavior ratings	Improvement on selected measures for experimental groups but inconclusive (no comparison scores for other measures reported)

Table B-8
Summary of Controlled Studies of Delinquency Reviewed by Wood (1978)

Author/Date	Clients/Subjects (N)	Presenting Problem	Study Design	Intervenor	Intervention	Dependent Variable	Assessment	Outcome
Berleman and Steinburn (1967, 1968); Berleman, Seaburg, and Steinburn (1972)	Lower-class black seventh-grade boys (N=102: experimental group, 52; control group, 50)	Delinquency	Matched/randomized/controlled experiment	M.S.W.s	Group work Individual casework Work with parents	Delinquency rate	Police records School disciplinary records	No significant difference between experimental and control groups
Tait and Hodges (1962)	Elementary school children, majority boys and blacks (N=165: experimental group, 108; control group, 57)	Predelinquent	Matched/controlled experiment	M.S.W.s Graduate students	Casework Psychotherapy	Delinquency rate	Police and court records	Higher rate of delinquency in experimental group than in control group

*Note: Following studies reviewed by Fischer (1973) are excluded here in the summary of controlled studies of delinquency reviewed by Wood (1978): Craig and Furst (1965); Meyers, Borgatta, and Jones (1965); Miller, (1962); and Webb and Riley (1970).

Table B-9

Summary of Controlled Studies of Intervention with Preadolescent Children Reviewed by Wood (1978)

Author/Date	Clients/ Subjects (N)	Presenting Problem	Study Design	Intervenor	Intervention	Dependent Variable	Assessment	Outcome
Levitt (1957); Levit, Beiser, and Robertson (1959)	Follow-up study of children and mothers who had received at least five interviews 1944–1954, mean age 10.5 yrs., 69% males (N=330: experimental group, 237 [treated], control group, 93 [defectors])	Social adjustment	Matched/controlled ex post facto quasi-experimental	MSW staff "Other professionals" Graduate students	Casework Psychotherapy	Psychological and social adjustment	Psychological tests School completion Evaluations of adjustment by parents, children, and interviewers	No significant difference between experimental and control groups

* Note: The study by McCabe et al. (1967) and reviewed by Fischer (1973) was excluded from this summary.

Table B-10

Summary of Controlled Studies of the Poor Reviewed by Wood (1978)

Author/Date	Clients/ Subjects (N)	Presenting Problem	Study Design	Intervenor	Intervention	Dependent Variable	Assessment	Outcome
Behling (1961)	Public welfare recipients (N=400: experimental group, 200; control group, 200)	Unclear	Randomized/ controlled experiment	B.A.-level caseworkers	Intensive casework Smaller caseloads	Status of case at termination of services	CSS Movement Scale "Chronicity score" Open versus closed cases Financial cost	Mixed and inconclusive results
Geismar (1971), Geismar and Krisbery (1966a, b; Geismar et al. (1972)	Young, low-income families with first child (N=352: experimental group, 177; control group, 175)	Family functioning	Randomized/ controlled experiment	B.A. workers under M.S.W. supervision	Intensive casework Brokerage Advocacy Smaller caseloads	Family functioning	Income status Family structure "Legal deviance" Use of community resources St. Paul Scale of Family Functioning	Mixed—generally no significant difference between experimental and control groups

(continues)

Author/Date	Clients/ Subjects (N)	Presenting Problem	Study Design	Intervenor	Intervention	Dependent Variable	Assessment	Outcome
Olson (1968, 1970)	New AFDC cases, young, single mothers, 87% white ($N=131$: experimental group, 66 in two groups; control group, 65 in two groups)	Individual and family functioning	Randomized/ controlled experiment	B.A.-level workers	High or low welfare grants Worker experience	Individual and family functioning	Judgments by interviewer from outside research firm re health, housekeeping, money management, morale, and individual and family functioning	Higher grant and experienced worker groups made more gains than other groups
Schwartz (1966); Schwartz and Sample (1967, 1972)	Public welfare recipients, 90% black ($N=314$: experimental group, 164; control group, 150)	Client functioning	Randomized/ controlled experiment	B.A.-level workers (Experience group workers supervised by M.S.W.s)	Team versus conventional delivery	Client functioning Personal morale	Absence and turnover rates CSS Movement Scale St. Paul Family Functioning Scale	Improvements for experimental service groups and low caseloads

| Wilkinson and Ross (1972) | Black AFDC mothers and children (N=181: experimental group, 125 in three groups; control group, 56) | Client functioning | Randomized/controlled experiment | B.A.-level workers | Work training and placement Supplemental income Adult education Individual counseling Intensive individual counseling Medical and dental services Clothing and educational supplies for children Group sessions on nutrition, money matters, adult education | Client functioning | Before and after interviews re employment status, nutritional habits, housekeeping standards, use of medical and dental services, participation in community activities, attitudes toward work, attitudes toward welfare | No significant difference between experimental and control groups |
| Wilson (1966, 1967) | AFDC families (N=314: experimental group, 163; control group, 151) | Welfare dependency | Not specified | B.A. workers with professional supervision | Intensive casework | Independent of welfare | Follow-up interviews Case records | Positive outcome for experimental group |

Note: Studies by Brown (1968), Geismar and Krisberg (1967), and Mullen, Chazin, and Feldstein (1970, 1972) and reviewed by Fischer (1973) excluded from this summary.

Table B-11

Summary of Controlled Studies Reviewed by Reid and Hanrahan (1982)

Author/Date	Clients/ Subjects (N)	Presenting Problem	Study Design	Intervenor	Intervention	Dependent Variable	Assessment	Outcome
Berger and Rose (1977)	Nursing home residents (N=27: 2 experimental groups, 9 in each; control group, 9)	Inadequate social skills	Randomized/ controlled experiment	Unspecified "social worker"	Skill training Group discussions	Social skills	Skill training scores Self-reports Role-play test	Mixed—statistically significant difference between skill group and other treatment and control group on only behavioral role-play measure No difference in three out of four measures at follow-up
Blatterbauer, Kupst, and Schulman (1976); Kupst et al. (1977)	Parents of children with cardiac disorders (N=84: 3 experimental groups, 21 in each; control group, 21)	Inadequate grasp of medical information	Randomized controlled experiment	Unspecified "social worker"	Medical information only Social information only Medical and social information	Medical knowledge	Medical information recall Anxiety ratings Service satisfaction	Statistically significant difference between treatment and control group Mixed—at follow-up, no significant differences on any measure

Study	Sample	Problem	Design	Practitioner	Intervention	Outcome area	Measure	Results
Feldman and Caplinger (1977)	Pre- and adolescent boys (N=2,104: 7 experimental groups, N1=362, N2=339, N3=283, N4=174, N5=290, N6=258, N7=229; control group, 214)	Antisocial behavior	Randomized controlled experiment	Unspecified "social worker"	Behavioral-authoritarian type socialization Traditional-democratic type socialization Nondirective–laissez-faire type socialization	Social behavior	Observations of appropriate social behavior	Mixed—statistically significant differences favoring behavioral and control group
Hogarty et al. (1973), Hogarty et al. (1974a, b), Goldberg et al. (1977)	Schizophrenic clients in state hospitals (N=374: 2 experimental groups, 192 and 190; 2 control groups, 182 and 184)	Social adjustment	Randomized controlled experiment	Unspecified "social worker"	Role therapy Drug therapy	Social adjustment	Rates of schizophrenia Hospitalization rates Adjustment ratings	Mixed—statistically significant difference for treatment and control groups Positive outcome for males in control group over role therapy treatment group
Jayaratne (1978)	Dysfunctional families (N=28: experimental group, 13; control group, 15)	Behavioral and academic problems	Randomized controlled experiment	Unspecified "social worker"	Behavioral contracting Instructions Modeling Reinforcement	Family functioning	Role play	Statistically significant difference between treatment and control groups

(continues)

Author/Date	Clients/Subjects (N)	Presenting Problem	Study Design	Intervenor	Intervention	Dependent Variable	Assessment	Outcome
Jones, Neuman, and Shyne (1978)	Families with children at risk of or in foster care (N=549: experimental group, 176; control group, 373)	Unnecessary and prolonged foster care	Randomized controlled experiment	Unspecified "social worker"	Intensive service	Length of time in foster care	Return rates to natural parents Worker ratings	Statistically significant difference between treatment and control groups
Lawrence and Walter (1978)	Clients in mental health agencies (N=35: experimental group, 18; control group, 17)	Personal and social relational	Randomized controlled experiment	Unspecified "social worker"	Behavioral group work Instructions Modeling Role playing	Social relations Personal problems	Problem rating Others not reported	Inconclusive—statistical significant difference between treatment and control groups reported for only one measure
Mayadas and Duehn (1977)	Married couples (N=30: 3 treatment groups, N1=10, N2=10, N3=10)	Communications	Randomized/No control preexperimental	Unspecified "social worker"	Verbal counseling Stimulus modeling (tape) Stimulus modeling (tape and video feedback)	Communications	Ratings of videotaped interactions	Statistically significant differences among treatment groups

Study	Sample	Problem	Design	Worker	Intervention	Outcome area	Measures	Findings
Piliavin and Gross (1977)	Clients on AFDC (N=441: 4 experimental groups, N1=70, N2=75, N3=72, N4=73; control group, 151)	Unspecified, unclear	Randomized/controlled experiment Two-by-two factorial design	Unspecified "social worker"	Services and grants administered by separate workers Services and grants administered by same worker Client-requested services Worker-initiated services	Effects of mode of social service delivery systems	Number of requests for financial services Client's worker ratings Frequency of contact with workers	Statistically significant differences of effectiveness among treatment groups No reported statistical findings comparing treatment groups and control group
Polster and Pinkston (1979)	Students in grades 7 and 8 (N=35: 2 experimental groups, 6 in each; control group, 23)	Academic under-achievement	Randomized controlled experiment	Unspecified "social worker"	Behavioral contracting Parent monitoring Self-monitoring	School achievement	G.P.A. Iowa Test of Basic Skills Time spent studying	Statistical significant difference between treatment and control groups on one measure Positive outcomes reported for treatment group—no significant level reported
Reid (1975)	Public school students, adult clients in a mental health clinic (N=32: 2 treatment groups, 16 in each)	Varied, unspecified	Random-ized/no control pre-experimental	Unspecified "social worker"	Task centered with task implementation sequence Task centered without task implementation sequence	Problem resolution	Achievement ratings Client and worker ratings of progress	Mixed—statistically significant difference between treatment groups on achievement problem ratings; nonsignificant positive outcome for treatment group with task implementation (no no-treatment control comparison group)

(continues)

Author/Date	Clients/ Subjects (N)	Presenting Problem	Study Design	Intervenor	Intervention	Dependent Variable	Assessment	Outcome
Reid (1978)	Psychiatric outpatients, public school students (N=86: experimental group, 43; control group, 43)	Unspecified, selected by research subjects	Randomized/ controlled experimental	Unspecified "social worker"	Task centered with task implementation sequence	Problem resolution	Ratings of audiotaped problems reviews	Statistically significant difference between experimental and control groups
Schinke et al. (1978)	Teenage mothers or expectant mothers (N=26: 2 treatment groups, 13 in each)	Job application skills	Randomized/ no control preexperimental	Unspecified "social workers"	Behavioral skills Group work Group discussions	Employment application skills	Ratings of employment application Ratings of simulated employment Other non-specified	Statistically significant difference between treatment groups (no treatment control comparison group)
Schinke and Rose (1976)	Social agency clients, subjects recruited through ads (N=36: 2 treatment groups, 21 and 15)	Social skills	Randomized/ no control preexperimental	Unspecified "social workers"	Rehearsal contracting Behavioral discussion	Social skills	Role-play test Overall assertive rating Affect rating Other non-specified ratings	Mixed—statistically significant difference between treatment groups; role-play test; other nonsignificant difference between treatment groups (no treatment control comparison group)

Study	Sample	Target problem	Design	Practitioner	Intervention	Outcome	Measures	Results
Schofield (1979)	Parents of children in grades 3–6 (N=42: 2 experimental groups, 14 in each; control group, 14)	Academic preproblem	Randomized quasi-controlled experiment	Unspecified "social workers"	Parent effectiveness training Behavior modification	Academic problems	Self-esteem scores Other non-specified	Mixed—statistically significant difference between parent and quasi-control groups; no significant difference in self-esteem scores between treatment groups; nonstatistically significant difference between behavior modification group and quasi-control group
Stein (1976); Stein, Gambril, and Wiltse (1978)	Natural parents of children in foster care (N=428: experimental group (N=227; control group, 2)	Long-term foster care	Nonrandomized/controlled experiment	Unspecified "social workers"	Behavioral contracting Routine service	Foster care	Length of time in foster care Return child to natural parents Problem resolution	Statistically significant difference between experimental and control groups
Stuart and Tripodi (1973)	Junior high students (N=94: 3 experimental groups, N1=26, N2=27, N3=26; control group, 15)	Antisocial behavior Truancy Motivational	Randomized/quasi-controlled experiment	Unspecified "social worker"	Behavioral contracting	School attendance School performance School behavior	Records of attendance Attitude measures Grades Observed behavior at school, home, and in community	Mixed—statistically significant difference on attendance for 90-day treatment group; improved attitude for 15-day treatment group; no statistically significant difference on eight attitude and behavioral measures among treatment groups; statistically significant negative outcome on grades for quasi-control group

(continues)

Author/Date	Clients/ Subjects (N)	Presenting Problem	Study Design	Intervenor	Intervention	Dependent Variable	Assessment	Outcome
Stuart and Tripodi (1974)	Junior high students (N=64: 2 experimental groups, N1=27, N2=22; control group, 15)	Antisocial behavior Truancy Motivational	Randomized/ controlled experiment	Unspecified "social worker"	Home-based contracting School-based contracting	School attendance School performance School behavior	Grades Client satisfaction Other unspecified	Statistically significant difference on grades between home-based and other treatment and control groups. Statistically significant difference on client satisfaction between two treatment groups. Statistically significant difference on 5 of 10 measures between home-based and control group
Stuart Jayarate, and Tripodi (1976)	Junior high students (N=60: experimental group, 30; control group, 30)	Antisocial behavior Truancy Motivational	Randomized/ controlled experiment	Unspecified "social worker"	Behavior contracting	School attendance School performance School behavior	Teacher evaluations Counselor evaluations Mother's marital adjustment Mother's adolescent evaluation Other unspecified	Mixed—statistically significant difference in only 4 of 13 measures between experimental and control groups; no significant difference on other unspecified measures

Study	Sample	Problem	Design	Practitioner	Intervention	Outcome Construct	Measure	Results
Toseland and Rose (1978)	Elderly (N=53, with 15 treatment groups)	Lack of social skills	Unclear	Unspecified "social workers"	Behavioral role play Social group work Problem solving	Social skills	Role-play test Other unspecified	Statistically significant difference—role-play test among treatment groups No statistical difference among treatment groups at follow-up (no no-treatment control comparison group)
Weissman, Geanakoplos, and Prusoff (1973); Weissman et al. (1974); Klerman et al. (1974)	Depressed females on drug therapy (N=150: experimental group, 75; control group, 75)	Social adjustment	Randomized/controlled experiment Two-by-three factorial design	Unspecified "social worker"	Psychotherapy Drug therapy	Social adjustment	Ratings of social adjustment Adjustment scales, work performance	Statistically significant difference on social adjustment between psychotherapy/drug and other treatment groups
Wells, Figurel, and McNamee (1977)	Middle-class couples (N=42: 2 treatment groups, N1=22, N2=20)	Marital conflict	Randomized/no control preexperimental	Unspecified "social workers"	Conjoint treatment Communications training	Marital conflict	Unspecified marital adjustment scale	No statistically significant difference between two treatment groups

Table B-12
Summary of Controlled Studies Reviewed by Rubin (1985)

Author/Date	Clients/Subjects (N)	Presenting Problem	Study Design	Intervenor	Intervention	Dependent Variable	Assessment	Outcome
Matson and Senatore (1981)	Mentally retarded clients in sheltered workshop (N not reported, experimental and control groups)	Deficits in interpersonal functioning	Randomized/controlled experiment	Unclear	Psychotherapy Social skills training	Interpersonal functioning	Ratings of two target behaviors (by independent observers) Two unspecified standardized rating scales of client performance	Social skills group had significantly better outcomes on 3 of 4 measures No statistics reported
Senatore, Matson, and Kazdin (1982)	Outpatients at a mental health and mental retardation clinic (N not reported, experimental and control groups)	Deficits in interpersonal functioning	Randomized/controlled experiment	Unclear	Social skills training Enriched social skills training with rehearsal	Interpersonal functioning	Behavioral ratings Observations during interview Videotaped role play Unobtrusive observations	Enriched social skills group did better than social skills only and control groups
Hogarty et al. (1979)	Previously hospitalized schizophrenic patients (N=105; 4 treatment groups, N not reported)	Interpersonal, personal, social, and rehabilitative needs	Randomized/no-treatment controlled experiment	Experienced M.S.W.s Unspecified medical personnel	Oral medication Injection medication Social therapy	Effectiveness of day treatment Role performance	Length of time patient remained in the community Unspecified standardized inventories	No significant difference in relapse for medication groups Social therapy significant in forestalling relapse in second year

Study	Sample							Results
Lin et al. (1979)	Discharged VA chronic schizophrenic patients (N not reported; 2 treatment groups)	Social interaction skills	Randomized/no no-treatment controlled experiment	Unclear	Social treatment Chemotherapy	Social interaction skills Effectiveness of day treatment	Length of time patients remained in the community Unspecified scales of social function, symptoms, and attitudes	No significant difference between two groups regarding length of time patients remained in community Significant difference favoring day treatment group on other measures No statistics reported
Stein Test (1980)	Chronically affected subjects seeking institutionalization (N not reported)	Pathological dependency	Randomized/ controlled experiment	Unclear	Training in community living (TCL)	Effectiveness of community-based treatment Independent living	Face-to-face interviews Unspecified scales to measure symptomatology, community adjustment, and self-esteem	Results significantly favoring TCL subjects No statistics reported
Velasquez and McCubbin (1980)	Mentally ill young adults (N=94: experimental and control groups)	Personality disorders	Randomized/ controlled experiment	Unclear	Milieu therapy	Effectiveness of community-based treatment Role performance/functioning	Six unspecified standardized rating scales Two unspecified self-report measures	Experimental group outcome better than comparison group No statistics reported

(continues)

Author/Date	Clients/ Subjects (N)	Presenting Problem	Study Design	Intervenor	Intervention	Dependent Variable	Assessment	Outcome
Tableman et al. (1982)	Women receiving AFDC and not receiving mental health services (N not reported: experimental and control groups)	Life stress	Randomized/ controlled experiment	Unclear	Stress management training	Effectiveness of training Life-coping skills	Unspecified standardized scales	Significant differences on 8 measures favoring experimental group No statistics reported
Reid et al. (1980)	Lower-income children ages 7–13 (N=21)	Academic, behavioral, and interpersonal problems	No control (one group) preexperimental	First-year M.S.W. students—part of field training in a task-center sequence	Contract with practitioner to work on at least two problems	Effectiveness of task-centered method for overcoming academic, behavioral, and interpersonal problems	Retrospective reports by client, teacher, or parent on frequency of target behavior	Significantly more improvements on problem being treated than on those not treated

Study	Sample	Problem	Design	Orientation	Intervention	Target	Measures	Findings
Akabas, Fine, and Yasser (1982)	Disability claimants, City of New York municipal workers (N not reported: experimental and control groups)	Disability	Matched/randomized controlled experiment	Unclear	Case management	Physical disabilities	Insurance carrier costs; Return to work; Physical self-perception; Service received and perception of those	56% of treatment group and 83% of control group returned to work; Positive outcome for treatment group for feeling better than before services and disability; No inferential statistical data reported
Boone, Coulton, and Keller (1981)	Orthopedic inpatients (N not reported: experimental and control groups)	Orthopedic	Randomized controlled experiment	Unspecified social work, medical, and nursing staff	Early comprehensive social work services	Social and psychological barriers in discharge	Length of stay in hospital	Experiment group averaged 1.25 days less than control group
Toseland, Sherman, and Bliven (1981)	Members of two senior service centers (N=40: 2 experimental and 1 control groups)	Mutual support	Randomized controlled experiment	Unclear	Group work: less structure, less directive; more structure, task oriented	Social skills	Unspecified standardized instruments	Inconclusive—structured treatment terminated due to a lack of participation; No significant findings
Roskin (1982)	Adults with two or more life changes (N not reported: 2 experimental groups)	Emotional health	A semi-crossover	Unclear	Cognitive-affective group work	Emotional health	Unspecified self-rated symptom checkist	Significantly greater improvement for treatment group on 3 of 10 comparisons

(continues)

Author/Date	Clients/ Subjects (N)	Presenting Problem	Study Design	Intervenor	Intervention	Dependent Variable	Assessment	Outcome
Berlin (1980)	Adult women (N=50: 1 experimental and 2 control groups)	Self-criticism	Randomized/ controlled experiment	Unclear	Cognitive-behavioral	Self-criticism	Frequency of self-criticism statements Self-criticism analog test	Inconclusive—questionable significant differences between treatment group and two control groups

APPENDIX C

Tables for Use in Conjunction with Chapter 5

Tables C-1–C-14   Agencies' Success Rates

Table C-15   Intercorrelation Success Outcomes by Worker Characteristics

Table C-16   The Rotated Factor Matrix

Table C-17   Correlation Matrix

Table C-18   Summary of Regression Analysis

In the tables that follow, the agencies have been designated as A, B, C, and D to preserve anonymity.

Table C-1
Agencies' Success Rates for Assessment: Effective Coping (in percentages)

Success	A	B	C	D
Yes	52.2	61.8	20.0	58.3
No	47.8	38.2	80.0	41.7
Total	100.0	100.0	100.0	100.0
	$\chi^2 = 12.63$	D.F. = 3	$p = .005$	

Table C-2
Agencies' Success Rates for Assessment: Minimal Blaming/Scapegoating (in percentages)

Success	A	B	C	D
Yes	15.4	62.1	18.5	50.0
No	84.6	37.9	81.5	50.0
Total	100.0	100.0	100.0	100.0
	$\chi^2 = 14.92$	D.F. = 3	$p = .001$	

Table C-3
Agencies' Success Rates for Advocacy: Seeking Own Resources (in percentages)

Success	A	B	C	D
Yes	41.7	87.4	25.0	50.0
No	58.3	12.6	75.0	50.0
Total	100.0	100.0	100.0	100.0
	$\chi^2 = 7.82$	D.F. = 3	$p = .05$	

Table C-4

Agencies' Success Rates for Empowerment: Use of Personal Power (in percentages)

Success	A	B	C	D
Yes	43.5	66.7	19.2	50.0
No	56.5	33.3	80.8	50.0
Total	100	100	100	100

$\chi^2 = 13.32$ D.F. $= 3$ $p = .004$

Table C-5

Agencies' Success Rates for Empowerment: Ability to Make Decisions and Pursue Personal Goals (in percentages)

Success	A	B	C	D
Yes	45.8	62.5	15.4	53.8
No	54.2	37.5	84.6	46.2
Total	100.0	100.0	100.0	100.0

$\chi^2 = 13.61$ D.F. $= 3$ $p = .003$

Table C-6

Agencies' Success Rates for Empowerment: Positive Self-Esteem (in percentages)

Success	A	B	C	D
Yes	41.7	64.7	27.6	78.6
No	58.3	35.3	72.4	21.4
Total	100.0	100.0	100.0	100.0

$\chi^2 = 13.99$ D.F. $= 3$ $p = .003$

Table C-7

Agencies' Success Rates for Individual/Family Work: Communication and Parenting Skills (in percentages)

Success	A	B	C	D
Yes	55.6	85.7	35.0	42.9
No	44.4	14.3	65.0	57.1
Total	100.0	100.0	100.0	100.0

$\chi^2 = 13.96$ D.F. = 3 $p = .003$

Table C-8

Agencies' Success Rates for Individual/Family Work: Personal Health and Hygiene (in percentages)

Success	A	B	C	D
Yes	72.7	92.3	46.7	83.3
No	27.3	7.7	53.3	16.7
Total	100.0	100.0	100.0	100.0

$\chi^2 = 11.06$ D.F. = 3 $p = .01$

Table C-9

Agencies' Success Rates for Individual/Family Work: Positive Self-Esteem (in percentages)

Success	A	B	C	D
Yes	33.3	69.0	35.7	76.9
No	66.7	31.0	64.3	23.1
Total	100.0	100.0	100.0	100.0

$\chi^2 = 12.47$ D.F. = 3 $p = .006$

Table C-10

Agencies' Success Rates for Individual/Family Work: Differentiation (in percentages)

Success	A	B	C	D
Yes	45.5	73.3	31.0	75.0
No	54.5	26.7	69.0	25.0
Total	100.0	100.0	100.0	100.0

$\chi^2 = 13.46$ D.F. = 3 $p = .004$

Table C-11

Agencies' Success Rates for Individual/Family Work: Competence (in percentages)

Success	A	B	C	D
Yes	40.0	66.7	38.7	64.3
No	60.0	33.3	61.3	35.7
Total	100.0	100.0	100.0	100.0

$\chi^2 = 6.76$ D.F. = 3 $p = .07$

Table C-12

Agencies' Success Rates for Group Work: Positive Self-Esteem (in percentages)

Success	A	B	C	D
Yes	40.0	87.5	20.0	
No	60.0	12.5	80.0	100.0
Total	100.0	100.0	100.0	100.0

$\chi^2 = 10.60$ D.F. = 3 $p = .01$

Table C-13
Agencies' Success Rates for Group Work: Differentiation (in percentages)

Success	A	B	C	D
Yes	45.0	75.0	16.7	50.0
No	55.0	25.0	83.3	50.0
Total	100.0	100.0	100.0	100.0
	$\chi^2 = 36.41$	D.F. = 3	$p = .00003$	

Table C-14
Agencies' Success Rates for Group Work: Competence (in percentages)

Success	A	B	C	D
Yes	41.2	87.5	25.0	50.0
No	58.8	12.5	75.0	50.0
Total	100.0	100.0	100.0	100.0
	$\chi^2 = 7.85$	D.F. = 3	$p = .05$	

Table C-15

Summary of Pearson Correlation Coefficients Between Worker Characteristics and Success Outcomes

Intervention Strategies	Worker Characteristics	
	Flexibility	Caring
Assessment		
Effective coping	.64 (N = 66) p = .0005	.54 (N = 68) p = .0005
Reduced scape- goating	.69 (N = 54) p = .0005	.64 (N = 55) p = .0005
Advocacy		
Seeking own resources	.61 (N = 42) p = .0005	.50 (N = 58) p = .0005
Empowerment		
Use of personal power	.75 (N = 65) p = .0005	.71 (N = 68) p = .0005
Ability to make own decisions	.75 (N = 65) p = .0005	.71 (N = 68) p = .0005
Positive self- esteem	.80 (N = 67) p = .0005	.72 (N = 68) p = .0005
Individual Work		
Able to budget money/time	.57 (N = 23) p = .005	.49 (N = 23) p = .018

Table C-15   *(continued)*

Intervention Strategies	Worker Characteristics	
	Flexibility	Caring
Exhibit communications skills	.82 (N = 53) p = .0005	.75 (N = 55) p = .0005
Exhibit health/ hygiene	.64 (N = 44) p = .0005	.57 (N = 46) p = .0005
Exhibit positive self-esteem	.90 (N = 61) p = .0005	.75 (N = 65) p = .0005
Exhibit differentiation	.78 (N = 64) p = .0005	.70 (N = 66) p = .0005
Exhibit competence	.82 (N = 65) p = .0005	.83 (N = 68) p = .0005
Group Work		
Exhibit positive self-esteem	.82 (N = 27) p = .0005	.66 (N = 28) p = .0005
Exhibit competence	.91 (N = 25) p = .0005	.80 (N = 27) p = .0005

Table C-16

Summary of Factor Loading for Each Dimension of Improved Overall Functioning

Dimensions	Factor 1	Factor 2
Effective coping	.38272	.68963
Minimal scapegoating	.58626	.48333
Seeking own resources	.35636	.69693
Use of personal power	.60554	.56858
Pursues personal goals	.50090	.65030
Positive self-esteem	.90933	.18659
Effective communications and parenting skills	.61695	.44228
Personal health and hygiene	.52451	.35520
Differentiation	.83242	.27689
Competence	.79374	.28252

Table C-17

Correlation Matrix of Overall Improved Functioning and Worker Characteristics

	Overall Improved Functioning
Overall improved functioning	1.00
Worker characteristic—flexibility	.8986**
Worker characteristic—caring	.8599**
Worker characteristic—positive reinforcement for education	.7754*

*Significant at <.05.
**Significant at <.01.

Table C-18

Multiple Regression Analysis of Overall Improved Functioning by Worker Characteristics

Dependent variable = Overall improved functioning Independent variable in the equation		*beta*	*T*
Worker characteristic—flexibility		.586032	4.160**
Worker characteristic—caring		.430759	1.839*
Positive reinforcement for education		−.025044	−.126
Multiple R	.94284		
R²	.88827		
Adjusted R²	.86529		
F	39.7494200**		

*Significant at <.05.
**Significant at <.001.

NOTES

Chapter 1. Overwhelmed Clients

1. Charles M. Sennott, "Finding Four Generations Sustained by Welfare," *Boston Globe*, February 20, 1994, pp. 1, 46.
2. W. C. Jones and E. F. Borgatta, "Methodology of Evolution," in E. F. Mullen and James R. Dumpson, eds., *Evaluation of Social Work Interventions* (San Francisco: Jossey-Bass, 1972).
3. Mullen and Dumpson, *Evaluation*.
4. B. J. Tidwell, "Research and Practice Issues with Black Families," in S. M. L. Logan, E. M. Freeman, and R. G. MacRoy, eds., *Social Work Practice with Black Families* (New York: Longman, 1990), pp. 257–272.
5. J. G. Hopps, "Effectiveness and Human Worth," *Social Work* (1985): 476.
6. B. Solomon, "Social Work in a Multi-ethnic Society," in M. Solemayer, ed., *Cross-Cultural Perspective in Social Work Practice and Education* (New York: Council on Social Work Education, 1976), pp. 167–176.
7. E. Erikson, *Childhood and Society* (New York: Norton, 1950); L. Chestang, *Character Development in a Hostile Environment*, Occasional Paper 3 (Chicago: University of Chicago School of Social Services, 1972); E. Pinderhughes, "Empowerment for Our Clients and Ourselves," *Social Casework* (June 1983): 311–338; W. J. Wilson, *The Truly Disadvantaged: The Inner City, the Underclass and Public Policy* (Chicago: University of Chicago Press, 1987); J. G. Hopps, "Whose Welfare," *Social Work* 31 (July–August 1986): 243–244; L. Chestang, "Work, Personal Change and Human Development," in *Work, Workers and Work Organizations: A View from Social Work* (Englewood Cliffs, N.J.: Prentice-Hall, 1982).
8. P. D. Cleary, "Gender Differences in Stress-Related Disorders," in R. C. Barnett, L. Brenen, and S. K. Tsaruch, eds., *Gender and Stress* (New York: Free Press, 1987); D. R. Brown, "Depression among Blacks: An Epidemiologic Perspective," in D. S. Ruiz, ed., *Handbook of Mental Health and*

Mental Disorder Among Black Americans (Westport, Conn.: Greenwood Press, 1990), pp. 71–93; "Single Women and Poverty Strongly Linked," *New York Times*, February 20, 1994, p. 35.

9. W. J. Wilson, "Race and the New Urban Poverty," unpublished manuscript (Chicago: University of Chicago, 1994), p. 10.

10. M. C. Basch, "Toward a Theory That Encompasses Depression: A Revision of Existing Causal Hypothesis in Psychoanalysis," in J. J. Anthony and T. Benedek, eds., *Depression and Human Existence* (Boston: Little, Brown, 1975).

11. M. Harrington, *The Other America: Poverty in the United States* (New York: Penguin, 1962); Children's Defense Fund, *The State of America's Children* (Washington, D.C.: Children's Defense Fund, 1991).

12. U.S. Bureau of the Census, *Money Income and Poverty Status in the U.S.: 1989*, Current Population Reports, Series P-60, No. 168 (Washington, D.C.: Government Printing Office, 1990); Children's Defense Fund, *The State of America's Children.*

13. S. M. Miller and Pamela A. Roby, *The Future of Inequality* (New York: Basic Books, 1970); R. Ropers, *Persistent Poverty: The American Dream Turned Nightmare* (New York: Insight Books, 1991); M. Harrington, *The New American Poverty* (New York: Holt, Rinehart and Winston, 1984).

14. J. G. Hopps, "Oppression Based on Color," *Social Work* 27 (1982): 4, and "Minorities of Color," in *Encyclopedia of Social Work*, 18th ed. (Silver Spring, Md.: N.A.S.W., 1987); F. Groskind, "Ideological Influences on Public Support for Assistance to Poor Families," *Social Work* 39 (January 1994): 81–89.

15. Hopps, "Oppression Based on Color."

16. J. Claude, "Poverty Patterns for Black Men and Women," *Black Scholar* (September–October 1986): 20–23; B. T. Dill, *Across the Boundaries of Race and Class* (New York: Garland Publishing, 1994); L. Davis and E. Proctor, *Race, Gender and Class* (Englewood Cliffs, N.J.: Prentice-Hall, 1989); D. Ellwood and L. Summers, "Poverty in America: Is Welfare the Answer or the Problem?" (paper prepared for delivery at a Conference on Poverty and Policy: Retrospect and Prospect, Williamsburg, Virginia, December 6–8, 1984).

17. Claude, "Poverty Patterns."

18. M. Abromowitz, *Regulating the Lives of Women: Social Welfare Policy from Colonial Times to the Present* (Boston: South End Press, 1988).

19. Ibid.

20. E. Ferguson, *Social Work* (Philadelphia: Lippincott, 1975).

21. G. Hoshino, "Money and Morality: Income, Security and Personal Social Services," *Social Work* 16 (1971): 16–24.

22. *Christian Science Monitor*, January 10, 1991, p. 20.

23. Ferguson, *Social Work.*
24. B. R. Schiller, *The Economics of Poverty and Discrimination,* 4th ed. (Engle-wood Cliffs, N.J.: Prentice-Hall, 1984). J. Jones, *The Dispossessed: America's Underclass from the Civil War to the Present* (New York: Basic Books, 1992).
25. Hopps, "Whose Welfare."
26. B. Harrison and L. Gorham, "Growing Inequality in Black Wages in the 1980's and the Emergence of an African-American Middle Class," *Journal of Policy Analysis and Management* 2 (1992): 235–253; U.S. Bureau of the Census, *Educational Attainment in the United States: March 1989 and 1988,* Current Population Reports, Series P-20, No. 451 (Washington, D.C.: Government Printing Office, August 1991), pp. 67–71; C. Jenks et al., *Who Gets Ahead? The Determinants of Economic Success in America* (New York: Basic Books 1979).
27. Claude, "Poverty Patterns"; A. Billingsley, *Climbing Jacob's Ladder* (New York: Simon and Schuster, 1993).
28. J. Claude, "Poverty Patterns."
29. Wilson, *The Truly Disadvantaged;* R. Staples, "Changes in Black Family Structures: The Conflict Between Family Ideology and Structural Condi-tions," *Journal of Marriage and the Family* 47 (1985): 1005–1013; R. Taylor, "Black American Families," in R. Taylor, ed., *Minority Families in the United States* (Englewood Cliffs, N.J.: Prentice-Hall, 1994), pp. 19–46.
30. D. F. Moynihan, *The Negro Family: The Case for National Action* (Washing-ton, D.C.: Office of Policy, Planning and Research, U.S. Department of Labor, 1965); G. Gilder, *Wealth and Poverty* (New York: Bantam Books, 1981); C. Murray, *Losing Ground: American Social Policy, 1950–1980* (New York: Basic Books, 1985); L. Rainwater and W. L. Yancey, *The Moynihan Report and the Politics of Controversy* (Cambridge, Mass.: MIT Press, 1967).
31. O. Lewis, *A Study of Slum Culture for La Vida* (New York: Random House, 1968); E. Liebow, *Tally's Corner* (Boston: Little, Brown, 1967).
32. Wilson, *Race and the New Urban Poverty.*
33. J. Rawls, *A Theory of Justice* (Cambridge: Harvard University Press, 1971). See also D. Iatridis, *Social Policy* (Pacific Grove, Calif.: Brooks/Cole Pub-lishing Co., 1994).
34. Claude, "Poverty Patterns"; Wilson, *Race and the New Urban Poverty.*
35. C. Williams, *Black Teenage Mothers* (Lexington, Mass.: Lexington Books, 1991).

Chapter 2. The Environmental Context for Clients: Environment, Isolation and More Entrapment

1. R. Reich, "Secession of the Successful," *New York Times Magazine,* January 20, 1991; A. Pertman, "Home Safe Home: Closed Communities Grow," *Boston Globe,* March 14, 1994, pp. 1, 6.

2. Compounding the problem of overwhelmed clients is the financial crisis confronting the cities in which they live in the form of deficits and poor credits. The recent recession resulted in reduced tax revenue, heightening a situation that never came fully to grips with earlier reduced federal aid and the inability or unwillingness to enact new taxes. The result is that spending outpaces revenue. For fiscal 1990–1991, Boston's budget was $1.3 billion, with a $21 million shortfall; for New York, $28 billion and $800 million, respectively; similarly, for San Francisco, $1.3 billion and $27 million; and for Chicago, $3.2 billion and $75 million. Cities are downsizing, cutting payrolls and physical services, including maintenance of infrastructures such as bridges, streets, and libraries, as well as human services programs, such as food and shelter for the mentally ill, drug addicts, and the homeless. Despite national affluence—the total GNP for 1990 was $5,465.1 billion, or approximately $20,000 per person—there seems little to expend for efforts directed toward human capital and neighborhood investments that would benefit persons like the overwhelmed clients in the study. M. Hinds, "Cities Take Painful Steps," *New York Times*, January 6, 1991; *Economic Indicators*, prepared for the Joint Committee by the Council of Economic Advisers (Washington, D.C.: Government Printing Office, 1991).

3. D. Caraley, "Washington Abandons the Cities," *Political Science Quarterly* 107 (Spring 1992): 1–30.

4. E. Anderson, *Hearing Before the Joint Economic Committee*, U.S. Congress, May 25, 1989.

5. Ibid.

6. W. J. Wilson, *The Truly Disadvantaged: The Inner City, the Underclass and Public Policy* (Chicago: University of Chicago Press, 1987), p. 58.

7. W. J. Wilson, "Race and the New Urban Poverty," unpublished manuscript (Chicago: University of Chicago, 1994), p. 1.

8. J. Fagan, "Drug Selling and Licit Income in Distressed Neighborhoods: The Economic Lives of Street-Level Drug Users and Dealers," in *Drugs, Crime and Social Isolation*, ed. G. Peterson and N. Harold Washington (Washington, D.C.: Urban Institute Press, 1993).

9. A. Hacker, *Two Nations: Black and White, Separate, Hostile, Unequal* (New York: Charles Scribners Sons, 1992).

10. J. G. Hopps, "Ghetto Economic Corporation Theory, Reality and Policy Implications," *Review of Black Political Economy* 3 (Spring 1973): 43–64.

11. R. A. Howe, "A Wake-Up Call for American Society or 'Have the Chickens Come Home to Roost'?" review of Charles Patrick Ewing, *When Children Kill: The Dynamics of Juvenile Homicide, Nova Law Review* 16 (Winter 1992). See also Federal Bureau of Investigation, *Crime in the United States 1992* (Washington, D.C.: Government Printing Office, 1992).

12. *Newsweek*, November 2, 1992, pp. 21–22.

13. C. Hedges, "In Brooklyn, Private Police as Violent as Their Enemy," *New York Times,* June 16, 1991.

14. *Christian Science Monitor,* January 10, 1991, p. 20.

15. R. Nisbet, *The Twilight of Authority* (Oxford: Oxford University Press, 1975).

16. *New York Times,* November 3, 1991; "The Word on the Street," *Dallas Post Tribune,* June 9–15, 1994, p. 1.

17. Howe, "A Wake-Up Call."

18. Ibid.

19. D. Arnold, "Getting Street Smart," *Boston Globe,* December 28, 1990, p. 1.

20. A recent study conducted by the Center on Addiction and Substance Abuse at Columbia University reported that a quarter of welfare recipients partake of illicit drugs or drink heavily. Among the youngest AFDC recipients, the rate of addiction and abuse is reported to be 37 percent. The U.S. Department of Health and Human Services challenged this finding, suggesting that only 4.5 percent of recipients have any substance abuse problems. "Study Says Quarter of Welfare Mothers Substance Abusers," *Boston Globe,* June 28, 1994, p. 5.

21. M. Waters, "The L.A. Disturbances Should Have Surprised No One," *Public Welfare* (Fall 1992); M. Zuckoff and P. Gosselin. "Area's Blacks Denied Loans at Triple the Rate of Whites," *Boston Globe,* October 22, 1991, pp. 1, 52.

22. E. Mulroy, "Single Parent Families and the Housing Crisis: Implications for Macro-Practice," *Social Work* (1990); 542–546.

23. Ibid.

24. E. Cox, "The Critical Role of Social Action in Empowerment of Oriental Groups," *Social Work with Groups* 14, (1991): 77–90; A. Mullender and D. Ward, "Empowerment Through Social Action Group Work: The Self-Directed Approach," *Social Work with Groups* 14 (1991): 125–139.

25. Marion Wright Edelman, quoted in R. Jordan, "Poll Shows Hope—If Society Listens," *Boston Sunday Globe,* June 12, 1994, p. 77.

Chapter 3. The Context for Practitioners and Clients

1. E. Pinderhughes, "Diversity and Populations at Risk: Ethnic Minorities and People of Color," in R. Reamer, ed., *The Foundations of Social Work* (New York: Columbia University Press, in press).

2. D. Wrong, *Power: Its Forms, Bases and Uses* (New York: Harper & Row, 1980); D. Heller, *Power in Psychotherapeutic Practice* (New York: Human Services Press, 1985); E. Pinderhughes, *Understanding Race, Ethnicity and Power* (New York: Free Press, 1989).

3. T. J. Goodrich, ed., *Women and Power* (New York: Norton, 1991), p. 10.

4. D. McClelland, *Power, the Inner Experience* (New York: Wiley, 1975); Wrong, *Power.*

5. M. Basch, "Toward a Theory That Encompasses Depression: A Review of Existing Causal Hypotheses in Psychoanalysis," in J. Anthony and T. Benedek, eds., *Depression and Human Existence* (Boston: Little, Brown, 1975), p. 513.

6. McClelland, *Power;* Pinderhughes, *Understanding Race.*

7. Wrong, *Power,* p. 3.

8. Pinderhughes, *Understanding Race.*

9. B. Solomon, "Social Work in Multiethnic Society," in M. Sotomayer, ed., *Cross Cultural Perspective in Social Work Practice and Education* (New York: Council on Social Work Education, 1976), pp. 165–176.

10. Pinderhughes, *Understanding Race.*

11. Goodrich, *Women and Power.*

12. J. G. Hopps, "Oppression Based on Color," *Social Work* 27 (1982): 4.

13. Pinderhughes, *Understanding Race.*

14. Ibid., p. 175.

15. M. Bowen, *Family Therapy in Clinical Practice* (New York: Jason Aronson, 1978); Pinderhughes, *Understanding Race.*

16. Bowen, *Family Therapy,* pp. 444–445.

17. Heller, *Power,* p. 16.

18. Pinderhughes, *Understanding Race.*

19. H. Robson, "Self-Esteem," *Harvard Medical School Mental Health Letter* (1991).

20. Pinderhughes, *Understanding Race,* p. 127.

21. Ibid., p. 143.

22. Ibid., pp. 145–146.

23. McClelland, *Power.*

24. L. Chestang, *Character Development in a Hostile Environment,* Occasional Paper No. 3 (Chicago: University of Chicago, School of Social Services Administration, 1972).

25. Ibid., p. 4.

26. L. Davis and E. Proctor, *Race, Gender and Class* (Englewood Cliffs, N.J.: Prentice-Hall, 1989).

27. E. Pinderhughes, "The Significance of Culture and Power in the Human Behavior Curriculum," in C. Jacobs and D. Boules, eds., *Ethnicity and Race: Critical Concepts in Social Work* (Washington D.C.: N.A.S.W., 1988).

Chapter 4. Research on Clinical Practice

1. A. Rubin, "Practice Effectiveness: More Grounds for Optimism," *Social Work* (November–December 1985): 469–476.

2. J. G. Hopps, "Effectiveness and Human Worth," *Social Work* (1985): 467.

3. E. F. Mullen and J. R. Dumpson, eds., *Evaluation of Social Work Interventions* (San Francisco: Jossey-Bass, 1972).
4. S. Briar, "A New Look at Social Casework," *Social Work* 19 (1974).
5. S. Briar, "Incorporating Research into Education for Clinical Practice in Social Work: Toward a Clinical Science in Social Work," in A. Rubin and A. Rosenblatt, eds., *Sourcebook on Research Utilization* (New York: Council on Social Work Education, 1979), and W. C. Sze and J. G. Hopps, *Evaluation and Accountability in Human Service Programs* (Cambridge, Mass.: Schenckman Publishing Co., 1973).
6. See E. Newman and J. Turem, "The Crisis of Accountability," *Social Work* 19 (1974): 5–16; M. L. Rosenberg and R. Brody, "The Threat or Challenge of Accountability," *Social Work* 19 (1974): 344–350; E. Tropp, "Expectation, Performance and Accountability," *Social Work* 19 (1974): 139–149; G. Hoshino, "The Problem of Accountability," *Social Service Review* 48 (1973): 373–383; and Sze and Hopps, *Evaluation and Accountability*.
7. Sze and Hopps, *Evaluation and Accountability*, p. 467.
8. Mullen and Dumpson, "Is Social Work on the Wrong Track?" in Mullen and Dumpson, *Evaluation of Social Work Interventions*, pp. 1–14.
9. Ludwig L. Geismar, "Thirteen Evaluative Studies," in Mullen and Dumpson, *Evaluation of Social Work Interventions*, pp. 15–38.
10. Steven Paul Segal, "Research on the Outcome of Social Work Therapeutic Interventions: A Review of the Literature," *Journal of Health and Social Behavior* 13 (March 1972): 3–17.
11. J. Fischer, "Is Casework Effective?" *Social Work* 18 (1973): 5–21.
12. Ibid., p. 14.
13. See Joel Fischer, *Effective Casework Practice: An Eclectic Approach* (New York: McGraw-Hill, 1978). The deficiencies associated with social casework were inefficiency of casework interventions; a lack of fully developed knowledge of procedures for changing the social environment; inadequate or insufficient use of clients' significant others; insufficient attention paid to intervention; preoccupation with talk therapy; clients minimally involved in the change process; unexplained client dropout rates; and differential perceptions of client and worker as to the goal to be accomplished. Fischer suggested that casework must undergo a major reconceptualization of its objectives, methods, and results toward a much greater degree of specificity, which would increase practice effectiveness.
14. K. M. Wood, "Casework Effectiveness: A New Look at the Research Evidence," *Social Work* 23 (1978): 437–458.
15. W. J. Reid and P. Hanrahan, "Recent Evaluations of Social Work: Grounds for Optimism," *Social Work* 27 (1982): 328–340.
16. Ibid., p. 338.
17. Rubin, "Practice Effectiveness." Of the thirteen studies reviewed, Rubin found seven studies with positive outcome and sound methods, three with

positive outcomes but questionable methods, and three with equivocal outcomes, concluding that there are grounds for optimism in practice effectiveness (pp. 470–472). Common threads found among the successful studies included well-explicated and highly structured forms of practice, identification of clients to be served, problems to be resolved, goals to be accomplished, interventions, procedures to be implemented, outcomes to be anticipated, and measurements (p. 474). A deficiency existed in the failure to identify clearly the intervenors and or the qualifications of workers in each study; the lack of specification relative to instruments assessing the dependent variable; or the lack of data on the total number of respondents and distribution of numbers between treatment and control groups.

18. Mark Ezell and C. Aaron McNeece, "Practice Effectiveness: Research or Rhetoric?" Points and Viewpoints, Social Work (September–October 1986): 401–402.

19. See the following studies listed in Appendix B: Powers (1949); Powers and Witmer (1951); Wiltse (1954); Behling (1961); Tait and Hodges (1962); Miller (1962); Craig and Furst (1965); Marin (1969); Meyer et al. (1965); Schwartz (1966); Wilson (1967); Schwartz and Sample (1967; 1972); Wilkinson and Ross (1972); Berleman and Steiner (1967); Geismar and Krisberg (1967); McCabe et al. (1967); Brown (1968); United Services of the Greater Vancouver Area (1968–69); Geismar et al. (1970); Olson (1970); Geismar (1971); Piliavin and Gross (1977); and Mullen et al. (1979), among others.

20. Milton M. Gordon, Assimilation in American Life (New York: Oxford University Press, 1964).

21. Gordon Allport, The Nature of Prejudice (Garden City, N.Y.: Doubleday, Anchor Books, 1958).

22. F. Reissman, The Culturally Deprived Child (New York: Harper & Row, 1962).

23. B. J. Tidwell, "Research and Practice Issues with Black Families," in S. M. L. Logan, E. M. Freeman, and R. G. MacRoy, eds., Social Work Practice with Black Families (New York: Longman, 1990), pp. 257–272.

24. William Ryan, Blaming the Victim (New York: Vintage Books, 1976).

25. Ibid.; N. Caplan and S. D. Nelson, "On Being Useful—The Nature and Consequences of Psychological Research on Social Problems," American Psychologist 28 (1973): 199–211. Some would argue that blaming the victim not only rationalized cruelty and injustice but it further freed the government, the private sector, the system of stratification, the system of justice, and the education system from any blame. This protection of the established social order against criticism increased the difficulty of trying to change the dominant economic, social, and political institutions.

26. Daniel P. Moynihan, The Negro Family: The Case for National Action (Washington, D.C.: Department of Labor, Office of Policy and Research, 1965); Edward C. Banfield, The Unheavenly City Revisited (Boston: Little,

Brown, 1977); Arthur Jensen, *Bias in Mental Testing* (New York: Free Press, 1980); Richard J. Herrnstein, *IQ in the Meritocracy* (Boston: Little, Brown, 1973).

27. D. Stanley Eitzen and Maxine Baca Zinn, *Social Problems* (Boston: Allyn and Bacon, 1994).

28. William P. O'Hare, "The Eight Myths of Poverty," *American Demographics* 8 (May 1986): 22–25; J. T. Tedeschi and D. O'Donovan, "Social Power and the Psychologist," *Professional Psychology* 2 (1971): 59–64, and S. J. Halleck, "Therapy Is the Handmaiden of the Status Quo," *Psychology Today* (April 1971): 30–34, 98–100, have viewed psychology and therapy as encompassing the use of social power and therapy as a handmaiden of the status quo, being as they are agents for transmission of Western values. T. S. Szasz, "The Crime of Commitment," in *Readings in Clinical Psychology Today* (Del Mar, Calif.: CRM Books, 1970), conceptualizes therapy as representing a slave-master relationship, a powerful political ploy against people whose values differ from those of the dominant society. Derald W. Sue, *Counseling the Culturally Different* (New York: Wiley, 1982), points out that the Western counseling framework is more appropriate for middle-class populations and communities and holds values characteristically different from those of groups from the Third World. Finally, Murray Bowen, *Family Therapy in Clinical Practice* (New York: Jason Aronson, 1978), refers to the societal projection process whereby workers perceive and treat clients as inferior or incompetent.

29. Wyatt C. Jones and Edgar F. Borgatta, "Methodology of Evaluation," in Mullen and Dumpson, *Evaluation of Social Work Interventions*, pp. 39–54.

30. Elaine Pinderhughes, "Empowerment for Our Clients and for Ourselves," *Social Casework* (June 1983): 331–338.

31. See James K. Whittaker and Elizabeth M. Tracy, "Family Preservation Services and Education for Social Work Practice: Stimulus and Response," in James K. Whittaker, Jill Kinney, Elizabeth M. Tracy, and Charlotte Booth, eds., *Reaching High-Risk Families* (New York: Aldine de Gruyter, 1990, pp. 1–11.

32. S. Maybanks and M. Bryce, *Home Based Services for Children and Families: Policies, Practice and Research* (Springfield, Ill.: Charles C. Thomas, 1979); M. Bryce and J. C. Lloyd, eds., *Treating Families in the Home* (Springfield, Ill.: Charles C. Thomas, 1981).

33. See Jill Kinney, David Haapala, Charlotte Booth, and Shelley Leavitt, "The Homebuilders Model," in Whittaker et al., *Reaching High-Risk Families*, pp. 31–64.

34. See Harvey Frankel, "Family-Centered, Home-Based Services in Child Protection: A Review of the Literature," *Social Service Review* 62 (1987): 137–157; Stephen Magura, "Are Services to Prevent Foster Care Effective?" *Children and Youth Services Review* 3 (1981): 193–212; Theodore J. Stein, "Projects to Prevent Out-of-Home Placement," *Children and Youth*

Services Review 7 (1985): 231–240 and Mary Ann Jones, *A Second Chance for Families, Five Years Late: Follow-Up of a Program to Prevent Foster Care* (New York: Child Welfare League of America, 1985).

35. Anthony McMahon and Paula Allen-Meares, "Is Social Work Racist?" *Social Work* 37 (November 1992): 533–539.

36. Elaine Pinderhughes, *Understanding Race, Ethnicity, and Power* (New York: Free Press, 1989).

37. Howard Goldstein, "The Knowledge Base of Social Work Practice: Theory, Wisdom, Analogue, or Art?" *Families in Society* (1990): 432–443.

38. Tidwell, "Research and Practice Issues with Black Families."

39. Goldstein, "Knowledge Base of Social Work Practice."

40. See W. W. Hudson, *The Clinical Measurement Package: A Field Manual* (Homewood, Ill.: Dorsey Press, 1982).

41. For example, in this evaluation research, the worker characteristics of caring and flexibility were found to be the best noninterventive predictors of success outcomes.

42. Juliet Cheetham, "Evaluating Social Work Effectiveness," *Research on Social Work Education* 2 (1992): 265–287.

Chapter 5. Empirical Findings on Clinical Effectiveness

1. Initially, 187 case files were randomly selected from a sampling frame of 2,369 cases. Sample size was reduced due to agencies' unawareness of duplicate cases and files with insufficient entries. These service records were excluded from the analysis, reducing the final sample size to 178, a size still well above the mean for most clinical research. See discussions of sampling procedures in Appendix A. The Client Service/Record Instruments was effective in extracting the desired data from each case file. Part A of the instrument generated data on a client profile and Part C on worker characteristics. Appendix A contains a copy of the instrument.

    Two licensed social workers who are also educators evaluated 178 closed case files. Judgments were made about the nature of interventions utilized and the outcomes. The operational definitions of the interventions and corresponding success outcomes are discussed in Appendix A. From each file assessed, the primary data extracted sought information as to whether there was sufficient evidence of change in client functioning attributable to a particular intervention strategy employed by the attending clinician.

2. This distribution is generally consistent with that found by R. Goetze and M. K. Johnson, *29 Page Profile: 1990 Census of Population and Housing from U.S. Census* (Boston: Boston Redevelopment Authority Policy Development and Research Department, March, 1993). Of the 28 percent defined as poor in the Boston neighborhoods, 45 percent are male and 55 percent are female.

3. See Diane R. Brown, "Depression Among Blacks: An Epidemiologic Perspective," in Dorothy S. Ruiz, ed., *Handbook of Mental Health and Mental Disorder Among Black Americans* (Westport, Conn.: Greenwood, 1990), pp. 71–93.

4. Goetze and Johnson, *29 Page Profile*, indicate a higher percentage of Hispanics (approximately 36 percent) over African Americans (approximately 26 percent) for whom poverty status was determined in Boston. Also while whites represent approximately 17 percent of Boston's poor, only 8.6 percent of clients who sought services from these agencies were white, obviously reflecting residential patterns.

5. Ibid. The age distribution of persons in the Boston neighborhoods for whom poverty status was determined indicates that approximately 35 percent are age seventeen years or under.

6. Black women outnumber black men, thus placing the black women at a disadvantage in the marriage market, causing a larger proportion of them to remain unmarried. See Reynolds Farley and Walter Allen, *The Color Line and the Quality of Life in America* (New York: Oxford University Press, 1987).

7. U.S. Bureau of Census, *Money Income of Households, Families, and Persons in the United States: 1987*, Current Population Reports, Series P-60, No. 162 (Washington, D.C.: Government Printing Office, 1989), pp. 49–52.

8. There is a period of cohabitation among adults prior to legally consummating marriages. See Henry Blackwell, *The Black Community: Diversity and Unity* (New York: HarperCollins, 1991).

9. Farley and Allen, *The Color Line*, p. 168. See David Alvirez and Frank D. Bean, "The Mexican-American Family," in Charles H. Hindel and Robert W. Habenstein, eds., *Ethnic Families in America* (New York: Elsevier, 1976), pp. 271–292, and E. Padilla, *Up from Puerto Rico* (New York: Columbia University Press, 1958).

10. Ludwig L. Geismar, *Early Supports for Family Life: A Social Work Experiment* (Metuchen, N.J.: Scarecrow Press, 1972).

11. The principal components method was employed here, and the test used for measuring the appropriateness of the correlation matrix was the Kaiser-Meyer-Olkin (KMO) measure of sampling adequacy. A value above .60 suggests that a factor analysis of the variables is appropriate. The KMO test result for the total sample in this investigation was .92. Three components were retained in every case and rotated to an orthogonal simple structure using the varimax procedure. See Marija J. Norusis, *SPSS-X Advanced Statistics Guide* (Chicago: SPSS-X, 1990). Cronbach's alpha reliability measure for Factor 1 was .847 and for Factor 2 .621.

12. Elaine B. Pinderhughes, "Empowerment for Our Clients and for Ourselves," *Social Casework* 64 (1983): 331–338.

13. To determine which worker characteristics would be entered in the regression equation, a correlation matrix was developed. See Table C-17 for a

summary of the correlation coefficients. Using the stepwise method, the following worker characteristics were treated as the independent variables: Flexibility, Caring, and Positive Reinforcement for Education and overall improved functioning as the dependent variable. See table C-18 for the regression equation and summary statistics.

Chapter 6. The Helping Education

1. L. Geismar, *Early Support for Family Life: A Social Work Experiment* (Metuchen, N.J.: Scarecrow Press, 1972).
2. E. Pinderhughes, "Black Genealogy: Self Liberator and Therapeutic Tool," *Smith College Studies for Social Work* 52 (March 1982): 93–106.

Chapter 7. Revitalizing Care

1. S. S. Gottscalk, *Communities and Alternatives* (New York: Wiley, 1975).
2. R. A. K. Shankar, "Asian Indian American," in *Encyclopedia of Multiculturalism* (1994), pp. 212–216. New York: Marshall Cavendish Corp.
3. A. Jackson, "'Black Single Working Mother in Poverty': Preference for Employment, Well-Being and Perception of Pre–School Age Children," *Social Work* 38 (1993): 26–34.
4. Shankar, "Asian Indian Americans."
5. A. Rubin, "Practice Effectiveness: More Grounds for Optimism," *Social Work* (November–December 1985): 469–476.
6. G. Auslander and H. Litwin, "The Parameters of Network Intervention: A Social Work Application," *Social Service Review* 61 (June 1987): 305–318.
7. W. J. Reid and P. Hanrahan, "Recent Evaluations of Social Work: Grounds for Optimism," *Social Work* 27 (1982): 328–340.
8. L. Weed, *Medical Records, Medical Evaluation and Patient Care* (Cleveland: Case Western Research University Press, 1969).
9. M. Bloom and J. Fischer, *Evaluating Practice: Guidelines for the Accountable Professional* (Englewood Cliffs, N.J.: Prentice-Hall, 1982).
10. In California the Healthy Start Support Services for Children Act, 1991, authorized $20 million for the planning and operation of school-linked services. Foundations also contributed funding. M. Wagner, *School-Linked Services: California's Healthy Start* (Los Altos, Calif.: Center for the Future of Children, David and Lucille Packard Foundation, 1993).

In New Jersey, the Department of Human Services initiated the School Based Youth Services Program, which linked education and human services in so-called one-step shopping centers in the thirty poorest school systems in the state. Mental health, family counseling, employment, and health services are available all days and weekends the entire year. C.

Maruzke and D. Both, *Getting Started: Planning a Comprehensive Service Initiative* (New York: National Center for Service Integration, Columbia University National Center for Children in Poverty, 1994).

In Connecticut, family resource centers offer extended day care, parent education, pregnancy prevention services, and training for providers of day care. See A. Melaville and M. Blank, *Together We Can: A Guide for Crafting a Profamily System of Education and Human Services* (Washington, D.C.: U.S. Departments of Education and Health and Human Services, 1993).

Goals 2000: Educate America Act (P.L. 103-227) passed in March 1994 and the Family Preservation and Family Support sections of the Omnibus Budget Reconciliation Act of 1993 include provisions for the coordination of education, social services, and health.

11. *U.S. Bureau of the Census, Statistical Abstract of the United States 1991* (Washington, D.C.: Government Printing Office, 1991).

The system of financing education in Massachusetts whereby affluent communities are able to allocate extensive resources to schools and poorer ones cannot was declared unfair and unconstitutional by the state supreme judicial court in summer 1993.

J. Kozol, *Savage Inequalities: Children in American Schools* (New York: Crown Publishers, 1991).

12. S. Walman, "The Stingy Politics of Head Start," *Newsweek*, Special Issue on Education (Fall–Winter 1990): 78–79. J. S. Coleman et al., *Equality of Educational Opportunity* (Washington, D.C.: Government Printing Office, 1966).

13. W. Winters, *African-American Mothers and Urban Schools: The Power of Participation* (New York: Lexington Books, 1993).

14. M. A. Drew, L. Penkower, and E. J. Bromet, "Effects of Unemployment on Mental Health in the Contemporary Family," *Behavior Modification* 15 (1991): 501–544. See also H. Brenner, statement on cost of unemployment, Hearings before the Subcommittee on Domestic Monetary Policy of the Committee on Banking, Finance and Urban Affairs, House of Representatives, 97th Cong., 2d ses., August 12, 17, 1982, pp. 33–59. Brenner documents that each 1 percent jump in unemployment results in a 3.7 percent increase in admissions to mental hospitals, 5.7 degree increase in homicides, and 4.1 percent increase in suicides. M. Merva and R. Fowles, *Effects of Diminished Economic Opportunities on Social Stress: Heart Attacks, Strokes and Crime* (Washington, D.C.: Economic Policy Institute, 1992).

15. E. Freeman and R. McRay, "Group Counseling Program for Unemployed Black Teenagers," *Social Work with Groups* 9 (Spring 1986): 73–89.

16. M. Breton, "Liberation Theology, Group Work and the Right of the Poor and the Oppressed to Participate in the Life of the Community, *Social Work with Groups* 15 (1992): 65–76; C. Garvin, "Barriers to Effective So-

cial Action by Groups," *Social Work with Groups* 14 (1991): 65–76; E. Cox, "The Critical Role of Social Action in Empowerment Oriented Groups," *Social Work with Groups* 14 (1991): 77–107.

Chapter 8. National Justice-Based Policies That Support Empowerment of Clients and Communities

1. W. P. O'Hare, "The Eight Myths of Poverty," *American Demographics* 8 (May 1986): 22–25.
2. E. Erikson, *Childhood and Society* (New York: Norton, 1950); L. Chestang, "Work, Personal Change and Human Development," in *Development in Work, Worker and Work Organizations* (1982), pp. 61–89.
3. J. Feagin and C. B. Feagin, *Social Problems: A Control-Power-Conflict Perspective*, 3d ed. (Englewood Cliffs, N.J.: Prentice-Hall, 1990); F. Piven and C. Cloward, *Regulating the Poor* (New York: Vintage Books, 1971).
4. Piven and Cloward, *Regulating the Poor*.
5. J. G. Hopps, "Minorities of Color," in *Encyclopedia of Social Work*, 18th ed. (Silver Spring, Md.: N.A.S.W., 1987), pp. 161–171.
6. S. A. Levitan and C. M. Johnson, *Second Thoughts on Work* (Kalamazoo, Mich.: W. E. Upjohn Institute for Employment Research, 1982); W. M. Young, Jr., *To Be Equal* (New York: McGraw-Hill, 1964); W. J. Wilson, "Race and the New Urban Poverty," unpublished manuscript (Chicago: University of Chicago, 1994).
7. Young, *To Be Equal*.
8. W. H. Beveridge, *Full Employment in a Free Society* (New York: Norton, 1945), pp. 18, 19; B. Kuttner, "The War Against Idleness and Want," *Boston Globe*, March 4, 1994, p. 23. See also L. E. Gary, B. R. Leashore, C. S. Howard, and R. R. Buckner-Dowell, *Help-Seeking Behavior Among Black Males* (Washington, D.C.: Mental Health Research and Development Center, Institute for Urban Affairs and Research, Howard University, 1983).
9. The earned income credit is a refundable tax credit for low-income working families. (Massachusetts working families received $137 million in 1993.) C. C. Saleh, "Tax Relief for Working Families," *Focus* (March 1994): 5.
10. D. Norton, "Diversity, Early Socialization and Temporal Development: The Dual Perspective Revisited," in D. M. Pearson, ed., *Perspectives on Equity and Justice in Social Work* (Alexandria, Va.: Council on Social Work Education, 1993), pp. 17–33.
11. S. Popkin, J. Rosenbaum, and P. Meader, "Labor Market Experiences of Low Income Black Women in Middle-Class Suburbs: Evidence from a

Survey of Gautieau Program Participants," *Journal of Policy Analysis and Management* 12 (1993): 556–573.

12. B. Harrison and L. Gorham, "Growing Inequality in Black Wages in the 1980's and the Emergence of an African American Middle-Class," *Journal of Policy Analysis and Management* 7 (1992): 235–253.

13. Ibid.

14. M. Brown and S. Eric, "Blacks and the Legacy of the Great Society," *Public Policy* (Summer 1981), pp. 299–300.

15. The Employment Training Act (CETA) was enacted as a manpower reform bill. During the 1960s, roughly seventeen categorical programs had been developed, under the 1971 Emergency Employment Act, each with different legislation funding sources. Ten thousand manpower projects under the Labor Department emerged out of these programs, some even competing for clients in the same locality. Under CETA, program control was transferred to state and local government. See W. Mirengoff and Lester Pindler, *The Comprehensive Employment and Training Act: An Interim Report* (Washington, D.C.: National Academy of Sciences, 1976).

16. Young, *To Be Equal*.

17. N. Dickerson, "Which Welfare Work Strategies Work?" *Social Work* 31 (1986): 266–272.

18. E. F. Mullen and J. R. Dumpson, "Is Social Work on the Wrong Track?" in E. F. Mullen and J. R. Dumpson, eds., *Evaluation of Social Work Interventions* (San Francisco: Jossey-Bass, 1972), pp. 1–14; Wyatt C. Jones and Edgar F. Borgatta, "Methodology of Evaluation," in Mullen and Dumpson, *Evaluation of Social Work Interventions*, pp. 39–54.

19. National Conference of Catholic Bishops, *The 1986 U.S. Catholic Bishops' Letter: Economic Justice for All, Social Teaching and the U.S. Economy* (Washington, D.C.: NCCB, 1986).

20. J. Winthrop, "A Model of Christian Charity," quoted in E. S. Morgan, ed., *Puritan Political Ideas, 1558–1794* (Indianapolis: Bobbs-Merrill, 1965).

21. G. Gilder, *Wealth and Poverty* (New York: Bantam Books, 1981).

22. C. Murray, *Losing Ground: American Social Policy, 1950–1980* (New York: Basic Books, 1985).

23. D. T. Ellwood, "The Changing Structure of American Families," *Journal of the American Planning Association* 59 (Winter 1993): 3–8.

24. H. MacAdoo, Presentation at the American Family Therapy Academy Conference, Baltimore, January 1993. (Unpublished paper)

25. J. Comer, *Beyond Black and White* (New York: Quadrangle/New York Times Book Co., 1972).

26. M. Kraus, *The End of Equality* (New York: Basic Books, 1992).

27. P. Drucker, *Post-Capitalist Society* (New York: Harper's Business, 1993), pp. 5, 20; L. Uchitelle, "The Nation: Good New Jobs, Same Old Salaries," *New York Times*, May 1, 1994, p. E3.

28. J. M. Gueron, *Reforming Welfare with Work: Ford Foundation Project in Social Welfare and the American Future*, Occasional Paper 2 (New York: Ford Foundation, 1987).

29. J. M. Gueron and E. Pauley, *From Welfare to Work* (New York: Russell Sage Foundation, 1991); J. Lurie and B. Sanger, "The Family Support Act: Defining the Social Contract in New York," *Social Service Review* (1991), pp. 42–67. See also Kraus, *End of Equality*.

30. M. Bane and D. Ellwood, *The Dynamics of Dependence: Routes to Self Sufficiency* (Cambridge: Harvard University, J.F.K. School of Government, 1983).

31. M. Greenberg, *Welfare Program in a Budget: What's Happening in JOBS* (Washington, D.C.: Center for Law and Social Policy, 1992); J. Hagen and L. Lurie, "How Ten States Implemented JOBS," *Public Welfare* 50 (1992): 12–21. J. DeParle, "In Welfare Debate, It's Now, Not 'How?' But 'Why?'" *New York Times*, May 8, 1994, sec. 4, pp. 1, 3; A. Flint and G. Negri, "Clashing Blueprints Offered for the Road from Welfare to Work," *Boston Globe*, May 15, 1994, pp. 1, 28.

32. J. DeParle, "Not 'How?' but 'Why?'"; A. Flint and G. Negri, "Clashing Blueprints"; L. Mead, "The New Paternalism," *Public Welfare* (Spring 1992); D. Bloom, V. Fellerath, D. Long, and R. G. Wood, "Ohio Boosts Attendance Among Teen Parents," *Public Welfare* (Winter 1994): 18–30.

33. W. D. O'Hare, "America's Welfare Population: Who Gets What?" *Population Trends and Public Policy* 13 (September 1987): entire issue; M. Rom, "Reversing America's Welfare Magnets," *USA Today*, March 20, 1992; J. DeParle, "Why Marginal Changes Don't Rescue the Welfare State," *New York Times*, March 1, 1992, p. 1A.

34. See *Budget of the United States Government—Fiscal Year 1995* (Washington, D.C.: Government Printing Office, 1994), pp. 205–229. While there is no substantial increase in the proposed 1995 budget for treatment and prevention, the total budget request for enforcement-related activities consumed approximately two-thirds of the administration's 1995 drug control budget request.

35. R. Jean Wilson, "Drinking and Driving: In Search of Solutions to an International Problem," *Alcohol Health and Research World* 17 (1993): 212–220.

36. G. C. E. Linbloom, *The Policy-Making Process*, 2d ed. (Englewood Cliffs, N.J.: Prentice-Hall, 1980).

37. B. S. Jansson, *Social Policy*, 2d ed. (Pacific Grove, Calif.: Brooks/Cole Publishing Co., 1994).

38. R. Morris, "Social Welfare Policies: Trends and Issues," in *Encyclopedia of Social Work*; M. Greenberg and J. Levy, *Confidentiality and Collaboration: Information Sharing in Interagency Efforts* (Washington, D.C.: American Public Welfare Association, Center for Law and Social Policy, Council of Chief State Schools Officers, Education Commission of the States, 1992).

39. M. Gibelman and P. H. Schervish, *Who Are We: The Social Work Labor Force as Reflected in the NASW Membership* (Washington, D.C.: NASW Press, 1993).

40. H. Specht and M. Courtney, *Unfaithful Angels* (New York: Free Press, 1994); R. Toseland and M. Siporin, "When to Recommend Group Treatment: A Review of the Clinical and Research Literature," *International Journal of Group Psychotherapy* 36 (1986): 171–201; J. Edleson and M. Syers, "Relative Effectiveness of Group Treatments for Men Who Batter," *Social Work Research and Abstracts* 26 (June 1990): 10–17; L. Gutierrez and R. Ortega, "Developing Methods to Empower Latinos: The Importance of Groups," *Social Work with Groups* 14 (1991): 23–43; J. Helper, "Evaluating the Clinical Significance of a Group Approach for Improving the Social Skills of Children," *Social Work with Groups* 14 (1991): 87–103; G. Fashimpar, "From Probation to Mini-Bikes: A Comparison of Traditional and Innovative Programs for Community Treatment of Delinquent Adolescents," *Social Work with Groups* 14:2 (1991): 105–118.

41. Specht and Courtney, *Unfaithful Angels*; P. R. Popple and L. H. Leighringer, *Social Work, Social Welfare and American Society* (Boston: Allyn and Bacon, 1990).

Appendix A: Investigative Procedures and Study Implementation of Clinical Practice Effectiveness

1. L. Ruttman, ed., *Evaluation Research Methods: A Basic Guide* (Beverly Hills, Calif.: Sage, 1977); R. Kaufman, R. Thomas, and S. Thomas, *Evaluation Without Fear* (New York: Viewpoints, 1980); and Peter H. Rossi and Howard E. Freeman, *Evaluation: A Systematic Approach*, 6th ed. (Newbury Park, Calif.: Sage, 1994).

2. Rossi and Freeman, *Evaluation*, p. 44.

3. Ibid.; Emil J. Posavac and Raymond G. Carey, *Program Evaluation: Methods and Case Studies* (Englewood Cliffs, N.J.: Prentice-Hall, 1980).

4. Duane R. Monette, Thomas J. Sullivan, and Cornell R. DeJong, *Applied Social Research*, 3d ed. (New York: Holt, Rinehart and Winston, 1994).

5. Fred Groskind, "Practice Evaluation: Essential for Social Work Clinicians and Educators," in P. Collins and K. Kayser, eds., *Clinical Practice Evaluation*, 2d ed. (Chestnut Hill, Mass.: Boston College Graduate School of Social Work, 1992).

6. John W. Best and James V. Kahn, *Research in Education* (Englewood Cliffs, N.J.: Prentice-Hall, 1993); Rossi and Freeman, *Evaluation*.

7. Mark Fraser, "Assessing the Effectiveness of Family Preservation Programs: Implications for Agency-Based Research," in *Family Preservation: Papers from the Institute for Social Education* (Detroit: National Association for Family Related Services, 1991), pp. 47–63.

8. Peter Gabor, "Sampling," in Richard M. Grinnell, Jr., *Social Work Research and Evaluation* (Itasca, Ill.: F. E. Peacock, 1993), pp. 154–170. Agency-based studies must guard against threats to external validity. Often single agency–based studies are limited in their generalizability capacity. Questions of whether the study sample represents a cross-section of the larger population always remain unanswered in such investigations. To minimize threats to external validity, this study developed a sampling frame of over 2,000 cases using information from four inner-city agencies. The utility of agency-based studies lies in the ability to generalize to other clients in other agency settings. With a sampling frame of 2,369 cases generating a random sample of 178, the pure and applied significance of this study is greatly enhanced.

9. Rand Corporation, *A Million Random Digits with 100,000 Normal Deviates* (Glencoe, Ill.: Free Press, 1955).

10. Marija J. Norusis, *SPSS-X Advanced Statistical Guide* (Chicago: SPSS, 1990).

INDEX

Advocacy, 19, 20, 24, 26, 27, 82, 220
African Americans, 6, 78
  credit and, 40–41
  economic restructuring and, 7
  education of, 78–79, 142
  exodus from cities of middle-class,
    30–31, 150, 152
  female role, 45, 53–54
  homicide rate and, 34
  male role, 114
  negative attitudes and stereotypes
    toward, 13–14
  in poverty, 11
  response to oppression, 60
  revitalization of care for, 130–132,
    134
  suitable home requirement and, 13
  unemployment rate of, 32
  wage rates and, 13
  work opportunities for, 12–15, 150
After-school programs, 37
Aggressive accommodation, 60
Aggressive passivity, 60
Aid to Dependent Children (ADC),
  12, 13
Aid to Families with Dependent
  Children (AFDC), 11–13, 138,
  154, 158–160
Aid to the Blind, 13
Alcohol abuse, 161
Ambition, 12

Anxiety, practitioner, 46–48, 50
Apathy, 55
Armed robbery, 32
Asian Americans, 132, 135
Assessment, 19, 20, 24, 26, 27,
  80–82, 96–99, 220
Atlanta, Georgia, 35
Automobile industry, 14
Autonomy, 52

Banfield, Edward C., 70
Banking industry, 40–41
Basch, M., 44
Beveridge, William, 151
Bilingual workers, 22
Black capitalism, 32
Blaming, 81–82, 89, 220
Body diagrams, 97, 100
Borgatta, Edgar F., 71
Bowen, M., 48–49
Bryce, M., 72
Bunker Hill Community College, 142
Burnout, practitioner, 49, 50,
  122–124

Cabrini-Green Housing Project,
  Chicago, 34
Camping, 37
Caribbeans, 6, 78, 114, 134
Case studies of interventions, 1–2,
  8–9, 29, 101–113

Cheetham, Juliet, 75
Chestang, L., 60
Chicanos, 134
Child therapy, 21
Civilian Conservation Corps, 153
Class in client-practitioner interactions, 62–63
Clinical practice: *See also* Practitioners
   agency and staff dynamics, 119–125
   case studies of interventions, 1–2, 8–9, 29, 101–113
   client behaviors resulting from interventions, 80–88
   cognitive-behavioral therapy, 19, 24, 26, 27, 33, 126
   collaboration with other helpers, 125–127
   constraints to, 15–19
   cross-system intervention, 139–140, 162–163
   culturally sensitive approaches, 22, 131–132, 134–136
   drug entrapment and, 31–32, 38–39, 116–119, 122, 161–162
   empirical findings on effectiveness, 77–91
   environmental context, 29–42, 121, 129–130
   family therapy approach, 21, 83–86, 126, 133, 222
   group work, 20, 21, 24, 26, 27, 86–87, 126, 132–134, 145, 165, 223–224
   individual treatment, 20, 21, 24, 26, 27, 83–86, 133, 222
   initial contact and engagement, 94–96
   investigative procedures and study implementation, 19–21, 167–184
   justice-based, 24–27, 143–166
   male clients and, 113–118, 144–145

   multilevel, multisystem approach, 136–138
   overinvolvement, 46–48
   philosophy on community, 127–128
   power conundrum: *see* Power
   psychodynamic approach, 9, 19, 24, 26, 27, 33, 126
   recording and information systems, 140–141
   research on, 65–75, 185–218
   revitalization of care, 129–146
   service coordination, 138–140
   sociodemographic profile of overwhelmed clients, 77–79
   systems theory, 19, 24, 26, 27, 126
   targeting most needful groups, 130–132
Clinton, Bill, 157
Cognitive-behavioral therapy, 19, 24, 26, 27, 33, 126
Colonial period, 12, 36
Communication skills, 83–84, 87, 89, 222, 227
Community, philosophy on, 127–128
Community building, 25, 27, 42, 49, 87, 127, 144–146
Community Reinvestment Act of 1977, 40
Companionate family model, 36
Competence, 86, 88, 89, 149, 223, 224, 227
Competence-behavior dimensions of clinical work, 24, 25, 27, 90
Comprehensive Employment Training Act of 1973, 153
Computers, 141
Control, 45
   practitioner need for, 46
Cooperation, 52
Cross-system intervention, 139–140, 162–163
Cubans, 134
Cultural group status assignment, 44, 51

Culturally sensitive approaches, 22, 131–132, 134–136
Culture
dynamics of power and, 56–62
of poverty, 18
Cunning, 52
Curfews, 35

Daley, Richard, 34
Dallas, Texas, 35
Dating, 20
Davis, Datrell, 34
Day care, 37, 152
Decision making, 45, 83, 88, 90, 221
Deferred power, 12
Dependency, 59
Detroit, Michigan, 35
Dignity, 16, 21
Domestic service, 12
Dominance-subordination relation-ship, 44
Dress of practitioners, 120
Drucker, Peter, 158
Drugs, 17–18, 31–32, 38–39, 116–119, 122, 161–162
Dumpson, J. R., 66, 71, 185–187

Earned income tax credit, 151
Economic Opportunity Act of 1964, 153
Economic restructuring, 7, 14
Edelman, Marion Wright, 42
Education, 16, 78–79, 125, 142–143, 158
Education, Department of, 162
Effective coping, 81, 90, 220, 227
Empathy, 22
Empowerment, 20, 24, 26, 27, 71, 82–83, 87, 128, 146, 221
Entrapment, practitioner, 46, 47
Environmental context, 29–42, 121, 129–130
Equality relationship, 44
Erikson, Erik, 149
Ethnic-sensitive practice, 71
Exhaustion, practitioner, 49

Expectations, 18–19, 21, 23, 61, 147, 157
Ezell, Mark, 69

Factor analysis, 89–90, 227
Family planning, 114
Family preservation services, 71, 72, 124, 139
Family solidarity, 16, 155
Family styles, 57
Family Support Act of 1988, 159
Family theory, 19, 24, 26, 27
Family therapy approach, 21, 83–86, 126, 133, 222
Fatalism, 52
Fatigue, practitioner, 46, 47
Feagin, C. B., 150
Feagin, J., 150
Fischer, Joel, 67, 185, 186, 197, 199
Flexibility of workers, 21, 164
Flynn, Raymond, 37
Food stamps, 10, 11, 32, 158
Full-employment policy, 150, 151

Gangs, 31, 32, 34, 115, 137
GED programs, 142
Geismar, Ludwig L., 66, 71, 185, 186, 188
Genogram, 81, 97
GI Bill of Rights, 153
Gilder, George, 154–155
Goals, personal, 83, 88, 90, 221, 227
Goldstein, Howard, 73
Goodrich, T. J., 44
Great Depression, 14
Great Society, 153
Group theory, 19, 24, 26, 27
Group work, 20, 21, 24, 26, 27, 86–87, 126, 132–134, 145, 165, 223–224

Haitians, 134
Hanrahan, P., 68, 140, 186, 206
Health and Human Services, Depart-ment of, 162

Health and hygiene, personal, 84, 88, 89, 222, 227
Heller, D., 44
Herrnstein, Richard J., 70
Hispanics: *See* Latinos
Homestead Act, 153
Homicide, juvenile, 33–35
Hopps, J. G., 65
Housing and Urban Development, Department of, 162

Identification with aggressor, 59
Income distribution, 10
Index of Self-Esteem (ISE), 74
Individualism, 12, 133, 154, 165, 166
Individual treatment, 20, 21, 24, 26, 27, 83–86, 133, 222
Inflation, 13
Initial contact and engagement, 94–96
Institutional racism, 40–41
Isolation, 5, 29, 53, 55, 56

Jackson, A., 134
Jensen, Arthur, 70
Job apprenticeship, 21
Joblessness, 5, 23, 25, 29, 31
Job Opportunities and Basic Skills Training Programs (JOBS), 159
Jones, Wyatt C., 71
Justice-based clinical practice, 24–27, 143–166
Juvenile homicide, 33–35

Labor, Department of, 162
Latinos, 6, 54–55, 78
    credit and, 40–41
    education of, 78–79, 142
    exodus from cities of middle-class, 31
    homicide rate and, 34
    male role, 114
    negative attitudes and stereotypes toward, 14
    revitalization of care for, 130, 132, 134

Learned helplessness, 18
Learning theory, 18
Living for today, 52
Lloyd, J. C., 72
Lumber industry, 14

MacAdoo, H., 155
Male clients, working with, 113–118, 144–145
Managed care, 22, 138, 141, 144, 146
Man in the house rules, 14
Manipulation, 57–59
Marshall Plan, 153
Maybanks, S., 72
McClelland, D., 59
McNeece, C. Aaron, 69
Mean streets, 33–35, 52
Medicare, 158
Milieu treatment, 120
Minimal family, 36
Minimum wage, 151
Mother's Pension, 12
Moynihan, Daniel P., 70
M.S.W degree, 123, 163
Muggings, 32
Mullen, E. F., 66, 71, 185–187
Murray, Charles, 155
Mutuality, 60

National Housing Act of 1949, 41
National Opinion Research Center, 13–14
Native Americans, 54, 132
Natural disasters, 7–8
Negro Family, The: The Case for National Action (Moynihan), 70
New Deal, 153
Nisbet, R., 35
Norms, 57

Old Age Assistance, 13
Old Age Insurance Programs, 13
Old Heads, 31
Openness, 60
Orlando, Florida, 35

Parental authority, 35–37
Parenting skills, 21, 83–84, 88, 89, 222, 227
Peer pressure, 23, 38
Personal goals, 83, 88, 90, 221, 227
Personal health and hygiene, 84, 88, 89, 222, 227
Personal power, 82–83, 88, 89, 135, 227
Pessimism, 55
Pimping, 32
Pinderhughes, E., 44, 57
Portuguese, 6
Post-Capitalist Society (Drucker), 158
Poverty level, 10
Power
    class in client-practitioner interactions, 62–63
    defining, 43–46
    dynamics of culture and, 56–62
    in overwhelmed client families, 51–56
    personal, 82–83, 88, 89, 135, 227
    practitioner role and, 46–51, 61
Powerlessness, 7–8, 12, 23, 43, 44, 49–53: *See also* Power
    systemic process of, 4–5, 7–8, 12, 23
Practitioners
    anxiety, 46–48, 50
    bilingual, 22
    burnout, 49, 50, 122–124
    characteristics, 19, 20–21, 88, 119–120, 225–228
    class in client interactions, 62–63
    compensation, 141–142
    dress of, 120
    entrapment, 46, 47
    fatigue and exhaustion of, 46, 47, 49
    flexibility, 21, 164
    hours, 80
    need for control, 46
    power in role of, 46–51, 61
    professional education, 163–165

Prescription drugs, 161
Preventive programs, 132–133
Privacy rights, 14
Private police, 34–35
Professional education, 163–165
Psychodynamic approach, 9, 19, 24, 26, 27, 33, 126
Public housing, 11, 16, 34–35, 38–41
Puerto Ricans, 78, 134, 135
Putative fathers, searches for, 14

Rawls, John, 24
Reaction formation, 57
Reciprocity, 60
Recording and information systems, 140–141
Regression analysis, 90–91, 228
Reid, W. J., 68, 140, 186, 206
Rent supplements, 11, 158
Rescue behavior, 48
Research on clinical practice, 65–75, 185–218
Residential environment, 29, 30, 34–37, 39–41
Rigidity, 53
Role entrapment, 6
Role models, 22, 30–31, 37, 119–120
Role play, 22
Role status assignment, 44
Roosevelt, Franklin Delano, 153
Roxbury Community College, 142
Rubin, Allen, 65, 69, 186, 214

Scapegoating, 81, 89, 220, 227
Segal, Steven Paul, 67, 71, 185, 186, 192, 193, 195
Self-differentiation, 19, 85, 86, 88, 89, 223, 224, 227
Self-disclosure, 60
Self-efficacy-personal mastery dimensions of clinical work, 24, 25, 27, 89
Self-esteem, 5, 12, 19, 55–56, 83, 84, 86–89, 221–223, 227
Self-hatred, 59
Self-sufficiency, 5, 17, 19, 84, 88, 159

Service coordination, 138–140
Shankar, R. A. K., 132, 134
Single-parent households, 6, 11
Smoking, 161
Social roles, 57
Social Security Act of 1935, 13, 153
Social Services, Department of, 95
Sociodemographic profile of over-
    whelmed clients, 77–79
Sociogram, 81
Spirituality, 52
SSI Patrol Services, 35
Steel industry, 14
Stereotypes, 13–14, 61
Strength, 52
Struggle, 52
Suicide, 116, 117
Suitable home requirement, 13
Super-stud syndrome, 59
Supervision, 21
Systems theory, 19, 24, 26, 27, 126

TAT (Thematic Apperception Test)
    projective test, 67
Teachers, 125, 142
Textile industry, 14–15
Tidwell, B. J., 70, 73
Time limits on welfare programs,
    159
Time-series records, 140
Toughness, 52
Transportation, Department of, 162
Trust, 46, 47
20/20 clubs, 23, 59

Underground economy, 31, 32
Unemployment rate, 32, 150
Unheavenly City Revisited, The (Ban-
    field), 70
Universal health care, 152
University-based professional educa-
    tion programs, 134
Uselessness syndrome, 6, 148,
    149–156

Values, 52, 57
Vandalism, 32
"Vanishing Family, The" (CBS Spe-
    cial Report), 70

Wage rates, 13, 14, 78–79, 151
War on Poverty, 14, 153
Welfare: See also specific programs
    delivery system, complexities in,
    16
    dependency, 17
    expansion of, 155
    man in the house rules, 14
    reform proposals, 156–160
    suitable home requirement, 13
Wilson, W. J., 6–7
Winthrop, John, 154
Wood, K. M., 67–68, 185, 186,
    201–203
Work environment, 30
Work opportunity, 149–156
Work referral, 21
Works Progress Administration, 153
Wrong, D., 44